15 St Michaels...

My darling B. We had quite a good move yesterday, 100 miles to Suwon & it kept fine, having rained all night. The roads were awful for the first 30 miles often quite reasonable. We had one truck in the ditch but for it out all night. So we arrived eventually with all our own vehicles (to the astonishment of the Americans who never do their trip from Pusan without a high % of write offs on their vehicles.) I was quite proud of that, especially as many of our vehicles are merely reconditioned ones & not often not too well reconditioned at that. We are ... just North of Suwon, the usual smelly Korean city but of more in... ... more as it is very old, with the old city wall & gates still ... site is not very good, as it is very wet but at least ... ... in that we get a little shade. To day is dull ...
... Cue Talks have been put in ...
... ... know where we stand
... ... selves ready ...

11TH (H.A.C.) REGIMENT, R.H.A.
Middle East Force

18th Feb.

My dear Mrs Tompson
              Just a line to send you my very deepest sympathy over the news. I know he must be a terrible loss to you; he is a great loss to the Regt. as a whole & to us in particular. I thought you might like to know that I do not think he suffered at all as he was badly hit in a dive bombing attack, & I ... to get him back to an ambulance in my car, but he unfortunately died on the way without ever really regaining consciousness. He was buried by

Col A. Band,
    Senior Chaplain
HQ. Middle East Force, ... who has said he would
    write to you.
    I was 2nd in land. dept to the ...
heard from his B.C. ...

FROM THE
FRONT LINE

To Jean

With love, gratitude and admiration

FROM THE FRONT LINE

Family Letters and Diaries –
1900 to the Falklands and Afghanistan

by

Hew Pike

Pen & Sword
MILITARY

First published in Great Britain in 2008 by
Pen & Sword Military
an imprint of
Pen & Sword Books Ltd
47 Church Street
Barnsley
South Yorkshire
S70 2AS

ISBN: 978-1-84415-812-6

A CIP catalogue record for this book is
available from the British Library.

Typeset in 11/13pt Sabon by
Concept, Huddersfield, West Yorkshire

Printed and bound in England by
Biddles Ltd

Pen & Sword Books Ltd incorporates the Imprints of Pen & Sword
Aviation, Pen & Sword Maritime, Pen & Sword Military, Wharncliffe
Local History, Pen & Sword Select, Pen & Sword Military Classics,
Leo Cooper, Remember When, Seaforth Publishing and
Frontline Publishing.

For a complete list of Pen & Sword titles please contact
PEN & SWORD BOOKS LIMITED
47 Church Street, Barnsley, South Yorkshire, S70 2AS, England
E-mail: enquiries@pen-and-sword.co.uk
Website: www.pen-and-sword.co.uk

Contents

List of Maps

Preface

And some there be, which have no memorial ...
And are become as though they had never been born ...
But these were merciful men, whose righteousness
hath not been forgotten ...
Their seed shall remain for ever, and their glory
shall not be blotted out.
Their bodies are buried in peace; but their name liveth for evermore.

Ecclesiasticus Ch 44, v 9

From the Front Line is a family as well as a military story, whose genesis has been a growing fascination with the diaries and letters that have for many years lain quietly in an old chest at home. Having always been conscious of my forebears, I increasingly came to realize that here was a wealth of original material that connected past campaigns with my own more recent soldiering experiences and those of my son Will. The book traces the story through four generations of the family, over the past hundred years or so.

In every family, children grow up surrounded by their relatives, both living and dead. We three – my two sisters and I – were no exception; we must have been pretty typical of our times. We were born in 1941 and 1943, our father was a soldier and our grandparents lived with their memories and sadnesses from the First World War. Uncle Frank, our Grandmother Bridget's brother, was killed in 1917, aged thirty-one, in command of an artillery battery during the Battle of Passchendaele; Uncle Hew, our mother Josie's brother, was killed in 1942 aged twenty-two, serving with the Honourable Artillery Company (11 HAC) in North Africa. Neither of them seemed to be much talked about, at least not with us children. Yet they were always a part of our lives and of family memories, and Hew's photograph as a young Gunner officer was always there on a table in the drawing room, a poppy pinned to its frame every 11th of November. Added to this, there is a strong military strain running through the family, especially on our mother's side, where everyone seems to have been either a soldier or a clergyman since time immemorial.

Indeed, it is the very 'ordinariness' of our family story, mostly one of lives well spent, many in the service of the country, that has compelled me to pull it together so that it is not forgotten, as one generation follows another into the mists of time. 'Out of a misty dream, our path emerges for a while, then closes within a dream', as the poet Ernest Dowson puts it. For these people, like tens of thousands of others, surely deserve to be remembered reasonably accurately, at the very least by their own families; and it is for my own family, past, present and future, that this book is primarily written. To claim that I have written it is in fact something of an impertinence, since in the main I have simply taken and edited the writings of others – a most enjoyable task. I hope they would all approve.

As is so often the case, perhaps the strongest role in the story is played by the womenfolk – our two grandmothers, Bessie, known universally as 'B', and Bridget, always Bridgy to her husband, Reggie Tompson. Bessie brought up her three boys after her husband Sydney, having survived the South African War, died following a cycling accident, leaving her with no money apart from a tiny widow's pension. Bridgy lived through both World Wars, losing her brother Frank Thicknesse at Passchendaele and her son, Hew Tompson, in the North African campaign. Her other brother, Cuthbert was also badly wounded as a chaplain on the Western Front, and makes a subsequent appearance in the story when, as Dean of St Albans, he was a passionate opponent of the bombing of Hiroshima and Nagasaki. Bridgy's husband Reggie Tompson served as a staff officer with the British Expeditionary Force (BEF), and then as an artillery battery commander on the Western Front from 1914 to November 1916, when he was badly wounded. Nor should one forget what Bridgy's daughter, our mother Josie, had to put up with through the Second World War and Korea, during our father Willie Pike's soldiering career. Much later in her life, Bridgy wrote a touching little reminiscence of the small country station at Bentley in Hampshire during the glorious spring weather of the Dunkirk evacuation, as Willie's return was anxiously awaited. Great stoicism was also demanded of my own wife Jean through the South Atlantic campaign of 1982, not to mention my intermittent absences in Northern Ireland and Bosnia. Will's wife Alison showed equal resilience during his four tours of duty with the Parachute Regiment in Macedonia, Iraq, and twice in Afghanistan.

I have included a brief factual summary of each person's life and tried to provide links in the narrative where necessary. But it is the people themselves who are speaking to us in the main, through their diaries, letters and operational notes. These have about them an immediacy and a freshness that I think brings both story and writer to life; they seem to weave a rich fabric not only of continual though rarely stated anxiety and occasional poignancy, but also of humour, love, impatience, frustration and loneliness, as well as acute observation and colourful scene painting. There are inevitably some very frank comments on individuals, too, which I have included, not to be unkind, but to show how some obviously cope better than others in war – that most difficult and uncertain of environments. It is these 'stickers', as Charles Bean, the Australian journalist at Gallipoli called them, who must as far as possible be advanced in peacetime, and this does not always happen. With Shakespearean insight into the demands of war, Edward Gibbon described Alaric the Goth as having 'that invincible temper of mind that rises superior to every misfortune, and derives resources from adversity'.

For reasons of context, I have taken the story back before the First World War, to my two grandfathers, neither of whom I knew, at the opening of the twentieth century – one serving in the South African War, the other in southern Nigeria with the West Africa Frontier Force. The narrative then follows one of my grandfathers, Reggie, with his new wife, Bridgy, through the First World War, whilst touching as well on her two brothers Frank and Cuthbert. After that we pick up the story of the next generation, with my father Willie at Dunkirk and then in North Africa, as well as the loss in action there of my uncle, Hew Tompson. Following Willie's service in Korea, we move to the next two generations, with my own service in the Middle East and in the Falklands, and my son Will's in Afghanistan. Striking and I suppose predictable patterns emerge, like the number of times we have all set off to war from Portsmouth or Southampton, the agony of partings, and the predominance of rumour over hard facts. I could have gone back further and revealed even more continuity. Will, for example, went off to Afghanistan with The Parachute Regiment in 2002 and again in 2006, hot on the heels of his great-great-great uncle, William Tompson (Reggie's much-loved uncle), who commanded the 17th Foot (later the Royal Leicesters) in the Second Afghan War of 1878–81. But if that William wrote letters and notes at the time, which we can assume that he did, they have not survived, as far as I can find. The diary to which Reggie refers covering the Aro Expedition in Nigeria has also long since disappeared, though happily one or two letters survive, as well as copious newspaper cuttings; but there are precious few letters from Sydney's time in South Africa. So what a lesson it is for our own generation and our children's, that without the letters, diaries and notes that have been so carefully kept over the years, often by our wives and mothers, there wouldn't be much immediacy in the story now. Certainly there would be few clues to character and attitudes.

There is a timeless quality to many aspects of this story, for the nature of soldiering, of relationships, of love and of life never changes. 'A nation is not merely a place where we happen to be,' writes Dr Jonathan Sachs of the traditions of Remembrance Day. 'A nation is also a narrative of which we are a part. Society is a contract between the dead, the living and those not yet born. Without that sense of duty between the generations, we would never make the sacrifice necessary to a future we may not live to see. We must make space to hear the call across the years.'

My hope is that this book helps to make that space.

Sources and Acknowledgements

Most of my sources come from within the family, but I should acknowledge with gratitude the following additional and essential books to which I have been able to refer, short extracts from some of which appear in the text:

de Rothschild, Edmund, *A Gilt Edged Life*, John Murray, 1998.
Gilbert, Martin, *The First World War*, Weidenfeld & Nicolson, 1994.
Hastings, Max, The Korean War, Michael Joseph Ltd, 1987.
Haywood, Colonel A. and Clark, Brigadier F.A.S., *The History of the West Africa Frontier Force*, Gale & Polden, 1964.
Johnson, Brigadier R.F., *Regimental Fire. The HAC in World War 2*, Williams, Lea and Co, 1958.
Pakenham, Thomas, *The Boer War*, Weidenfeld & Nicolson, 1979.
Williamson, Hugh, *The 4th Division 1939–45*, Newman Neame, 1951.

My thanks must go to Suzanne, the Archivist at Winchester College for providing me with a striking portrait photograph of Frank Thicknesse, and to Dr David Kelsall of St Albans Abbey for a charming photograph of Frank's brother Cuthbert at the door of the Abbey, introducing the Verger, John Watkins, to Her Majesty The Queen in July 1952, only five months after her Accession. He also generously gave me access to documents and photographs in the Muniments Room at the Abbey.

I am very grateful to Brigadier Henry Wilson, Publishing Manager of Pen & Sword Books Ltd, for his encouragement, and to Ricky Capanni – by chance a fellow parachutist – and Peter Wilkinson of HL Studios (Cartographers), at Long Hanborough, Oxford, who prepared the maps. Bobby Gainher has been an invaluable guide and mentor as Editor to a novice author, and I acknowledge most sincerely his unfailing commitment to the undertaking, manifest not least in his eagle eye for detail.

I have used a number of Falklands photographs taken originally by Tom Smith, then of the *Daily Express*, by Max Hastings and by Graham Colbeck, then of 3 PARA. I gratefully acknowledge their skill and bravery in capturing some graphic and memorable images of war.

Particular thanks are due to the wonderful Mrs Trudi Papps, PA to the Headmaster at Treloar School, Upper Froyle, who skilfully tackled the family tree for me on her computer. Geoff Sear of the Prince Consort's Library, Aldershot has also been most helpful in tracking down source material for me.

Above all, I must thank my two daughters Arabella – herself in the publishing world – Emma, and especially my son Will for their support and advice, and to Jean my wife for patiently giving way to me so often on the computer, as well as for all her help and interest in the undertaking.

THE PIKES, TOMPSONS AND THICKNESSES (EXTRACT ONLY)

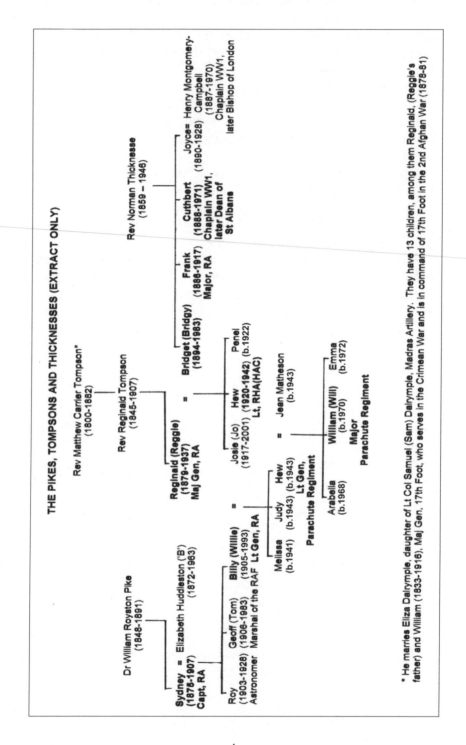

* He marries Eliza Dalrymple, daughter of Lt Col Samuel (Sam) Dalrymple, Madras Artillery. They have 13 children, among them Reginald, (Reggie's father) and William (1833-1916). Maj Gen, 17th Foot, who serves in the Crimean War and is in command of 17th Foot in the 2nd Afghan War (1878-81)

Chapter One

Reggie Tompson – Aro Expedition, Southern Nigeria, 1901–2

On 30 September 1902, the 23-year-old Reggie Tompson writes to his father from southern Nigeria, where he is serving with the West Africa Frontier Force:

My dearest father,

I am this day the proudest and happiest fellow in the whole wide world. The mail has come in today, bringing the welcome news that I am in the Gazette as a member of the Distinguished Service Order! I need not say how thoroughly unworthy and undeserving I am of this great honour, but still they have thought fit to give it me and I am so pleased I hardly know what to do. Brass dogs with ten arms and legs aren't in it for pleasure and conceit! Now at last I don't mind letting out a long held secret, viz that after that water picquet business the Colonel sent for us and told us we should be recommended for the VC and although he said it was unlikely we should all get it, however he considered it worthy and we should consider ourselves equally entitled even if only one got it. [In fact no one did] Of course we never expected it, and to tell the truth I didn't expect a DSO but that's the whole story.

You will be glad and perhaps surprised to see that I am back in Bendi. This will catch the same mail as the last letter I wrote, so you will be relieved to hear I am safe, but it is only by some wonderful Providence that my life has been spared once more. On Sunday 28th September we were fighting six hours, heavier fighting than all the Aro show put together. The bushmen fought with the utmost bravery and stood up magnificently. It was a far bigger rising than we ever thought and although we had gone out prepared for a fortnight's operations we returned in two days having expended 5 or 6 thousand rounds, and as it was a tiny column, with the following losses which were heavy:

Killed 4

Very severely wounded 6

Slightly wounded 2

I have written a fullish account in my diary [not found amongst the family papers] which will interest you, but amongst other instances of luck I may say that on Monday I was serving my gun right in the front in a narrow path and out of the bush about an arm's length off a man let drive and the fellow standing by me rolled over choking, shot dead with 3 slugs in him. I was covered with the powder but was unscratched. Again, we were caught in a narrow defile, a cutting and they put a gun over the top and loosed off. I don't know where the bullets went. They ought to have blown my brains out. They had entrenched the road for miles and miles. The operations must start again soon when we get more men. It was a grand fight. How good comes out of evil. If I hadn't had fever I should have been sent on the Enyong show, which probably won't have a shot fired. The fever is absolutely gone as is proved by the fact I was marching and fighting all that time without inconvenience.

Best love Reggie DSO

Reggie is the oldest son of Canon Reginald Tompson, who holds the living of Woodston Rectory, Huntingdonshire and is also Rector of St Mary Stoke, Ipswich, where they live. He is educated at Winchester and Merton College, Oxford, where he reads theology and is Captain of the College Boat Club. He is commissioned into the Royal Artillery in 1900, aged twenty-one. After his death from cancer in 1937, his sister Margaret (Sister Margaret Teresa, a nun) writes from St Dunstan's Abbey, Plymouth to the *Peterborough Advertiser* correcting a reminiscence of Reggie that had been published, and stating that 'My brother went up to Oxford firmly resolved to take Holy Orders ... A few months before his finals he became convinced that his vocation was to be a soldier. This change was certainly at the moment a disappointment to his father, but it was the mature decision of a thoughtful young man and not that of a "lively boy who did not want to visit old ladies".' (This had been suggested in the reminiscence.)

Disappointed at missing the South African War, he volunteers for service with the West Africa Frontier Force, which he joins at the end of 1901. The objects of the Aro Expedition in January 1902 are 'to suppress the slave trade actively carried on by the Aro section of the large Ibo family in the entire territory belonging to, or dominated by them. Further, to abolish the fetish known as the "Long Juju" which, by superstition and fraud, causes many evils amongst the Ibo tribe and all outlying tribes who constantly appeal

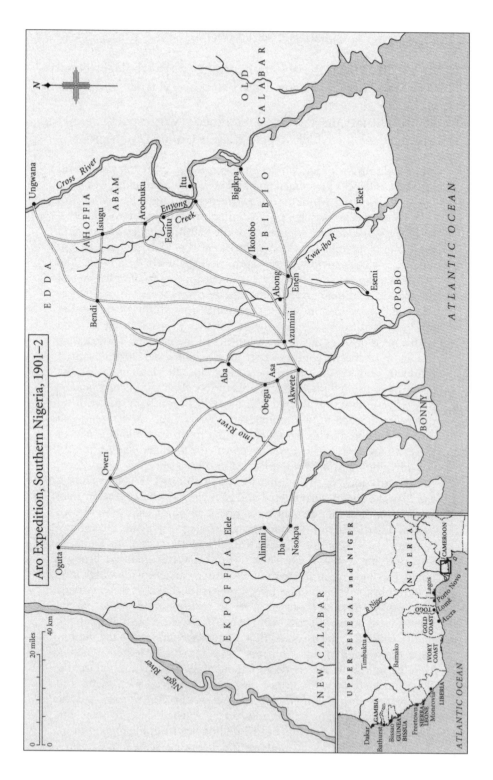

Aro Expedition, Southern Nigeria, 1901–2

3

against it.' It also has the object of opening up the whole Ibo country between the Niger and Cross Rivers to peaceful trade and freedom from bloody massacres.

On 15 February the *Morning Post*'s Special Correspondent reports on the incident for which Reggie is awarded his DSO thus:

No. 2 Column under Lt Colonel Heneker, followed at a day's interval by No. 4 under the personal command of the Commandant, Aro Field Force (Lt Colonel Montanaro), proceeded through the Ibibio into Qua country. Consisting of a 75-millimetre gun and two Maxims, half the scouts and two companies of the Southern Nigeria Regiment, the Column marched from Arochuku on the 15th January to Itu, whence it struck inland on the 16th, taking the road to Enen. The presence of so many troops in the country appears to have frightened the Ibibios, and many rifles, guns and revolvers were surrendered at Itu. The Ibibios are a miserable race, eaten up with the worst form of the most loathsome disease, the very babes in arms being covered with a mass of sores due to the iniquities of the parents. Though they live in magnificent country, rich in oil, palms and other natural products, they are an utterly effete race. On 22nd January, when the columns continued their march, a waterless country was met, and as mile after mile was traversed and daylight began to wane, with no prospect of reaching a camp near to water, our carriers suffered much from thirst. This led to one of the most dramatic episodes of the campaign, as I will presently relate. On January 22, 23 and 24 considerable fighting took place. On the latter day Lt Colonel Montanaro and No. 4 Column joined Lt Colonel Heneker: and on the 25th the enemy surrendered and gave up 250 guns. Heneker then went on to Ikotubo, a small town about seven or eight miles north east of Enen, where he found the white flag displayed. He formed camp here and sent out Captain Knowles, with most of his Force, to visit outlying districts. Then the inevitable water question brought about the incident aforementioned. Thirty carriers with water jars, escorted by Lt Wayling and fifteen men, proceeded to the waterside some 600 yards from the town. A report was sent to Heneker that the enemy were holding it in force. He could spare no men and, relying on the white flag, he assumed that a palaver would settle the matter. So, accompanied by a few officers and a Maxim, he joined Wayling. Here he found the waterside commanded by high ground on the far side, and held by many armed men. He palavered with them, and they promised to give up their guns, but were trying to surround the small force all the time. The interpreter warned them to stop, but they only jeered and commenced a galling fire from the high ground, the bullets falling all around us and breaking several water jars.

Wayling and six men crossed the stream to try to clear the heights, led across with the greatest dash and gallantry by Sergeant Major Ojo Ibadan. They reached the high ground with two men wounded and in a serious predicament. The Maxim, choosing as always the worst possible moment, jammed with a broken spring. We were now attacked heavily from the left front and right flank, and the position became untenable. One carrier was killed, four wounded, and the rest stampeded. On the far bank, Wayling was hotly pressed. The situation was critical. It was necessary, above all, to rescue Wayling and his wounded from their dangerous position. Major Hodson, Indian Staff Corps, dashing forward with a cheer, rushed across the stream, closely followed by Captain Goldie and Lieutenant Tompson. They reached Wayling untouched, though the water all round them was alive with bullet splashes; and, with the aid of their carbines, the pressure was for a time relieved. Heneker now sounded the 'retire'. Tompson seized the soldier who was too badly wounded to walk, and carried him back across the stream. The others rushed across in pairs, Hodson and Goldie covering the retreat and being the last to leave the heights. Once across, camp was regained in safety. Nothing could be done until Knowles' return at 7pm. Then the tables were turned, Knowles' leading section scouting down the water road, followed by the 75-millimetre gun and all the carriers laden with every conceivable vessel for carrying water. Knowles found the enemy on his side of the water, for emboldened by their temporary success, they had crossed the river and had now themselves to withdraw across under a shrapnel and case shot fire, with which Tompson raked them. Knowles charged after them, and they bolted headlong. Two men only were wounded on our side, and the long desired water was obtained at last.

The Columns converge on Akwete some days later. Thirteen Europeans have been wounded in the enterprise, and of the native soldiers of the West Africa Frontier Force, twenty-seven have been killed and 140 wounded; seventy die of disease. As well as Reggie, Hodson, Heneker, Goldie and Knowles are all awarded the DSO (the Military Cross (MC) is not introduced as an award for gallantry until 1914). Sergeant Major Ojo Ibadan is awarded the Distinguished Conduct Medal (DCM) for his gallantry.

Reggie's grey-flannel Aro shirt, identified in his wife's writing as the 'Aro shirt' by a luggage label attached to the collar, lies in a family trunk to this day – still unwashed.

Chapter Two

Sydney Pike and Bessie Huddleston ('B') – South Africa, Mauritius and Blackheath, 1900–7

From the *Kentish Mercury*, 9 February 1907:

At Greenwich, on Tuesday, on the body of Captain Sydney Royston Pike, aged 31, of 73, Granville Park, Blackheath, who died in the Blackheath and Charlton Cottage Hospital on Saturday. The Coroner explained that on January 21st Captain Pike was riding a bicycle in Charlton Road, Blackheath, when, apparently, his machine collapsed. His left thumb was injured, and at the hospital it was found necessary to amputate it. Death followed from tetanus.

Police-constable Ricks, 629R, said that Captain Pike was travelling at about 8 miles an hour at the time. The front forks of the machine broke and he was thrown heavily. He got up, but witness saw that he was bleeding very much from the face, and he complained of his thumb. His face was dressed by Dr Hooper and then he was removed to hospital in a cab. Mr John Bennett, solicitor, of Chapel-en-le-Frith, brother-in-law of deceased, said that the bicycle had B.S.A. fittings, and it had been given heavy wear for three years. Dr Hooper said that the thumb was fractured in two places, and it was reduced while Captain Pike was under chloroform. On January 28th a slight stiffness of the jaw was noticed and tetanus was diagnosed. The thumb was amputated, carbolic injected, and other precautions taken. Next day Captain Pike appeared to be doing very well, but on Wednesday and Thursday the spasms were more numerous. On Friday he was worse and another operation was performed, but he died of exhaustion on Saturday in consequence of the tetanus. The Coroner said that this was a most unhappy occurrence, but the jury would agree that everything possible that human skill and aid could do to save the unfortunate officer's life was done. The jury returned a verdict of 'Accidental Death'.

The funeral took place, with full military honours, on Wednesday at Shooters Hill Cemetery, the Rev. R. Armitage, DSO, Chaplain to the Forces at Woolwich, officiating. The coffin, covered with the Union Jack, was conveyed on a gun carriage, drawn by six horses, furnished by the 29th Brigade, Royal Field Artillery, and the firing party, numbering one hundred, was under the command of Captain F.D. Logan, with whom were Lieutenants P.A. Meldon and R.A. McClymont. The firing party and the Royal Artillery Band (under Serjeant Major Foster), met the cortege at the junction of Marlborough Lane and Shooters Hill Road, and preceded it to the cemetery, where the usual three volleys were fired, and the buglers sounded 'The Last Post'. The various troops in Woolwich Garrison were represented, among the officers present being ... & etc., & etc.

Of Sydney's wife Bessie ('B') and their three small boys, Roy, Billy and Geoff, aged three, eighteen months and seven months, there is, however, no mention in this conscientiously detailed little report on a sudden death that left a young family struggling and fatherless.

Sydney Pike is the son of Royston Pike, a doctor with a large practice in Southsea, who dies of overwork and exhaustion aged

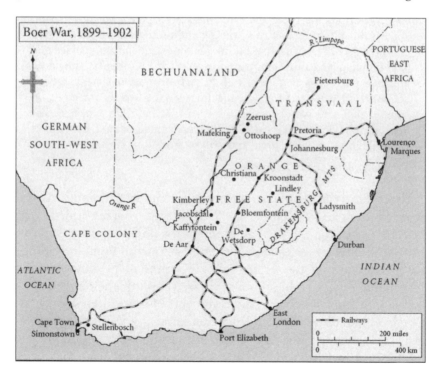

forty-three, when Sydney is fifteen. Sydney is commissioned into the Royal Artillery from the Royal Military Academy, Woolwich ('The Shop') in 1895, aged nineteen. A small man, he is a good footballer, playing for The Shop and for the combined RMA Woolwich and Royal Military College (RMC) Sandhurst IX. In 1899 he joins the Army Ordnance Department as an Ordnance Officer (4th Class), and for much of this year he is stationed in Gibraltar. In April 1900 he marries Elizabeth (Bessie) Huddleston, three years his senior, the daughter of William Huddleston, a dissenting minister, of Ely, Cambridgeshire. They honeymoon at the Albany Hotel, Hastings, from where Sydney writes a dutiful letter to his new mother-in-law:

My dear Mrs Huddleston,

I am just writing to tell you how we are getting on ... I need hardly tell you that we are very happy together here and enjoying ourselves very much ... How well the wedding went off, didn't it? Nothing could possibly have been nicer and there was no hitch of any sort. But the amount of confetti about us was something disgraceful. The floor of the railway carriage was simply inches deep in it, and as I daresay you know they were so unkind as to gum it on the carriage windows, to say nothing of tying on little flags etc . We are going to an entertainment on the pier this evening and tomorrow we are going to go to Battle Abbey by coach. I think Hastings is a charming place and am very glad we came here. I suppose everyone has departed by now and that you are very quiet. I feel an awful robber in having carried off Bess for I know from my own feelings what a loss she must be, but I know that you won't look upon it in that light but will feel that instead of having lost a daughter you have gained a son. Bessie unites with me in sending her best love to you all.

Yours Affectionately Sydney

Shortly after his marriage he leaves for the war in South Africa, which had started in October 1899. Separated from his bride for the next two years, he works as an ammunition and weapons inspector, travelling extensively by train in support of operations in the Orange River Colony and the Transvaal. He writes polite but generally rather dull letters to his mother-in-law (like the one above), with occasional hints of humour and comments of more interest, such as: 'We have had the great Lord Kitchener knocking about this place all last week stirring things up. I was not at all favourably impressed by him' (from Kroonstad, 5 July 1900). After the disastrous early months of the war, Lord Roberts ('Bobs') succeeds Sir Redvers Buller as Commander-in-Chief (C-in-C) South Africa in December 1899, with Kitchener as his Chief of Staff. Ladysmith is relieved in February 1900, Mafeking in May, and by 1901, with Kitchener now the C-in-C, British power begins to prevail, although the irregular warfare, conducted with such skill by the Boers, continues. Concentration camps for Boer women and children displaced by his drives against the guerrillas are introduced by Kitchener in March 1901. With over 100,000 detained in the camps, the death rate from disease and malnutrition is running at one point at nearly 35 per cent for all white inmates (the majority) and almost double that for children. With this bitter and disgraceful legacy of neglect, the war ends with surrender terms signed at Pretoria on 31 May 1902. No letters to Bessie can now be found, but these are extracts from a few surviving ones from Sydney to his mother-in-law:

Kroonstadt. 5 July 1900.

My dear Mrs Huddleston, I expect Bessie will have told you most of my news. I was at Port Elizabeth for 10 days on my first arrival where I stayed with the Martins who were really most kind to me. They have a beautiful house in Port Elizabeth with a very good garden, and I was quite at home and most comfortable. Next I went to Bloemfontein where one felt one really was campaigning a little, and then came on here, in charge of a little show of my own. There is a slight difference between life here and living with the Martins in Port Elizabeth, I can tell you. We carve our meat here with a carpenter's putty knife and think ourselves very lucky to have that. My servant is a very good cook and so we do very well. There is one thing about it, it does not cost one much to live here. We have been very busy here. The men are in a shocking state, some of them have the very thinnest clothing and that all in rags, with no underlinen to speak of, and literally no soles at all to their boots. So sleeping in the open must be dreadful for them. Their delight at raising a jersey or an overcoat is astonishing. There has been heavy fighting going on these last few days. There has been a very stiff fight at Lindley, which is quite close. A despatch rider has just come in with the news. I believe the Boers are defeated in the end and driven off towards the Drakensburg, but it is impossible to tell what really happened. We get practically no news at all here beyond rumours. I think S Africa seems a poor sort of country, principally consisting of desert. I don't think much of the people, either colonists or Boers I must say ... I wonder how much longer this war will last. There do not seem to be very many signs of it stopping just yet in my opinion, but it might end quite suddenly.

Kroonstadt. 29 November 1900.

Very many thanks for your most welcome letter. I am just writing to wish you and Mr Huddleston and all at the Manse a very happy Christmas. As you may be sure I am more than disappointed at not being home to spend it with you all. This will be the first Christmas Day I have ever spent away from home, and I sincerely hope it will be the last. We have been having very hot weather here ... We are all keeping in very good health here I am glad to say and have only one man in hospital and his is not a serious case. I am looking forward to the pudding you are sending very much. I sincerely hope it won't meet with any accidents on the way and get bagged by the Boers. I see today that the garrison of De Wetsdorp has surrendered to the enemy which is simply sickening. It is high time that sort of thing was stopped. [General Christiaan De Wet, whose 'eyes were his one remarkable feature: brown and very bright – a hunter's eyes', was one of the Boers' most brilliant commando leaders, who 'plundered and burnt garrisons with apparent impunity'. De Wetsdorp, a small town named after his father 50 miles south-east of Bloemfontein, fell on 23 November.] All the fighting nearly seems to be going on south of Bloemfontein on the borders of the Colony. The Boers are trying to penetrate south I believe, to induce the colonial Dutch to rise, but I don't think they will succeed now ... I don't like the heat at all. We had quite a swarm of locusts over the camp the day before yesterday. They are most curious creatures to look at. The ants are getting a frightful nuisance and fly over everything – or else crawl – according to which particular breed they belong to. There seem to be plenty of varieties of ant in this charming country. Also a large assortment of beetles and other creeping things.

Kroonstadt. 12 March 1901.

Bessie will have told you I expect that I have had a touch of fever, of a very mild sort ... One is very much out of the world in Kroonstadt, in every way. It has been raining steadily for 4 days on end now so you can imagine everything is pretty damp. It is a horrible country this! And as for the inhabitants – they are beyond words, both Dutch, English and foreigners. We hear rumours that Botha is still negotiating for surrender, and that an Armistice has been proclaimed in the Transvaal pending the result. I am afraid it sounds much too good to be true. It is very seldom we hear a true rumour in this place, and everyone has got into a state in which they believe nothing until it is officially announced ... I can't tell you how I long to be home again and see you all. I seem to have been out here for years and years. There is another absurd rumour started today that De Wet has been captured.

De Aar. 21 August 1901.

As Bessie will have told you, I expect, I have been a sort of wandering Jew lately, wandering up and down the line between De Aar and Mafeking, travelling in mail trains, goods trains, armoured trains and in fact nearly all sorts of trains that have been invented, to say nothing of going out with columns or on my own to Zeerust, Ottoshoep, Christiana, Jacobsdal and Kaffyfontein etc. I ought to begin to know something of this country soon, oughtn't I. I am glad to say the war seems to be going on most satisfactorily, and I am very sanguine about it, in fact I am expecting to be home before Xmas arrives...They have stopped the circulation of all papers of whatever description in De Aar, so you may imagine news is a wee bit scarce in the place. We hear that De la Rey was badly smashed up by Methuen the other day, losing 400 killed and wounded, he himself being badly hit. Prisoners have been rolling in in very large numbers lately, particularly along the Western Line. My cabin trunk that you gave me was sent here for me the other day from Port Elizabeth; so I have just seen it and my kit for the first time for 15 months. I am almost afraid to open it lest everything should have been destroyed by moth.

Your affectionate son-in-law, Sydney.

A tiny 1901 diary survives, intermittently filled in with details of travel and inspections, but rather reminiscent of a schoolboy's desultory attempts at diary keeping. Pathetically, it even includes at the front a note of his bicycle number – 1695.

By April 1902, however, things are looking up and Bessie is on her way, unaccompanied, to join her husband in Mauritius, where he has been posted from South Africa. The character and self-reliance of this 'daughter of the Manse' begin to emerge from a letter she writes to her parents in Ely from the ship on 16 April:

My dearest father and mother,

... I made a great mistake in thinking there was nothing interesting to be seen at Port Said for it is the queerest place imaginable; we reached there yesterday about half past six in the evening and directly after dinner there was a general rush for the shore. I went with another lady and her husband who offered to escort me as I couldn't go alone. We were rowed ashore in a small boat and landed on a funny little landing stage from which after paying 6d each for our journey we walked into the town ... there were lights all along the streets and we went in to several of the shops and bazaars and made one or two small purchases. The shopkeepers come out into the streets and beseech you to go in and look at their wares and when you get inside ask about ten times what a thing is worth, they generally end though by taking about a quarter of the original price and even then they don't do badly for they are most unblushingly impudent in their demands and quite expect you to offer much less than they ask. It was a beautiful moonlight night and the queer houses, funny little trams and quaintly dressed people altogether looked most weird, there was the usual swarm of little children dressed in garments like nightdresses of various colours and they kept following us and bothering us to buy their dirty little wares and every now and then a policeman (in a most wonderful uniform!) would come and flourish something at them and utter some dreadful sounding threat and off they would scutter like rabbits till his back was turned and then back they would come again; there are people of all nationalities and colours to be seen in the streets and all kinds of queer costumes about, altogether it was quite an experience to have seen the place and I am very glad to have done so. This morning we are passing through the Canal, it is not very interesting, mostly a high sand bank on each side, with signal stations at intervals, we passed one queer little building which proved to be a Hindu temple but I didn't see any worshippers there! We reached Suez by and by. I must tell you what it is like when I have seen it. Until today the weather has been rather cool, but now we seem suddenly plunged into summer, the ladies have all appeared in cotton dresses and the soldiers in their uniform, officers in khaki, men in white things. We have a huge awning stretched right across the deck to keep off the sun but nearly everyone today is sporting a huge white helmet (lined with green) as well; the heat today is just about like what it was at home last August ... I have had an interruption to my letter here in the shape of a young man who came up and asked if I were Mrs Pike, he introduced himself as a Capt Hofferman (or some such name), who is returning to Mauritius after being home on sick leave, he is in the Royal Army Medical Corps (RAMC); he speaks very enthusiastically of Mauritius and says he is sure I shall like being there very much; ... he has been giving me most amusing descriptions of various notabilities in the Island. We have just reached Suez, it is rather a pretty little place, low houses with trees along in front of them, we only stop here for about an hour, so no one is allowed to go on shore, but a tribe of natives ('bum boatman' they have on their caps) are swarming on the deck with all sorts of things to sell ... Our next stopping place is Djibouti, which I hear is nothing but a cluster of little houses and huts dumped down in the middle of a large district of sand. I have had to change to 1st Class as I really couldn't stand second, it was fortunate that I had enough money with me to pay the difference, it leaves me rather short but I shall have just about enough to manage alright ... There are one or two other English people on the boat, about six altogether. I have got to know them all now, but I don't like any of them nearly as much as my little French friend (Mlle Harel) and her father, the more I see them the better I like them, they are so simple and unaffected and yet so kind and thoughtful to me in every way. They have a dog on board (it is shut up and not allowed on deck poor thing) which has come from England and they are taking back to Mauritius with them, I went with them to see it yesterday; it is a pointer, the poor animal doesn't understand French and seemed so pleased when I talked to it in English ... Last night a piano was brought on deck and we had quite a little concert after dinner, and afterwards they started dancing; one of the French officers came up to me and asked if I danced and I rashly said 'Un peu' and before I knew it he had seized my hand and whisked me off; as there are about three men to each lady, all those who could dance were very much in request and directly one dance was over my late partner would bring up another man and off we would go again, till at last I was so hot and tired that I felt like a walking grease spot; there are about 18 or 20 of these French officers on board and some of them dance awfully well. I expect we shall be at it nearly every night now.

One of the poor Tommies escaped early on Tuesday morning; we were going down the Canal when suddenly the boat stopped and everybody crowded to the side to see what was up. It turned out that one of the soldiers had slipped overboard and swum ashore. They launched a boat and sent some men after him but did not succeed in capturing him, the poor wretch lost his helmet in the water and as we were about 50 miles from Port Said, I am afraid the poor man would have rather a bad time of it, for with no covering in that burning sun he would probably die of sunstroke or starvation, so he had better have stayed on board, but evidently he had no wish to see Madagascar. I will save my letter again for a day or two, how I wish I could just pop in this morning for a chat with you!

Sunday afternoon.... The Captain told me last night that he thinks we will get to Mauritius on May 10th ... I am enclosing menu from Dejeuner this morning so that you can see how we fare ... I am just going to have some iced lemonade, the quantity I drink is appalling yet I'm always thirsty – Well goodbye now, with my dearest love to you all from Your Loving Bessie.

Reunited at last, Sydney reports on 8 June to his mother-in-law at The Manse in Ely that Mauritius:

is a very pretty island and the climate up in the hills where everyone lives is very healthy and always cool at night. It is a very great change for me from South Africa, as you may imagine. The absence of bustle and hurry is especially strange. Bessie is looking very well and happy. She is quite putting on flesh!! As for me, I am disgracefully fat already and am seriously thinking of having to go in for some sort of training to keep myself small enough to fit my present stock of clothes!!! My work here is not very arduous. There are several dissipations about the 26th June in Honour of the Coronation [of King Edward VII] amongst the rest a ball at Government House which we shall have to go to.

By the following January Bessie is pregnant with Roy, and writes to her mother about the house they are taking from 1 March, that they now have a horse and carriage, and that:

I had a little luncheon party on Sunday; don't be shocked, it is the only thing to do that day and the only day, as a rule, that the husbands can accompany their wives and I don't think there can be much harm in having people in quietly to lunch and staying for an hour or two's chat afterwards ... I find the mornings rather long sometimes ... so I amuse myself with sewing and reading and pottering about arranging the flowers. But I often wish that I could just come in and spend the morning with you, doesn't it seem a long time ago since we used to have our after-breakfast talks together in your bedroom!!

After two years in Mauritius they return to Woolwich with baby Roy. Sydney passes his Advanced Course at the Ordnance College and becomes an Assistant Inspector on the Royal Arsenal's Inspection and Experimental staff. William (Willie, as he was to be generally called in the Army, although Bill or Billy in his family) is born in June 1905 and Thomas Geoffrey (Tom, as he was to be known in the RAF and by his wife Althea, but always Geoff to his mother and brothers) in June 1906.

In the March 1907 edition of the monthly RA Institution Leaflet, the following notice appears:

Captain S.R. Pike R.A., died on the 2nd February from lockjaw, following an accident caused by the breaking of his bicycle.

He was an Officer of great promise, had passed the Advanced Class, and at the time of his death was employed as an Assistant Inspector at Woolwich Arsenal, having previously done 5 years as a 4th Class Ordnance Officer. He was employed in South Africa during the War and possessed the Queen's [South Africa Campaign] Medal with 3 clasps and the King's [South Africa Campaign] Medal with 2 clasps.

His mother spent capital on his education and latterly he was giving her an allowance.

He was not insured and did not belong to the R.A. Marriage Society.

He unfortunately leaves a widow and three small children, all boys under 4 years of age, who, with the exception of the pension and shares valued at about £200, are unprovided for, and without prospect of any provision in the future.

We therefore appeal to the Regiment to assist this most distressing and deserving case.

Any money subscribed will be handed over to the Secretary R.A. Charities for investment as a Trust Fund for the benefit of the widow and orphans.

This appeal is strongly supported by Field Marshal the Right Hon. Earl Roberts, VC, KT.

By the autumn of that year, hundreds have subscribed, their names and the sums given all listed in the RA Institution Leaflet month by month. When the Fund is closed, over £1,600 has been raised and invested, and Bessie submits her sad and dignified little note for inclusion in the Leaflet:

Mrs Pike desires to convey her very sincere thanks to all those officers and friends who have expressed so much sympathy with her in her bereavement. She deeply appreciates the great kindness and generosity shown to her and her children and values them most highly as expressive of the esteem in which her late husband was held.

Though Sydney's failure to make better provision for his family may still surprise us, especially after his own father's early death and Sydney's service in the Boer War, the generosity of all these good people is not wasted. Bessie never re-marries, but settles in Bedford and devotes herself to raising her three boys, all of whom remain utterly devoted to her and make her a proud mother.

From Bedford School Roy gains the Henry Skynner Scholarship in Astronomy and Mathematics to Balliol College, Oxford. A slim blue book published after his own early death from meningitis aged twenty-five, summarizes his short life:

In 1924 he crowned a brilliant University career with a First Class in the Final Honour School of Natural Science. After a year of research in Oxford, he was appointed Assistant Lecturer in Physics at the University of Leeds, where he soon showed his capacity for original work by a series of papers on astro-physical subjects. Whilst at Leeds, he became engaged to be married to Miss Ruth Garstang, daughter of Professor Garstang of Leeds University.

In 1928 he was awarded a Research Fellowship by the International Education Board, and, being granted a year's leave of absence by the University, went out to work at the Mount Wilson Observatory, California. There, after a brief fortnight of active research, in which his brilliantly original work and his great personal charm won the admiration and love of his fellow workers, he was seized with meningitis following a severe chill. On hearing of his illness, his fiancée went out to him, but, though everything possible was done, and the ablest specialists were called in, he died in hospital at Pasadena on 22 November 1928. Nothing can surpass the sympathy of his American colleagues, both to the sufferer and to those to whom he was especially dear. Their many acts of personal kindness were crowned by the courteous action of the authorities of the Observatory in granting him a final resting place on the slopes of Mount Wilson, near the great Observatory.

On his headstone are these words: 'Seeking afar a watchtower in the skies, beneath its stars for evermore he lies.'

Ruth Garstang lives a long life, but never marries.

From Bedford School Willie gains a scholarship to Marlborough College, after which he follows his father to the RMA Woolwich 'The Shop' and then into the Royal Artillery. Willie's fortunes as a soldier are described in Chapters 6, 9 and 11.

Having been tempted to emigrate to Australia, Tom joins the Royal Air Force from Bedford School, where he does not excel academically, being more interested in machinery and motorbikes. He has a distinguished wartime career as a fighter pilot, including a period in command of No. 219 Night Fighter Squadron – Beau-fighters based at RAF Tangmere. He is awarded two Distinguished Flying Crosses (DFC) during the War, and goes on to become Chief of the Air Staff and a Marshal of the Royal Air Force. He remains the most modest and unassuming of men, at his happiest with his family and when he is either making or mending something mechanical.

'B' proves to be resourceful and careful in all things (she has to be!), and very determined. She is bright, too, with a good sense of humour and a nice chuckle; in later years she enjoys her bridge, and of course proudly follows the fortunes of her sons, whose love and deep respect for the manner of their upbringing remain undimmed by time, stubbornness and infirmity. She dies in 1963, aged ninety-one, and is buried with her husband in Shooters Hill Cemetery at Woolwich.

Chapter Three

Reggie Tompson and Bridget Thicknesse, Western Front, 1914–16

When war is declared on 4 August 1914, Reggie, now aged thirty-five, is a student at the Army Staff College, Camberley. As a Staff College trained officer he is prevented from returning to regimental duty and instead moves at once to France on the Railway Transport staff of the British Expeditionary Force (BEF). He starts a diary on 4 August which he then maintains assiduously until his final illness with cancer in 1937. In small weatherproof notebooks or 'page-a-day' diaries, he records in a neat hand not only personal feelings, but family and professional events, relationships and the scenes he witnesses. Each daily entry normally fills a page, occasionally spilling over to a spare space at the back of the book. He also likes to include little diagrams, newspaper cuttings and even tiny photographs. The wartime diaries 1914–1919 are now held in the Liddle Collection at the Brotherton Library, Leeds University.

By 1914 he is also engaged to Bridget Thicknesse (Bridgy), aged twenty, the daughter of the Reverend Norman Thicknesse, Rector of St George's, Hanover Square. They marry there very quietly during his leave, in February 1915. Thereafter he agonizes constantly in his diary about the relative advantages of working on the staff, which he sometimes dislikes but is better for his career, or returning to front-line soldiering (on worse pay) and possibly leaving Bridgy a widow. In late 1916 he finally returns to regimental duty as a battery commander, and is almost immediately badly wounded. After he recovers, he spends the rest of the War on the staff again. Despite his great happiness with Bridgy and his children – Josephine (born 1917), Hew (born 1920) and Penelope (born 1922) – he seems to suffer bouts of stress from overwork and serious depression.

18

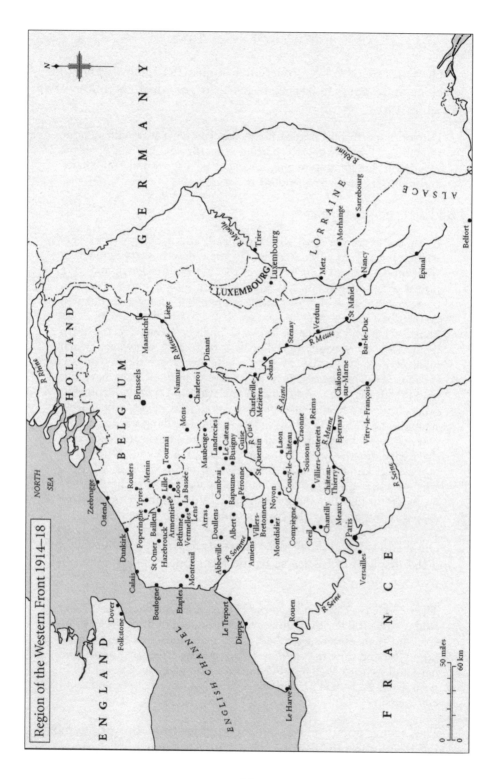

Region of the Western Front 1914–18

He writes twice to his mother on 4 August 1914, mostly about his packing and what is to happen to his 'gear', of which there seems to be quite a lot:

I'm sorry the Bishop prayed for peace. I hope it was with honour though ... I had a ghastly parting from Bridgy last night, she is wonderful though and longing for me to go – it's wonderful what a grasp she has of the tremendous issues at stake.

And at 11pm that night:

If you could see me now! Room stripped, and packing cases every-where. Juggins and Rik (terriers) in their new baskets wondering what on earth is up ... I went over to Yateley after lunch and have just said goodbye to Bridgy. Poor mite, it's hard that she should have to go through all this, terrible for her, but I hope everyone will do their best to look after her and see that she is all right ... Goodness knows what will happen to Rik and Juggins. I shall try and leave them with my servant. It is hopeless to suggest anywhere which involves a train journey as they would never get there ... I am nervous about politicians in war. I suppose most of them have not read the history of the American War, Jefferson Davies, Lincoln and other notorious historical examples. Would they had. Still, I trust Asquith and Grey and all of them I think. The danger is that if the Navy takes a knock they will run into the fatal trap of keeping the Expeditionary Force at home to 'defend' England. Whereas as every child knows the only form of 'defence' is 'offence'. That is where we may go on the rocks, but I pray we don't ... There will be no peace till that blooming Deutsche Flotte is at the bottom of the deepest pool, and may the Navy soon send them spinning there.

On Wednesday, 5 August the diary starts, mostly about packing and the disposal of his horse to the Remount Depot at Arborfield Cross:

Then I rode over on a bike to the Hartford Bridge flats where I met Bridgy, and for the third time we said goodbye. Bridgy was more splendid than ever and we had quite a precious time, and almost forgot for the time the sadness of the goodbye. It came on to rain hard and we took shelter in the garden of a cottage on Cricket Hill. I went back at 7pm. I'm glad the saying goodbye is over and can't come again.

The 'saying goodbye' of course continues to be one of the most painful and constant features of the war for tens of thousands of people, and certainly for Reggie and Bridgy. On 6 August he travels from Farnborough to Southampton by train, noticing that 'each station had a squad of Terriers [Territorial Army – TA] in charge of it and every bridge was piquetted.' On Sunday, 9 August they embark for France, Reggie commenting:

> We were a mixed crew. Dreadful looking 'dug out' officers from the Reserve. At 5pm we got off from an empty quayside, but as we left, the stevedores and crews of liners alongside the quays crowded the sides and burst out cheering, and it made the lump rise in one's throat to feel one was off – the first British soldiers to the continent going to help France.

They arrive at Le Havre early the following morning.

> As we entered Havre, the scene was very remarkable ... although it was 1 o'clock in the morning there was quite a crowd on the pier head. They seemed to go frantic with joy, and cheered across the water at us. As the boat sailed dead slow up the harbour, the crowd followed, running round the harbours and catching up with us again and again. Cries of 'Vive les Anglais', 'Vive le Roi Angleterre' were passed from quay to quay. Windows flew up and people waved in their nightshirts ... The whole thing seemed more like a dream than a reality... The men rose to the occasion thoroughly – Atkins always does. They seemed to take it all as perfectly natural, and to meet the occasion stood packed on the lower deck and in sepulchral tones to the words 'la-la-la' solemnly went through the Marseillaise.
>
> We left Havre station at about 11.30 amidst terrific enthusiasm and from there till 1030 pm our progress was remarkable. I think it will always remain the most memorable day of my life. As the train crept along stopping at every station, the people at the stations and the Guard Civile stationed along the line saw us. The expressions were a study: indifference at the train, surprise at seeing strange uniforms, curiosity to discover what they were, joy at realising they were English, frenzy when the truth soaked in. Practically from the start at Havre to our night's destination at Amiens the bursts and torrents of cheering never ceased. As we ran into a station, the men on guard left their occupation of standing stolidly at their post day and night and hurled themselves at the carriages and footboards ... The station gates barricaded and guarded were holding back crowds of men, women and children, waving, shouting, singing, kissing their hands and allowing the overpowering enthusiasm of their joy to over-come all feelings of restraint or reserve ... One had it brought back to one as it had never been before, 'How this nation can hate!' ... every

21

soul burning with hatred against the German. One could never have believed that any cause could have gone so deep into the soul of the individual, but here the individual is France.... And one looked at the filthy old red pantaloons, and the dirty old coat buttoned back at the thighs, and the old caps which hardly deserved the name of uniform. And behind these unshaven, dirty, unsmart, dilapidated and battered old reservists one almost saw the fury and passion underneath. One old man in a perfect dumbshow ... went through the motion of firing, the bayonet (a very long and savage looking thing, going to a sharp, needle-like point), brought to the engage, the thrust, the cutting of the throat, and truly French, the final kick up the backside ... The 40 years since 1870 piled up with a long tale of German bullying has pickled the rod for the Prussians to a terrible extent ... At Rouen Cathedral lots of people were at their devotions, when out of the corner of their eyes they caught sight of the khaki uniforms. All attention became fixed, the faces solemn in prayer suddenly lit up with a radiant look of joy and enthusiasm. And soon they discovered that so and so's soul might wait, but 'Les Anglais, les anglais sont arrives!'

August 11th Tuesday. Amiens.

I smoked a cigarette, the first I have smoked since July 1904, ten years ago.

In the days that follow, the BEF begins to arrive. Naturally things do not always run smoothly, and Reggie's forthright and often entertaining comments to his diary on the shortcomings of others come to the fore:

August 18th, Tuesday. Amiens.

A train arrived with 9th Battery (41st Brigade RFA). Had about an hour's sleep before this. Lushington (Colonel) a perfect old ass ... and as incompetent and useless as they make them, was there with his Adjutant, an excitable and rather stupid Captain with spectacles. The detraining was pandemonium. Lushington for the time being became an indifferent Sergeant and acted the part to perfection. Brusson, his Adjutant, lost his head and was futility itself, becoming obstructionist.

The 'organized chaos', as familiar to every generation of soldiers as the 'incompetent enthusiast' just described, continues unabated. So too does the general discomfort and the feeling of isolation from family and loved ones.

August 22nd, Saturday. Busigny.

THREE LETTERS, the first I had had since landing. One from Irene [his sister], one from Mother and one from Bridgy. They had all been to Southampton and had been marked 'gone away'. I'm afraid I was nearly silly about these letters. It was such a treat. I don't remember ever experiencing such a feeling of delight. I read them through and through and loved them.

The reality of the war is also closing in. The retreat from Mons begins on 23 August, the delaying action at Le Cateau takes place on the 26th, and the defensive battle on the River Marne that halts the German advance, is fought in the early days of September:

August 24th, Monday. Busigny.

At about 6 I got up and a lovely morning it was too. Blue sky and fleecy clouds and swallows high, and for the first time as I stood on the station platform I heard the guns firing to the north. They were a continuous thud-thud-thud. There must have been an enormous expenditure of ammunition proceeding, and one could imagine the perfect plastering of iron which must have been going on. But it was an eerie, curious sensation with which one listened to it and wondered.

August 25th, Tuesday. Written in train retiring to St Quentin.

Refugees from Belgium keep pouring through, the station is choked with them. They all look as if they had dressed in a hurry and had snatched what they could and left. Poor hunted looking creatures, of all classes packed into such few trains as they could get hold of ... some people were half wild with thirst ... our men were of course very good and kept running to fill their bottles ... one woman had been separated from her two small children, but concluded they were on the train, and found they were not! Many people had dogs, which were obviously an awful bore, but it showed a nice spirit not leaving them behind ... At 2 o'clock wounded began to go through and news began to leak out. There has been a disaster. All accounts are very confused and probably exaggerated, but boiled down the rumours agree that part of the English army has taken a severe knock. They say that infantry were surprised, that the artillery had not got up in time and that they were unsupported and consequently suffered seriously under German artillery fire. The Middlesex Regiment is said to have been practically annihilated, and others, Scots Fusiliers and a Guards Regiment destroyed. There is probably a good bit of

23

truth in the general purport but it is impossible to find out any details. Anyhow there is a sort of air of disaster hanging over the place. Le Cateau, about 3 miles up the line, is being entrenched.

August 28th, Friday.

At Rouen Station there were a batch of German prisoners ... they had two ranks of men with fixed bayonets all round them and they walked in the square in the middle. The fury of the people is awful to see. They would certainly lynch them and the faces of the prisoners is an awful sight. There is one officer of Cuirassiers, a boy of about 18 ... his face was terrible, just like an animal at bay, staring, cowed and shamed and with an awful look of animal fear ... The women are the most terrible, but perhaps because they suffer most from war ... after speaking to several I find the sentiment almost universal demanding the massacre of women and children. They say the children will only grow up and attack us again. Therefore kill them ... One wounded German pointed to his bandaged foot and expostulated that he could not march. But the French were compelling him to limp to his feet and try, when two of our soldiers dashed in through the crowd and picked him up and carried him. Even the French applauded.

We left Rouen at 1245 pm, going round by Paris (nearly). Reached Creil at about 6.30 pm.

The news tonight is awful. The 2nd Army (3rd and 5th Divisions) was said to have ceased to exist. General Snow (4th Div) was reported killed and the whole British Army had had such a hammering that it was practically crippled. The question arose, 'Where *is* the French Army?' The evacuation of St Quentin was a thing of horror yesterday afternoon. Stragglers, wounded and fugitives poured in having had no sleep for about 4 nights, heavy fighting and little food. They marshalled train after train and huddled them in as best they could, some staggering on and refusing to give in along the road but overcome and falling out when their strength gave out ... The Hospital was abandoned, trusting the Germans to respect it, but one does not know. A doctor who was kneeling beside a wounded man (Royal Irish?) was approached by a German officer who at 3 yds range blew the doctor's brains out ... However the Royal Irish captured about 16 prisoners who put up their hands but they shot the lot and small blame to them. The doggedness and silent grit of the remnants of the 3rd and 5th Divisions during the debacle of St Quentin was a thing which one will never forget. Our men may be blighters in many ways, but they are magnificent.

August 30th, Sunday. Creil.

Doubt seems to be arising as to the quality of the French troops. This, if true, is our last hope gone. Apparently they will not stand and fight, they manoeuvre and manoeuvre (especially cavalry), 'keeping the enemy under observation' but do nothing ...Things are looking blacker every day.

There is a little time for habitual practices, like Holy Communion on a Sunday:

September 20th, Sunday. Creil.

In the large workshop on the concrete floor we had the Celebration. The altar was a table with a towel on it, but it was nicely done in spite of everything. We had altar lights, and a crucifix and it was quite real although the bread was in the top of a mess tin and there were no carpets or benches, and though in one corner of the room was the London Scottish guard room with all the prisoners under the sentry and in other parts were men getting up, washing and talking and having their breakfast. All jumbled up together in the same great shed, but it was none the less real, perhaps more real for all this. We just knelt round anywhere as best we could. I hadn't made much preparation I'm afraid, but perhaps that won't matter so much this time as it was the only chance we have had.

The following Sunday Reggie has a 'day off' and heads for Meaux in 'the motor' with two colleagues, Hildyard and Binny.

September 27th, Sunday.

The main road over the Marne came to an abrupt end as the bridge, an old stone one, was shorn clean away, blown up by the French ... We went on to Meaux. The great valley was very beautiful as we ran down into it. Large 'posts' seemed to be established in all the villages and trenches and earthworks were cut everywhere. It looked so curious to see turnip fields with huge redoubts turned up in them, and fences and houses flattened regardless, to improve the field of fire ... We were now on the northern bank [of the River Marne] and there were remnants of fighting; broken down motor vans lying disconsolate by the road with wheels off with such inscriptions as 'Gurneys best Stout' and 'Daily deliveries to all parts'. Thoroughly English looking! We passed many newly made graves, dotted about everywhere.

September 29th, Tuesday. Creil.

Had a very sweet couple of letters from Bridgy. Wonder if I shall ever see her again. Goodness I never knew how much I loved her, nor what she meant to me, and I have sometimes been cross with her. Ye Gods!

October 9th, Friday. Creil.

Hundreds of wounded go through every day (French from Arras). One sight went past, a half-naked corpse on a stretcher, a German. I suppose they had been trying to save his life? However he was covered with blood and much bashed about. As one looked at him, one couldn't help thinking that there was probably someone to whom this belonged, and there he was. I suppose died in a truck with not so much as a friend within miles.

November 13th Friday. St Omer.

Heard that Bobs [Lord Roberts] was here.

November 14th, Saturday. St Omer.

Heard that Bobs was dead. Great grief.

November 17th, Tuesday. St Omer.

Lord Roberts funeral. There was a feeling that death could not be better, or come in a better way. The Prince of Wales was at the funeral. I was standing quite close to him. I was much struck by his smallness and fragile appearance. But he certainly looked very nice. He looked about 15. Hard to believe he is 20. Saw some British tommies practising an attack. One can't help being struck with the way our troops on arrival here drill and practise and keep themselves fit – in contradistinction to the French ... who do nothing but slope about when they aren't cooking food, at which occupation 90% of their time seems to be spent.

November 23rd, Monday. St Omer.

There seems a chance that we might get a couple of days in England. Heavens if this came true what joy would it be. Think of two days with Bridgy.

December 1st, Tuesday. St Omer.

Great excitement because the King arrived ... The so-called battle of Ypres seems to be finished for the present ... In the evening there was a big crowd to see the King and Poincaré (the French President) arrive back. I saw the King quite well. He was standing on top of the steps in the house facing Sir John French's billet. Joffre (the French C in C) was there and all sorts of big people. The King was in Service Dress. There were (apparently) no precautions. He stood practically *in* the crowd and everyone was surging round the house.

December 4th, Friday.

Had a very rough and soaking wet passage. I was provided with an oilskin, otherwise I would have been soaked through. Got some awful duckings at Folkestone as the water was breaking over the pier onto the ship ... Arrived at Victoria and found Bridgy looking her very preciousest ... A very happy afternoon and evening.

December 5th, Saturday.

The joy of getting into evening clothes (which precious Bridgy had provided from nowhere) was delicious. Also clean white shirt etc.

December 7th, Monday.

Rained all afternoon but went out to exercise dogs in evening. London appears to me exactly the same as in peace. It is hard to believe it is wartime. So different in every way from France.

December 8th, Tuesday.

Went with Bridgy to the War Office in the morning to see if I could do any good about helping Frank [Frank Thicknesse, Bridgy's brother, is a Regular Army officer (a Gunner) and a Mandarin linguist who has spent the past seven years in Hong Kong and is pressing to return in order to serve on the Western Front]. Made some final purchases, tobacco, whisky etc and left for Victoria about 12 noon. Bridgy was very good on the platform, and never cried or anything, dear brave little darling, though I know she felt like it.

December 12th, Saturday.

The following in the Times rather appealed to me:

THE ONE O'CLOCK WAR TRAIN. STIRRING SCENES AT VICTORIA STATION.

A stirring if a touching sight is the departure of the 1 o'clock train each day from Victoria Station, taking back to the front officers and men who have been spending their short leave at home. A great mass of people throngs the station, but double barriers keep from the platform itself all but the travellers and the friends who have come to see them off. Even so the platform is crowded, and to an onlooker ignorant of the cause of the gathering, it would seem as if it must be some occasion of unusual festivity.

There are tears, of course, shed unaffectedly, and partings at the last moment from which one can only turn away. There are anxious women's faces, but the men themselves are in – or gallantly assume – such laughing spirits that anything like general or sustained depression is impossible. Extraordinarily fine men they are, too, many of them in equipment which shows unmistakable evidence of recent hard usage; and the mixture of regiments and uniforms makes the assemblage doubly interesting.

RE, RA, RFA, you can read the lettering of almost every branch of the Service – Grenadier and Coldstream Guards, South Wales Borderers, Lancashires, Highlanders in kilts, airmen and staff officers of every degree; ribbons on the breast which tell of service in South Africa, in the Sudan and on the Indian frontier; and every man looks fit and, outwardly at least, is as happy as a schoolboy going for his holidays.

It seems impossible, as the whistles blow, that out of all the clinging leave-takings, all the passengers can really get on board. But somehow, swinging into open doors and clustering on carriage steps as the train is already moving, they are safely off, still shouting back laughing 'Goodbyes'. As the train slides away a deep-voiced cheer rises from it, to be answered by another less deep-voiced from the throng left upon the platform, the air above which is a forest of waving hats and umbrellas.

It is all very British, the casualness of it, and the masking under laughter of the deeper emotions. Certain reflections must occur to any-one who witnesses the scene. The first is of the splendid quality of the sacrifice which we are making. To British eyes, it seems impossible that any men whom other nations are offering on the battlefield can be quite as fine as these, our own. Next, one must wish that every man who hesitates about joining the Army could go to see the train pull out; for no man could help being happy and proud to be one among such comrades in such a leave-taking.

The reality is, of course, much less appealing. The first Battle of Ypres, which follows the German retreat from the Marne to the Aisne, ends in a stalemate that causes both sides to feel for the open flank, by moving troops northwards in what becomes known as 'the race to the sea'. By the end of the year, the war has gone to earth. Sir John French, commanding the BEF, tells the King that 'the spade will be as great a necessity as the rifle, and the heaviest types of artillery will be brought up by either side.' Reggie comments on the battle:

December 14th, Monday. St Omer.

The attack was to begin today and great anxiety prevailed. Messines is the stumbling block which is strongly held. To take this it is first necessary to take Wytschaete [both objectives south of Ypres]. This is strongly held also, but a certain amount of progress was made ... two woods were captured. And many guns are massed to support the attack. The German line makes a considerable bulge in our front, and they want this straightened out first ... the amount of barbed wire is awful. This pending attack must have been awful. The troops have been staring across the gap for weeks, knowing that the time must come when the gap must be crossed.

December 16th, Wednesday. St Omer.

I got Rudkin (18th Royal Irish) to talk about Le Cateau and those times, and one could see that his whole nerves had been terribly shaken. The 18th lost perhaps more terribly than anyone. It appears that after the French cavalry (which was supposed to be covering the front) had evaporated without a word to anyone, and after the French troops on the right and left of the British (who were supposed to advance up to the alignment held by the British, but did nothing except to retire leaving the British in the salient exposed to the full force of the attack of five Army Corps and two Cavalry Divisions), they were utterly outflanked and almost annihilated. The Le Cateau-Condry road was a sunken road a few feet down and in this all the wounded were stacked. When the Germans outflanked the position, they swept this road with shell and machine guns killing most of the wounded. Apparently a battery in retirement went full gallop down the road over the dead and living and the scenes seem to have been too horrible. He mentioned particularly their Mess Corporal, the whole of the lower part of his face was blown away by a shell, and he had his hands up to his face and his eyes peeping over his fingers, rushing about screaming. Fortunately he died in about a quarter of an hour. He told me how many men had gone raving mad and instanced what he said with the case of a sergeant of his, who rushed into a farm and shouted, 'Come out at once, there are four dead men there, you can see them up there.' This sergeant died in an hour absolutely unwounded. If the history of that retreat is ever written, it will make horrible reading.

December 23rd, Wednesday. St Omer.

No news and gloom and depression is eating into one's soul. On this day perhaps more acutely than other days, as this is, or was to have been our Wedding Day. It is all very deadly, but after all one is better off than many, but the dullness and monotony of day after day is awful.

December 25th, Friday. St Omer.

Christmas Day was about the most doleful I had ever experienced. It was cold and wretched ... The firing in certain parts of the line ceased by mutual consent, according to accounts ... The Essex Regiment are said to have arranged a football match with a Bavarian regiment ... by sort of tacit consent men came out of the trenches and took the opportunity to remove corpses which were hanging over the barbed wire entanglements on both sides. Cigarettes and food were exchanged.

1915

January 2nd, Saturday. St Omer.

Complete stagnation continues. The reason is, I firmly believe, one of ammunition. The supply is short in England and there is no reserve. The late Master General of the Ordnance (Haddon) is the flat catcher who ... is responsible almost entirely for this. He persuaded [the Government] that economies could be effected and here is the result ... Strong rumours about the war coming to an end suddenly are in circulation. Hope they are untrue. Our only chance is to stick it out now while we have the chance.

On 23 February, Reggie travels home to marry Bridgy:

February 24th, Wednesday.

Mrs Thynne's car came at twenty to eight and picked us up and Mother and I went to St George's, Hanover Square. I waited at the bottom of the Church for a bit and then the Bishop of London sent for me in the Vestry and had a talk for a minute or two. Then I went and sat in the top seat and waited for Bridgy. The service was exactly as we wanted it, very simple and very dignified. Cuthbert [Bridgy's brother] acted as Bishop's chaplain and carried his crozier ... There was one hymn as Bridgy came in, 'Come gracious spirit Heavenly dove'. There were only boys in the choir ... It was a beautiful morning with snow on the ground and sunny. Bridgy looked more beautiful in her wedding dress and veil than ever she had looked before. Everyone admitted she was the most beautiful bride who had ever been seen in the Church. The Bishop gave a short and very nice address ... Jolly played most beautifully all through.

After a night at the Grosvenor, they set off by train for Torquay, accompanied by Jug and Rik; 25 February is 'a heavenly day, spent in absolute bliss'. They stay at The Grove guesthouse.

February 26th, Friday.

The whole place is absolutely perfect, and a more blissful time could not have been invented. Mrs Eales looked after us and we were otherwise quite alone. In the afternoon we walked down to Babbacombe beach, and everything was just one long dream of happiness ... Bridgy at once began to look prettier, healthier and better, and I felt twice the man I was. The dogs improved almost instantly, and a happier day would be hard to imagine.

March 1st, Monday.

Another perfect day ... Walked over Oddicombe beach and up the cliff. Lost Jug and Rik. Former soon found. Latter utterly lost. Spent a good half hour whistling and shouting. Finally went down the cliff to see if anything could be seen of him that way. Twice thought I heard a sound, and Bridgy who remained on top thought so too. The cliff here hung over perfectly sheer, and I thought he was lying at the bottom with a broken back or leg having missed his footing. Once again heard a distinct whine and took off coat, cap and gloves and started to go up the cliff face in the direction of the sound. A lot of roots and over hanging branches made progress difficult, but helped to give hand and foothold, though many were rotten. At last got to a point where I saw Rik perched (and terrified) where he could not get up or down. He had blood on his leg. Could not reach him. Bridgy worked her way along the top to a point where she could see him, but neither of us could quite reach him. Eventually got him by the scruff and put him on shoulder, where he clung trembling, as I had no hand to spare, and let myself down. Got safely down and so home arriving at 6.

March 4th, Thursday.

Our last day of the happiest week of our lives ... Our bills for the 8 days came to £4–16s–11d which considering we have done ourselves slap up is not bad.

March 5th, Friday.

Bridgy very good girl at station and did not cry. Hope this is the last time one will have to go through this business, it isn't very pleasant ... Wrote a letter to say goodbye to Bridgy. Gangway being pulled up as I took it on deck. Mrs Lloyd on the pier. Tried to throw it to her but it didn't carry and fell into the water and was lost. Scribbled another short line and got that ashore as the boat was shoving off. Hope that Bridgy may get that.

March 10th, Wednesday. St Omer and Bethune [Opening of the attack to capture Neuve Chapelle, north of La Bassée].

Terrific bombardment going on ... all troops very cheerful and confident ... Heard that Neuve Chapelle had been taken by us at 8am. The Canadians were holding their own. Middlesex had got caught on the barbed wire and had suffered heavily ... No reply from the enemy's artillery to the artillery fire from 7th Div ... rung up by Gray to say he had filled his Ambulance train and had still 700 cases and they were still pouring in. Ordered an improvised train. [Heard that] a fellow in the Scottish Rifles had told Gray that they had got tired of making prisoners and had bayoneted a lot. Everyone very content. Apparently more was achieved than had been hoped for. 1st and 2nd Divs had not achieved much. Probably their losses heavy. Saw that Goldie had been killed (accidentally with a bomb). He got his DSO the same day as I did [Aro Expedition 1902].

March 11th, Thursday. St Omer.

Casualties very heavy ... At Bailleul 2nd Cheshires were parading after their 7 days rest to go back to the trenches ... I thought they looked shocking, worn and tired.

March 17th, Wednesday. St Omer.

Got a piteous letter from Bridgy which distressed me. Poor darling. But I wrote to comfort her, a second letter as I had written. Still there wasn't much time for this.

March 30th, Tuesday. St Omer.

Bishop of London [Arthur Winnington Ingram, famous in his day and known as the 'Bishop of the Battlefields', who in one address to 5,000 Territorials tells them, 'We would rather all die, wouldn't we, than have England a German province?'] at the Hotel du Commerce ... had asked for me, so went and looked him up after dinner. He was changing and just going to have a bath. I went in by his insistence and sat talking to him while he had his bath. He only had a sort of dish to wash in and of course it all slopped over on the carpet and I helped mop it up. He was quite interesting and talked about Bridgy.

'A rattling fine sermon' is Reggie's verdict when he hears him preach that Sunday, 4 April. 'Bridgy sent me Horace Odes which I was delighted to get,' he notes on the 22nd.

After a further period on the staff at GHQ, St Omer, Reggie is posted to be DAQMG on the staff of HQ 7th Division, forward of Bethune, with responsibility for the logistic support to the fighting units of the Division. 'Such a relief I have never felt before in my life,' he comments on his new role, now much more directly involved in front-line realities. 'Some trolleys were taking up little wooden crosses with names painted on by the artificer ... to be planted,' he notes on one of his first visits to unit trenches. His Divisional Commander is Major General Hubert Gough, soon to be succeeded by Major General Tommy Capper, described by Reggie as 'quick, clear and decided'. On 25 September the Battle of Loos begins, following careful preparations for the use of gas, in which Reggie is closely involved, with the wind direction the main anxiety. On the 26th Reggie reports: 'things not going too well. Troops all utterly exhausted in the heavy rain and appalling mud.' And later on: 'General Capper went forward into Breslau trench during the attack by the Worcesters on the Quarries ... and to everyone's great dismay and grief he was badly wounded through the lung. He could not be got back till night.' On the 27th: 'Heard with great sorrow that the General had died during the night. Everyone rather cast down but it was known that it was the ambition of his life to be killed in action, which is some consolation. A braver man and a better general never walked.' His replacement is Major General H.E. Watts.

On 29 September Reggie is visiting Bethune and Vermelles, where there is heavy shelling.

> I saw some men standing round a car, and one said to me, 'Will you tell the Prince of Wales that his chauffeur's body has been put into this house.' Apparently the Prince of Wales had got out of his car and the car had gone on a few yards and was reversing when a shell got the car and killed the chauffeur. Can't think why the Prince of Wales is allowed to be in Vermelles at all. Don't suppose he is.

1916

The year of 'the Somme battle' as Bridgy would call it in years to come.

Sunday 2 January. Cavillon.

> Got a parcel from little Bridgy containing a pair of socks, a book and a piece of good soap, which was precious of her to have sent. A wretched day, wet and windy.

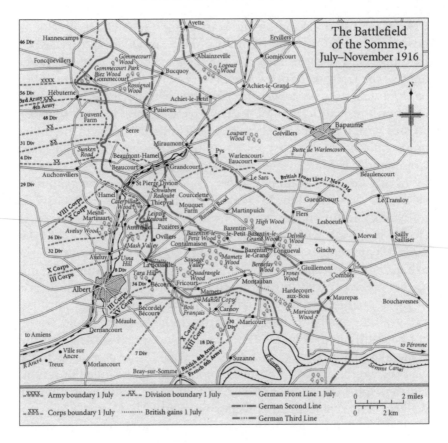

The Battlefield
of the Somme,
July–November 1916

⋯XXX⋯ Army boundary 1 July	⋯XX⋯ Division boundary 1 July	—— German Front Line 1 July
⋯XXX⋯ Corps boundary 1 July	⋯⋯⋯⋯ British gains 1 July	—·—·— German Second Line
		—··—··— German Third Line

0 ___ 2 miles
0 ___ 2 km

Friday 7 January. Cavillon.

Argylls wrote in demanding my servant Piper Jones back ... it was
clear he was all for going back. He very rightly pointed out that after
the war when he went back he would be looked on askance ... Gave
him a sovereign and shook hands with him, but he was rather upset
at going. Gallipoli evacuated.

Thursday 17 February. London–Boulogne.

Had about 20 minutes dumb agony at Victoria ... Bridgy splendid as
usual, but it gets worse and worse this going back.

Thursday 24th February. Treux [on the 7th Division's sector of the
Somme front].

Reached fire trench and saw over with periscopes ... Walked up into
the Tambour. It was heavily knocked about. Saw German corpses
lying out by our wire. Didn't go to the end of Tambour as they were

34

digging out the missing Borders and as the last body came out minus a head, I didn't much want to see it. Bitterly cold.

Thursday 9th, March. Treux.

Walked under the cover of the hill to Citadel [nickname for a forward location]. A trench mortar had recently burst and two Manchesters were being carried away on wheeled stretchers. As we walked down to the Citadel we passed one of the little cemeteries, and the two bodies were lying there all alone on the place where their graves would be, in the row of graves. Very pathetic. Went up the other trench tramway ... a trolley was going up pulled by a horse with the tea.

Friday 17th March. Treux.

Everyone apparently despondent in Germany and it is said that the War is being maintained to prevent internal troubles ... [The view is that] Germans must go on attacking at Verdun [against the French Army. The battle there had opened on 21 February] ... failure means absolute defeat.

Saturday 25th March. Treux.

We are to be ready by 15th April ... 1000 rounds per gun are to be dumped for Field Artillery, and other figures are so bewildering one could not take it in. What a show we are going to have ... I can't see how there can be much trenches or Germans left – <u>if</u> they don't clear out first.

Tuesday 18 April. Treux.

A chaffinch woke me up at 4.45am by singing on a tree outside. He stayed a long time and I got field glasses on to him to make sure what he was.

Wednesday 19th April. Treux.

The Germans made a raid on Mansel Copse. The poor 2nd Borders got it again. The trenches were absolutely flattened, not a trace of them was left. The Bosche put about 6000 shells into this little sector and did great damage ... About 20 killed and 40 wounded. A disastrous show ... but no one could have done more than the Borders actually did.

Sunday 23rd April. Treux. Easter Sunday.

Not an interesting day, although it was: Easter (English), Easter (Russian), Shakespeare Tercentenary, Cervantes ? Centenary, St Georges

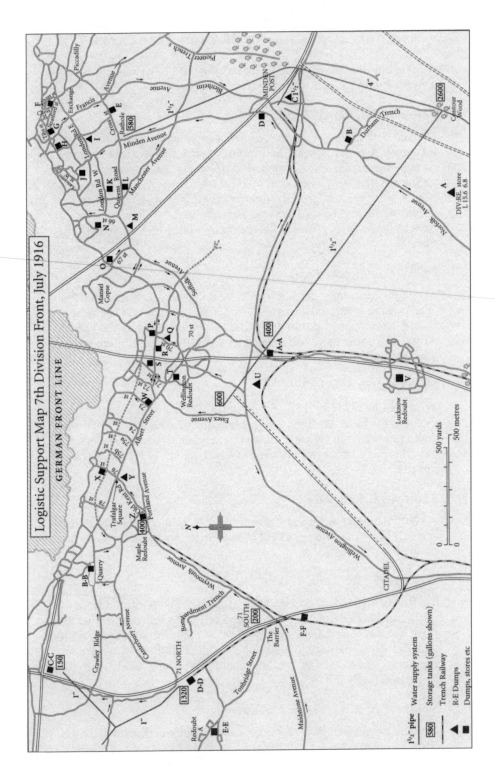

Logistic Support Map 7th Division Front, July 1916

36

Day. All this ought to have produced something but didn't. [But see 2 May!]

Tuesday 25th April. Treux.

Heard first Cuckoo. Nightingales singing, but not like the Ipswich ones.

May 2nd.

News bad today. A Russian reverse, Dublin [Easter rising] and Kut [Kut al Amara, on the Tigris River in Mesopotamia, where the besieged General Townshend surrenders to the Turks] combined.

The next two months are a busy time, mainly taken up with the preparations for the 7th Division's part in the Somme offensive, which finally opens on 1 July. Bridgy is now living at Handford Cottage, Yateley which they have rented. The preparatory bombardment begins on 24 June and on Monday, 26 June Reggie notes:

Treux.

The result up to date is fair. We seem to have a rather undue number of dud rounds but the wire has most successfully been cut in certain parts though not in others. Patrols sent out last night found the trenches strongly manned; so evidently the Bosche is not shaken yet.

Wednesday 28th June. Treux.

At 2pm the thunderclap burst – the whole show was put off for 48 hours. We couldn't believe it for a time ... The effect on the Infantry will be enormous, nothing but bad. Orders came at 3pm for the artillery to slacken fire. The 9.2 inch (our best gun) have been told that no more ammunition can be expected after allowance now with guns is expended. 8 inch are a little better off but not much. 6 inch ammo is plentiful but 30% are 'duds' ... Great depression everywhere.

Thursday 29th June. Treux.

Bombardment slackened slightly but not much. When the universal annoyance had subsided about the postponement, everyone seemed to be rather glad. The roads and trenches had become so appalling that it is very questionable whether troops and certainly wagons could have got across and up in time. Today was finer and things dried up a lot.

Saturday 1st July. Grovetown [nickname for one of the forward tactical locations].

Assault delivered at 7.30am.

The diary then notes the developments of the day on the 7th Division's front in considerable detail, including the usual raft of contradictory reports, especially relating to the situation around Mametz Wood. At 4.45 pm the diary records: '9th Devons report that they have no officers left. All reserve officers ordered up.' The 7th Division, attacking on the right flank of Sir Henry Rawlinson's Fourth Army, with the 18th and 30th Divisions on their right, capture all their early objectives in the morning and after hard fighting take Mametz village in the afternoon (captured by the Manchester Pals). Such is the success on this flank that Congreve, the Corps Commander, presses Rawlinson to allow a further advance supported by Indian cavalry. The refusal by Rawlinson to agree to his request remains one of the controversial aspects of the battle on this crucial first day.

A cousin of Bridgy's, Lieutenant Colonel J.A. Thicknesse (John) is killed in command of 1st Somerset Light Infantry in the 4th Division.

Grovetown ... to Citadel and Fricourt Cemetery.

It was a curious sensation going over the hill 'in full view' and looking over the country which one had never properly seen except through chinks and periscopes. Then to Ludgate and walked from there over the German trenches. The sight beggars all description. No trace of the trenches is left, craters took their place, dug outs were visible but fallen in and blocked. A good many British dead lying about just as they fell. None had been looted I'm glad to say. Went down to Mansel Copse where there were several bunches of dead. Saw heaps of German equipment and clothes where the bodies had disappeared. Realised that this had been 'no man's land'... I think the sight was the most impressive I have ever seen.

Monday 3rd July. Grovetown.

Went up to Mametz at 3pm to superintend the burial of the dead. Stuck it for some time, but was eventually nearly sick. The 9th Devons were buried in a trench by Mansel Copse. They held this trench, they hold it still ... The ground was mapped into 4 or 5 areas and the bodies buried in one trench in each area.

Tuesday 4th July. Grovetown.

A rather awful day. At 1pm a deluge came down and the whole valley was underwater. In a short time the whole place was a sea of mud ... There is more labour and worry about the evacuation of captured ordnance to 4th Army HQ than anything else. It would appear that the photographing of the captured ordnance is more important than getting on with the fighting.

The diary records the well-known story of repeated attacks at enormous cost and of hopes for a breakthrough dashed again and again.

Thursday July 20th. Minden Post [a forward tactical location].

Bombardment intensive for one hour before 4am, to which hour the time of the assault was changed. Our objective the road south east of High Wood. Everyone had great mistrust in this operation, as it seemed to be going back to old errors about attacking on small fronts. Losses were very heavy ... our objective was held for a time but was quite impossible to retain. At the end of the day we had gained nothing and lost heavily. It was a horrible day.

And so the Somme offensive grinds on, with 7th Division's operations recorded in some detail day by day:

Sunday 3rd September. Fricourt.

Bombardment continued, becoming intense at about 11am. Assault at noon. Very little news obtainable. Situation most obscure, but it seems certain that at one time we were right through Guinchy but that Ale Alley and the Eastern corner of Delville Wood were never taken. This was probably in great measure the cause of the rather terrible losses and almost failure of the operation. 22nd Brigade lost very heavily and ceased to exist as a fighting unit.

Monday 4th September. Fricourt.

20th Brigade carried out a relief but are still losing very heavily. The loss is becoming absolutely tragic. There is now no chance of the Division taking part in the big show on the 12th. They are very nearly done. Attack after attack was carried out with very little to show for it, but the corner of Delville Wood was taken which was something. 9th Devons and 2nd Borders had heavy casualties. The Gordons, one last unused up battalion, are going to make a final effort in a night attack tonight.

Tuesday 5th September. Fricourt.

One of the blackest days we have had. We were pushed out of Ale Alley and the losses against Guinchy are very appalling, and nothing whatsoever was accomplished as far as one can see. The GOC went to see the Corps Commander to protest against the way in which the Division was being butchered for no purpose. Everyone very depressed. Two officers of Royal Irish came in having been in Stout trench holding out for three days without water or food. The description of our loss was rather terrible. However they were able to give most valuable information.

Wednesday 6th September. Fricourt.

Asquith came and visited Fricourt. One shell went over while he was there. He merely looked like a stuffed owl and made a few remarks.

Monday 11th September. Ribemont. Albert. Hallencourt.

Went to the Loop at Bray, as we had heard that the new caterpillar landships were there. Found them and was enormously impressed. They are 30 ft long, armoured all over with ½ steel plate, travel 7mph on good roads and about 2mph in trenches and craters. Have a crew of nine, including one officer and two mechanics. The 'males' have 2 Hotchkiss, one on each side, and the 'females' two machine guns in their place. They were just like little battleships in miniature, most wonderfully and perfectly made, and I hope will be a complete surprise to the Bosche.

On 11 September, a cousin of Reggie's is killed, Second Lieutenant Ronald Carrier Tompson of the Grenadier Guards.

Saturday 23rd September. Bailleul.

Bad fit of depression all day. Prospects so frightfully gloomy. Probably one will have to go back to a battery which is an easier life and less work, but after over two years hard work at this job with nothing to show for it, it comes very hard to start again, as no credit will be given presumably for past work in another line. Also the prospect of dropping about £300 a year does not seem a very pleasant reward for any good one may have done. Altogether most depressing.

On Sunday, 22 October, Reggie joins 166 Battery at Hebuterne, supporting the 33rd Division. 'How anyone escapes the shelling I can't think. I got into a shelter and hoped for the best' is an early comment.

Other extracts include the following: 'A very wet night. Wet clothes and dugout full of mud.'

'Went up to forward OP which took about an hour and a half to reach. Mud and water in trenches. Very bad. Heavy shelling but OP was comparatively left alone.'

'Two of our aeroplanes came down, one in flames. It was a ghastly sight. The men jumped out at a great height.'

'We had a bad doing with gas shells. Bosche put over a continuous stream from a gun battery. We had three men badly gassed. Two were sent to the Dressing Station after we had dosed them with whiskey and ammonia. About midnight we had a still heavier shelling. Two more of our best Sergeants were gassed. This is getting serious ... the gas was very poisonous and strong.'

'Went to the forward OP at about 2. This was most unpleasant. The Bosche was shelling most uncomfortably.'

'Went down to the OP in the Quarries and for the first time it was shelled. Stuck it for a bit but it was so persistent and all round that I cleared the signallers out and went down the trench for a bit. Had hardly got back when they dropped a 4.2 about 10 yds from our OP, smothering us with mud and stones.'

'Everything seems to be indefinitely postponed, and the wet and mud are awful.'

'Each battalion one meets seems to be totally ignorant of their trenches, let alone the Bosche line, having only just arrived. Everyone always seems to have just arrived [in the front line]'

'Can't make out whether the show which was to take place is to fizzle out or not. The front trenches are so bad that it is practically impossible to assault from them. They are over the thighs in water. Wish we could know one way or the other, as then one would know better how much work to put in on this place.'

On Monday, 6 November, after only two weeks in command of his Battery, Reggie is wounded:

Got up at 6.30 and went to OP near Quarries. Came back to breakfast at 1030am. Was seeing about things in the Battery and dugout when got hit in the side. Felt just as if someone had swung at and hit me with a sledgehammer, knocked down. Pain in side (left). Stretcher party was at hand at once and was carried off. Was very frightened while being carried over such a regularly crumped part. Turner hit in chest and Higgins in leg by same shell. First field dressing put on by

41

gunner and was dressed at Dressing Station in Hebuterne with many others in deep dugout. Put on one side in a row with others.

Reggie is moved by Motor Ambulance to Couin and the next day to Saulty, thence by ambulance train to Le Treport.

In a perfect fever of anxiety as to what is going to happen to me, as there was some talk of some being marked for England. In the evening the Doctor came and told me he had marked me. I thanked him all I knew how, but I had a lump in the throat from delight. Could have cried for joy, in fact nearly did.

Reggie is allocated to Queen Alexandra's Hospital, Highgate. On arrival: 'Had Bridgy telephoned for and she came at once. It was the climax of a long and not unhappy journey to get her at the journey's end.'

There is shrapnel close to Reggie's spine and the doctors seemed to be divided three ways on whether to remove it from the front, the back or the side. Then on 20 November comes a visit from Queen Alexandra that only seems to add to the confusion:

The Queen arrived at about 3.45 and Bridgy about the same time. At 4.15 the Queen still had not arrived (in the Ward) and my precious time which I get with Bridgy was slipping by. Got very cross and told Nurse, who seemed to think that this visit was the most enormous treat, that I'd sooner see Bridgy than fourteen Queens. This yarn apparently went through the Hospital! At about 4.30 Queen Alexandra came into my room. I bowed in bed and she came up and held out her hand to shake. She spoke very indistinctly and foreign and was difficult at times to understand. She is very deaf and one had to shout. She got hold of the wrong end of the stick and would have it that the shrapnel had been taken out. I tried to explain for some time, but by remarks she made I could see she hadn't got it, so at last I gave in and pretended the shrapnel was out. Just then Miss Knollys explained to her and we had to begin again, amidst much laughter! Dr Patterson showed her the X ray photograph and she was much interested, very sympathetic and most kind and gracious. One can understand why everyone loves her so much. Shortly after she left and went to the next ward, but Princess Victoria, Miss Vivian and Miss Knollys remained talking to me, all being most charming. While they were talking it somehow transpired or rather they found out that Bridgy was being kept out till they had gone. At once they were all distressed and said 'send for her at once, and let her come in'. Bridgy was outside and came in immediately but as they had told her that only Miss Knollys was with me she was a good deal non-plussed to find Princess Victoria, whom naturally she did not know or recognise, and didn't know whether it was anybody or nobody. However the Princess didn't seem to mind that she didn't curtsy or anything, and was very charming and nice to her which I liked. Bridgy was allowed to stay extra time till about 5.25 owing to having had only short time.

A few days later comes the operation to remove the shrapnel and by early December Reggie is on the road to recovery, although there is a considerable wound that needs time to heal.

Wednesday 6th December.

Mother turned up unexpectedly with Bridgy to my great delight. Asquith resigned. Bucharest in extremis. Bridgy brought me some bananas.

On the 7th, the death occurred of Reggie's uncle, Major General William Dalrymple Tompson. Reggie writes in his diary: 'Was very sorry about it, as I feel I have now lost the one standby who was always there for advice. He died without pain, poor old man, one of the kindest and most selfless men that ever lived.

On 20 December the diary comments: 'Read Lloyd George's speech with great satisfaction,' and on the 22nd: 'President Wilson's extraordinary note published, everyone amazed and angry.' On 24 December, 'Peace Sunday', Reggie responds with: 'Peace be blowed!' as he marks the day when he gets up for the first time and feels very weak. Bridgy meanwhile is feeling unwell and faints in church. She is pregnant. On the 28th, Reggie records that he 'made a dummy in my bed which Nurse Davies came and tried to rouse, saying she wanted to make the bed. I was outside the window. She went to fetch another nurse saying she couldn't get me up. Great success.'

1917

Thursday 4th January.

(Dr) Paterson came in the evening and had a long talk. He told me some amusing stories of Sir John French's visit to the hospital. Apparently his brain did not rise to more than one remark only in the twenty-two rooms he visited. This remark was 'Capital place you have got here.'

Sunday 7th January.

After lunch walked down to the tram to meet Bridgy and walked round the ponds with her, she came back and stayed as usual till 5 – the last time of so many faithful and loving visits.

Reggie leaves hospital the following day and they travel to Bussage near Stroud, where they stay until 9 February in a guest house run by Mrs Griffiths. Reggie's growing enthusiasm for bird-watching is fostered, while in the evenings he reads to Bridgy and plays the piano while she sings. They spend a weekend at Byford near Hay on Wye, where Reggie's sister Winnie's husband is the Curate. Irene, his youngest sister, is also there (another clergyman's wife!).

Sunday 28th January. Byford.

We all went to the 11 o'clock. A very nice little church, looks as if it were Norman inside. Winnie played ... The small boys who formed the group of 'singers' round the organ at the bottom of the Church were a source of great amusement. One child had a voice like nothing on earth, a penetrating rasp. Irene called him the Bee. During one hymn she asked Winnie gravely at the organ, 'Shall I stop the Bee, or shall I keep him on for his volume?'

Back at Mrs Griffiths', Reggie records that her soldier son bicycles 52 miles from Warminster in cold January weather to see her, and 52 miles back the following day. He also notes his battle with the geyzer: "Had a go at the geyzer and though it worked fairly correctly, the water was barely tepid. They are the most loathsome things geyzers and I wanted to smash it.'

On Friday, 9 February they travel by train to Newbury and spend a night in the Lidden Hotel before taking over Paddock Cottage, Newtown, where they will live for the rest of the War and where their first child, Josephine, is born in July. Their brief stay at the Lidden Hotel has its moments:

Went up to our room and then down for tea. Found ourselves in a sort of general sitting room and exchanging pleasantries with the guests, a genteel, pink-eyed Mrs Rolland and a rather seedy old man. The former presided over the teapot. At the earliest opportunity we escaped ... decided we could not bear supper though finally decided they would be hurt ... but the gentility was awful, and one could not talk their talk. 'I noticed how wondrous lustrous the stars are tonight,' for example.

While Reggie struggles with the bureaucracy of medical boards, they settle down in Paddock Cottage, Newtown.

Thursday March 22nd.

Went at 7 to the chicken farm and met Mrs Sumples carrying 3 clucking hens. Dogs excited and snapping at them. Went into her house, one brown hen got out, pursued by Jug. Collared Rik and held him. Went to call Jug but no reply. Had heard what might have been a chase through the bushes ... After selecting our hens, we went back and Mrs Sumples started looking for her missing hen. I had a torch and searched for it. Saw in field some way off what might have been Jug ... found him standing eating amidst a disembowelled hen. Carried Jug home, put in stable and thrashed.

In April Reggie returns to France and spends most of the rest of this year on the staff in Lyon and Paris, before being posted in November 1917 to Tortona, 50 miles south of Milan, on the staff of the Italian Expeditionary Force, following the Italian defeat by the Austrians at Caporetto. He is on leave in Newtown in October during the final weeks of the Battle of Passchendaele, where his brother-in-law Frank is serving as a heavy battery commander.

Chapter Four

Frank Thicknesse, Passchendaele, 1917

'Miles Pacificus
Strenuus Fidelis
Et Deo Devotus'

Grave No. XXV.K.14
Lijssenthoek Military Cemetery
Near Poperinghe, Ypres

Reggie's diary for Monday, 22 October 1917:

Bicycled into Newbury and caught 8.40 train. At Paddington saw Mr Thicknesse on the platform and saw at once that something was wrong. He said in a very broken voice, 'He's gone, Reggie.' I said 'Not Frank, don't say Frank,' and he said 'Yes, he was killed on the 19th. The telegram came whilst we were at church, and Joyce and Henry [Montgomery Campbell, Bridgy's sister and brother-in-law] who had been to another church found it on their return. Joyce told Mrs Thicknesse and Henry told me.' I went with him in the Tube as far as Oxford St and there he left. He was utterly broken and crying terrible sobs. I arranged to tell Bridgy when I got back, poor darling, but I'd sooner tell her than let her get a wire ... Caught the 7.30pm back and bicycled home. Bridgy met me and I pushed the bike into the bathroom, wondering how I could tell her. But she knew at once something was wrong, so I took her into the study and told her as gently as I could. Poor treasure she was heartbroken. I led her up to bed ... and told the nurse that she couldn't nurse Josie again just yet ... Poor Bridgy cried all night and got very little sleep. I tried to comfort her as best I could but couldn't do much.

Frank, Bridgy's oldest brother, is born in 1886. He is a Scholar at Winchester College (3rd on the Roll) and passes 2nd into the RMA

Woolwich in 1904, subsequently joining the Royal Artillery. He serves in Hong Kong between 1907 and 1915, passing examinations in colloquial Chinese (two dialects) and in Hindustani, Lower and Higher Standard. After much lobbying, he gets to the Western Front in May 1915 and commands 122 Heavy Battery for the next two years. The Battery takes part in many of the great battles, Frank is twice mentioned in despatches and is awarded the DSO in June 1917.

He is hit by a splinter of high explosive when up looking for a new OP in the Ypres neighbourhood, and dies that night in the Casualty Clearing Station (CCS) at Lijssenthoek, where he is buried. It is now the second largest Commonwealth War Cemetery in Belgium. A slim leather-backed book is printed by his family, from which these letters, written to his mother and father, are taken:

The Revd H.S.S. Clarke writes from the CCS:

I am very sorry indeed to have to tell you that your son, Major F.W. Thicknesse, died in this Hospital last evening at 11.20pm.

He was brought here about 9.30 – very badly hit. I have just had a talk with the admitting medical officer who says that he was so bad that it was impossible and useless to examine him thoroughly ... He was, I understand, just conscious for a time, and died quietly at 11.20. Unfortunately I had left the ward at 8 for mess, and had two hours correspondence to see to before going back to the camp: and when I arrived at 11.20 I found your son had just that minute passed away. I was very sorry.

I did two little things I thought perhaps his people would like; I cut a little lock of hair from his brow, and put to his lips a little crucifix – both of which I enclose with this letter. I also enclose a little cutting of verbena which as coming from this place you may care to have.

A subaltern in your son's unit – Cotteril – came down this morning (he had great difficulty in finding out where he had been taken) and stayed for the funeral which I took this afternoon in the soldiers' cemetery, Lijssenthoek by name...

It was to this same Hospital that your other son was brought when he was wounded, I understand [Cuthbert, an army chaplain]. I need not say how deeply I sympathise with you and Mrs Thicknesse in your loss ... Later, if I am still here, I can see if you like to have the grave being kept tidy.

In a subsequent letter written by the Revd Clarke on the following day, he says that Frank was 'quite calm, brave and uncomplaining', and talks about the cemetery as 'a quiet and beautiful place where thousands of little crosses speak of sacrifice and victory'. He goes on to say that 'You will not mind my saying perhaps that the medical officer who operated on your other son [Cuthbert] says that he has never known so bad a thigh do so well, and he partly attributes his good recovery to his coolness and grit.'

Other letters:

John Leigh, of 122 Heavy Battery:

I am writing to offer you and Mrs Thicknesse the deepest sympathies of all officers and men in the battery on the death of your son. We have served under his command for over two years now and cannot give him sufficient praise as a soldier or a man. His death is a loss to the battery that can never be made up ... One of his subalterns lies close to him.

Major Douglas Clapham:

It was with great sorrow that I saw your boy's name in the casualty lists last week. Though I cannot claim to have been an intimate friend, I knew him well from the time he joined till 1912; and in common with all others who knew him looked on him as a man of quite exceptional ability and promise, added to a strength of character which made him a great influence for good wherever he served. I know no one of his contemporaries whom we could so ill afford to lose: he was a very perfect gentleman.

Lt Col C.H.W. Owen:

I only saw about your great loss in a belated paper, and as your son was under me from the time he left Ypres until he again left the Somme to return to Ypres, I feel I should like to let you know what a very high opinion I had of him. He was a first class soldier and battery commander, absolutely fearless, and one could always leave him a job to do knowing it would be done well ... We can ill spare officers like him from the Royal Regiment [RA].

A.G. Haig:

I don't suppose anything I say can add to the pride which you already have in him, but his vigorous personality and habitual gallantry had made him well known throughout the Artillery out here, and had earned a great reputation for the battery of which he and I were so proud.

Captain Arthur Roberts RE to Mrs Thicknesse:

He was a very dear friend of mine, and you better than anybody can understand why, nor is there need for me to say more, only those who knew and understood him can appreciate their loss ... I saw much of him in our careless care-free days in China, he and Bagnall spent many cheery days in my quarters at Shelung, and I used to put up at the R.A. Mess when I went to Hong Kong: our friendship grew up amongst dogs and ponies – our own and each others – and we always understood one another and them. There are a thousand of the little incidents and amusing things one meets as one goes through life we shared in common, and that will remain to me as very dear memories of him. And there are many friends of his and mine that will always share them with me, and share too my deep sorrow at his loss.

Second Lieutenant Maurice Gelli:

I have just heard with deepest sorrow and regret of the death of my Major. He had been my Commanding Officer from the early part of this year until six weeks ago, when I was sent home with a smashed arm.

I was hoping to serve under his command again shortly, but recent events have made 122 Heavy Battery too bitter a memory for me to return there for choice.

... He was certainly one of the bravest men I ever met, and his sense of duty, and method of carrying it out, was a great example to all officers and men.

As Battery Observation Officer, my work during the last two months carried me into more than average danger, but never any danger that my O.C. did not willingly share, an example which did an enormous lot to help me in my work. I know that there are many, many sad hearts in France at the loss of a gallant soldier and friend. If there is a finer O.C. Battery in France I should like to serve under him, but I doubt it ...

England has lost one of her finest soldiers, and I have lost the most highly honourable and most gallant O.C. I shall ever have.

Molly Hancock, almost as if she is in love with him, to Mrs Thicknesse:

I know how many, many letters you will have, but just some day, will you write to me, or one of your daughters, and tell me all you can about Major Thicknesse? I do so long to know everything about him, and how his very gallant life ended. For you, who have given your great sacrifice, I feel there must be a wonderful happiness in having made anything so fine, and dear, and human and so wholly what a man should be. Such a vivid and living personality to his friends, and such a consummated soldier's life, filled, in its short span, with so large a share of life's experiences, <u>lived</u> anyhow, before he died. The very finest type. He loved you so much, and found you wonderful and perfect, and was so extraordinarily nice to women because of you. I saw what mothers could be, and what they meant, and how they coloured a man's life, through him. It is a great piece of life's work, well accomplished. For the desolation and blank, my heart aches. I feel so dreadfully sad in thinking of you all. Dear Mrs Thicknesse, it seems unbearable and unbelievable. We loved him. I feel he is not far from us all. He saw my tiny new babies, he used to come and dine with us on Sunday evenings in Hong Kong, and my eldest little girl and I used to watch him play polo, and pet his horses, and take no interest in any of the proceedings if he was not there. She is so devoted to him that I cannot write and tell her at school, but I must wait till I have her with me, and comfort her. He used to sing on those evenings when he dined with us, and I have such happy memories of him, and a thousand jokes, and human, happy things. It is such a grief and heaviness. This sort of friend it is a bitterness to lose, one does not make them again. I wish I could see you and talk to you. Do you remember when he, Marybud (my little girl) and I came to tea with you last winter? Our love to you and all thoughts. May I come and see you some day? It would be comforting.

Major Harold Paris, 138 Heavy Battery, RGA:

Dear old 'Copper' as he used to be to us in Hong Kong, was always one of my very best friends ... We never had the luck to run across each other out here, but only a short time ago I heard news of him from a mutual Hong Kong friend, and he confirmed to me the opinion which had reached me from many sources before, that your son's battery was <u>the tip top</u> heavy battery, and that he had made a great name for himself out here .He was every inch a soldier, and in his life and death has set us all a fine example, and it is up to those of us who are fortunate enough to be left to carry on, to see that his great sacrifice is honoured, and that we carry right through to the very end the cause for which he has so nobly died.

H.S. Cotterill, 1/1 Nottinghamshire Yeomanry, attached to 122 Heavy Bty:

This is not a letter from a commanding officer to a father upon his son being killed in action, it is the other way round. Your son was my O.C., and I feel I must write and tell you just what he was to all of us, his subalterns, and to me in particular. I shall miss him most tremendously, long after peace has come again, for though he was my O.C. he was a very dear pal of mine. We had planned many an outing together for 'after the war'. If my grief is so great at losing him that I find, though I have started this letter, I have nothing to say, yours must be terrible.

I was in time to give him a last salute. The captain and another officer arrived a few minutes after, for unfortunately these things have to be done at once out here. The loss to the Battery is immense, and it is such a great loss to his country – his country he served so well, so gallantly, so eagerly. And I have lost a pal as dear as a brother ... I will see that a fitting cross is erected in his memory. It makes me hate this war a thousand-fold more than ever that it should take such splendid sportsman and gallant capable officer as he. I know he would have gone very far in his profession.

On 9 December, T.M. Harland writes to Reggie from 434 (Siege) Battery, about Frank's last day before being mortally wounded, out looking for new OP positions in support of his guns:

I am very pleased to be able to write again in answer to your letter. And I understand how valuable to you all the little incidents of that day are, for to me there was nothing anyone here ever said more treasured than my Major's last words to me. They epitomise his whole attitude and his point of view in life at that time. And since, I have always thought of them with one little incident which occurred on our outward journey. I slipped on a mule track near a passing pony and the Major at once stooped to help me up again with a smile and the words 'Not hurt surely?' – he was always cheery! Two incidents of the time we spent on the ridge stand out above others. One was the crawling across the main Passchendaele Road as close to the ground as we could, just to drop into a shell hole on the other side in time: and then only to get out of that one, two minutes before a shell dropped just where we had been. As we crawled away to the right the Major remarked that we appeared to have discovered a very unhealthy spot. Eventually we re-crossed the road in a similar manner but without drawing any fire and pushed on towards the village and the spot where the line crossed the road. We tried numerous spots from which to observe but found nothing satisfactory and were stood folding up the map when a Bosche plane dropped out of the clouds and turned his machine gun on us. When he had gone the Major rose quickly and with a smile said 'Let's push on from this spot. I don't like it.' Before getting in sight of the duck-boards again we stumbled across an Australian bivouac. The Major stopped and spoke to the men and asked them what the nights were like, and when we left called out as we turned away, 'Good day, you fellows, good luck to you!' The knowledge that I have been some little help to you is a joy for me and though I hope I never have another day like that day, I am glad I served with one, who will ever draw my admiration, and served with him at the last also.

Frank is remembered, too, in the War Cloister at Winchester College.

Chapter Five

Reggie and Bridget Tompson, 1918–37

At the beginning of 1918 Reggie is still based in Tortona, south of Milan:

January 10th Thursday.

Caught the train to Padova at 1155. Had a sleeper ... But Smith slept in the bottom berth and wasn't aware of the unwritten but irrevocable law that the man in the top berth <u>must</u> turn in first. So I sat on him while undressing which is the inevitable result of breaking this rule.

February 11 Monday.

Had a disastrous letter from Bridgy saying all the drains were wrong and that the sewage had leaked into and of course polluted the well. She and Josie are clearing out at once to the Cottage. The whole business is most alarming and nerve shattering as I can do nothing here and am very anxious.

February 14th.

Sent Bridgy a Valentine – my Leonardo da Vinci postcard off my looking glass.

February 21st Thursday.

During the journey to Turin, I got, for a time, one of the trap seats in the passage. I stood up for a minute and an Italian promptly sat down in it pretending to take only half. I was furious and sat down on a corner and wormed my way bit by bit on to the seat. At last I got him off and as soon as I had got the seat I called an Italian woman who was down the passage and made her have the seat, thereby scoring heavily off the Italian.

Sunday 10th March. [Returning after leave.]

Bridgy just the same as always on these occasions, refusing to show what it is meaning. Somehow I felt this time as if this were the last time possible I could do it. I feel I've borne this going away as far as I can.

Friday 15th March.

In the evening there was a party of 12 to dinner at the Chateau Brunskill and great fun it was. We tobogganed down the stairs in the bath, danced, played blind man's buff, and Up Jenkins and I don't know what. Mrs Monty Browne and the two Italian girls, Maria and another, and an American (Elsie) were there. It was a regular romp. The odd thing is that the Italian girls would no more have come if it had been Italian officers than flown, but there is no doubt that they trust the British officer in quite a different way. [An unbiased view of course!]

The German spring offensive is under way. Their attacks continue intermittently for the next three months, but by July the offensive is spent, and in late July and August Allied strategy coalesces under Foch's command, with the Americans under General Pershing at last beginning to weigh in heavily.

Friday 22nd March.

Got the wire that the Bosche attack had begun yesterday morning on a 50 mile front north and south of the River Somme ... It seems to have had limited success with very heavy losses.

Thursday 4th April.

Felt rotten all day, the old feeling of being rattled and overworked is coming over me.

On 23 May he leaves Italy and joins GHQ at Montreuil.

Tuesday 28th May.

The news not good. The Bosche made good his attack on the Chemin des Dames [on the line of the River Aisne between Soissons and Craonne] and has penetrated about 12 miles ... 9th Corps has lost 120 guns. They fought well and were especially praised ... It is rumoured that the Bosche has concentrated 50 divisions! Our Intelligence is left gaping again!

Wednesday 29th May.

The Bosche is in Soissons. Goodness where is he going to stop!

Friday 31st May.

Bosche aircraft succeeded in cutting the bridge at Etaples and doing a lot of wretched civilians in. All women and children killed in one house and 3 children of 7, 5 and 18 months (a whole family) in another, the mother and father being unhurt.

Wednesday 12th June.

Find the old man living here and his 2 small daughters and small son come from Bethune. 'Bethune n'existe plus' they say ... A perfectly heavenly day, cool and delicious, another golden day utterly wasted out of one's life by this grinding wretched war.

Sunday 7th July.

Saw Hughie Ellis who described the great success of his tanks at Hamel [on the Somme]. Everyone got back, only 14 men wounded and one killed. None destroyed. The tanks had carried up 40 tons of ammunition onto the final objective. He stated that the German infantry surrendered fairly easily, but the machine gunners refused to surrender and had to be driven over and squashed. Even when wounded they refused to give in.

Friday 12th July.

Felt so miserable, that I lost interest in everything. Utterly wretched and apart from wanting to see Bridgy and Josie, I don't think my brain will stand it. It's been a question for some time whether I'll stick another week without breaking down.

Sunday 21st July.

Went to celebration at 7am, taken by a truly dreadful person who sounded his aspirates with great and pronounced efforts and did not light the candles.

Saturday17th August.

End of leave. Black day of black days. It's never been worse than this time but its got to be stuck somehow. Josie came down dressed in her best as a treat and sat at our table at breakfast next to me and Bridgy in her high chair which her Granny gave her. She wasn't a bit afraid of me in uniform and picked at my bright medal ribbons ... The usual heartbreaking time, and I was almost glad when the train left.

Friday 23rd August.

A day of great excitement. News wonderfully good. Bosche in a very bad way. The first signs of a crack appear to be visible. A Bavarian division opposite the French broke and fled yesterday, carrying another German division with it. All their guns were left and captured.

Tuesday 27 August.

Canadians and part of 1st Army have got for the first time into ground where we have never been since the War began ... everyone on tenterhooks awaiting the Yankee push.

Friday 13th September.

News magnificent. The Americans have really succeeded in biting off the St Michel salient and have captured 20,000 prisoners ... Got a very sad letter from Bridgy which made me miserable.

Saturday 21st September.

Afternoon, got attack of nerves. Had too much work and couldn't compete with it.

Friday 27th September.

Telephone message arrived during the morning that Bulgaria had asked for an armistice (which was refused) and for PEACE. The whole place was electrified. It is not yet confirmed but it is believed to be true. Infinite possibilities can easily be foreseen. If Bulgaria, then Turkey must be cut off and Austria eventually threatened.

Sunday 6th October.

Great excitement owing to its becoming known that the Bosche had wired by Holland to President Wilson with a view to opening an Armistice to discuss peace on the terms of President Wilson's 14 Points.

Friday 11th October.

Had a sudden inspiration to make a long round to see Frank's grave. I knew it was near Poperinghe so made for there. Roads very busy and congested. Got Town Major to phone the Graves Commission to find out where it was, and went off again and found it. Brought some flowers away from the cemetery which was a bewildering mass of graves.

Sunday 13th October.

Things moved fast today. Yesterday Wilson's 14 Points were accepted by the Bosche in principle; anything may happen now. Pray God he doesn't get off too cheap, after all he has done. Rumour that Foch's terms for an armistice is for half the Bosche Army to lay down their arms, for all to retire to the east of the Rhine, to give up three bridge-heads on the Rhine and a belt of 30 miles beyond. If true of course he can never accept.

Saturday 26th October.

Heard to my great grief that Du Boulay AQMG 3rd Army had died suddenly as a result of influenza. It is very serious, eight or nine men have died in the French Mission.

Sunday 27th October.

Wireless says Ludendorff has resigned, everyone fell to speculating what this might portend. News from Hungary and Austria is also curious. Persistent reports of riots, insurrections, demands for peace, etc ... Some bold spirit offered to bet that the last round of the war would be fired within the next 168 hours.

Monday 4th November.

A very big attack was let off today, 3rd, 5th and 1st Armies and they achieved great success. Rumour has it that there were 14,000 prisoners and a big advance. Simultaneously the Americans have really achieved great success in the Argonne. Can't help thinking a break will come soon. Austria concluded an armistice at 3pm, so that only Germany is left. The Bosche published the most priceless piece of impudence (through Switzerland) proposing that all bombing behind the line should cease as they have done (sic!) to save historical monuments. Lovely!

Tuesday 5th November.

The operations went with a swing today. In fact touch with Divisions was all but lost, they are advancing so fast. Likewise the Americans, and disaster is staring Germany in the face.

Thursday 7th November.

The German parliamentaire is expected to cross the line at 12 noon and to be at Foch's Headquarters at Senlis at 4pm to receive the terms of the Armistice. All firing ceased on the road to Guise by which he is expected from about 10 am. The air was thick with rumours, and with them came the news of the mutiny of the German Fleet at Kiel, shooting their officers and taking charge of the ships. Altogether a thrilling time and the end is close.

Saturday 9th November.

Our troops are close to Mons and very little of France remains German. The time for accepting or refusing the Armistice expires at 11am on Monday (Nov 11th). The German wireless reports the abdication of the Kaiser and Crown Prince, so the game may now safely said to be up. What a headlong termination to what has for four years looked like a deadlock.

Sunday 10th November.

Situation looks very like Bolshevism, but not quite. Intercepted German wireless directed delegates to sign Armistice and ask that food stuffs in German territories might not be taken or German population would starve ... an inglorious end for the Bosche.

Monday 11th November.

Armistice signed at 11am. We don't know the terms, but I believe they are pretty awful for the Bosche. The bells began ringing early in the morning, and people turned out and started to cheer. Flags appeared from every window and the whole atmosphere changed with an electricity of utter relief and thankfulness. There was a tremendous amount of work and one's very soul turned from it all, but it had to be done ... A very cheery evening but it was spoilt by the idiocy of the Administrator of the Women's Auxiliary Army Corps (WAACs) who refused to let them dance. The Canadians and certain RAF officers became rather obstreperous and made things worse but the room was eventually cleared ... A very boisterous evening.

Tuesday 12th November.

The Bosche is more thoroughly smashed than anyone imagined I think. Think of the thousands who have said Germany can never be defeated, best make what terms one can ... the crowned heads in the states of Germany are falling like ninepins and at present the moderate Socialists hold what power there is. The possibility is that following the precedent of France '89 and Russia last year, the extremists will succeed to power and then the trouble will begin.

Saturday 21st December.

Am about at the end of my tether. Can hardly take in anything or understand anything. Brain absolutely fagged out and done. However there is only one more day before I get to Bridgy who will make all the difference.

Monday 23rd December.

London very different, lighter and happier altogether.

Wednesday 25th December. Paddock Cottage, Newtown.

Church at 7.30. Hard frost and everything looking absolutely lovely. It was not light yet and there were the most wonderful colours blue and black and red in the sky and woods. Christmas Dinner (the first Christmas Day I have spent with Bridgy). This was a great success. Josie [now 17 months old] came down for tea, and afterwards we went and lighted up her little Christmas tree and played with her till 5.30 when she had her bath and was put to bed. A very happy Christmas day.

Tuesday 31st December.

Dined early and at about 8 Molly Henecker and Jack Burnett called for us in a taxi and we went to Mrs Justice's dance, arriving first. Quite a good dance, the first I've had since the war and therefore the first I've danced with Bridgy as my wife.

Reggie is mentioned in despatches six times during the War, and is awarded the CMG (Commander of St Michael and St George) in 1918, as well as the Italian Holy Order of the Crown (4th class) and the French Croix de Guerre. He remains in France on the staff, now as a brevet Lieutenant Colonel working on the demobilization process, accompanied by Bridgy and Josephine from April, until October 1919. They live at Wimille, near Wimereux and Boulogne. Reggie serves on in the Army until his death from cancer in 1937, including a period as Deputy Commandant of the RMA, Woolwich ('The Shop') between 1921 and 1926. William Pike (Willie) is a cadet there from 1923 to 1924, and first meets his future wife Josie, then aged seven, when he is invited to tea by Colonel and Mrs Tompson.

Reggie maintains his diary for the rest of his life, which includes happy family times at Rawalpindi, Chester and Benson in Oxfordshire. Hew is born in 1920 and Penelope (Penel) in 1922. On their way down the Red Sea to India in 1928, they receive by telegram the news of the death of Bridgy's sister Joyce from pneumonia, following the birth of her youngest daughter. Joyce's husband, Henry Montgomery Campbell, who had won a Military Cross as a chaplain on the Western Front, never remarries, going on to become successively Bishop of Willesden, Kensington, Guildford and London, and remaining very close to Bridgy throughout his life. Reggie is a Major General in command of the 1st Anti-Aircraft Division (TA) in London when he is taken ill in 1937. His diary entry for 25 May records: 'Got Ogle to take the divisional conference as I felt too

59

bad.' The entry for the next day is in Bridgy's writing and just says: 'B returned'. Thereafter there are records of his medical progress, the last entry for 19 August simply states: 'Left Millbank (Hospital)'. The diary thereafter is blank. He dies on 11 October 1937.

In General Sir Frederick Pile's memoirs of his time in Anti-Aircraft Command, he recalls General Ironside, the CIGS at the time, saying to him as another war loomed: 'Pile, your predecessor, Tompson, killed himself because he never took a day off. I do not want you to kill yourself. You will need some leave, and I suggest you take it by going down to the TA Practice Camps.'

Reggie's great sense of humour and pithy turn of phrase is well illustrated in his notes for a speech made at a Merton College dinner in October 1934:

> You have done a great honour not only to me, but also to my brutal and licentious and much maligned profession by asking me to propose this toast ... My only claim to scholastic fame during those wonderful three years of my life was the winning of a prize for an essay entitled 'Erasmus. His attitude to the Reformation'. I read that famous essay over again last week, and I was much surprised. I won a £5 prize, with which I bought a bulldog with four legs. The only way I can account for this is that there was only one other runner, and he unfortunately exceeded the time limit, which I remember having had the utmost difficulty to reach ...
>
> The toast I am giving you needs delicate handling. If I were to refer to any individual, some forty others might quite rightly feel they had been overlooked ... For the two unforgivable crimes in an after dinner speech are (a) boring your listeners (b) hurting anyone's feelings. Then there are the reminiscences of the speaker. These usually come under (a) and are the most deadly dull of all subjects. One might so easily say, 'There was A. He became a Diplomatist. Then there was B. He was a fool too. C became a great financier. D is also in prison. How well I remember E. He won a Croix de Guerre. F never heard a shot fired either.'
>
> But all these are things of long ago. The Domestic Bursar wrote to me and said that Mertonians wanted to hear my views. But he did not say on what. And as it is popularly supposed that all British generals are solid bone from the eyebrows upward, it is improbable that they possess any 'views' ... The Army is a very small affair today, and there are many in this country who would like to have it so small that it could not be seen. They grudgingly admit the necessity for an army of sorts but they are inclined to deny it the implements to carry out

its job. I sometimes wonder whether these good people, if about to undergo an operation for appendicitis, would desire that the surgeon should be equipped only with a rusty table knife.

On his death, a number of generous tributes were published, from which these are extracts:

From *RA Regimental News*, November 1937, written by W.S and R..B.:

His character was so straightforward, clean and honest, his humour so pungent and witty, his laugh so spontaneous and unaffected that he was universally loved, honoured and respected. Thus he was very human, utterly unselfish and devoid of any suspicion of side. His work in those days was marked by the thoroughness and enthusiasm with which he tackled it, by the drive with which he carried it through, and by the cheerfulness which always pervaded everything he did ... His friends in the Regiment can only regret that after he passed the Staff College, his periods of Regimental duty were all too short. He was captain of the Merton Boat Club and earned his oar ... He had the knack of getting the best out of any crew in which he rowed, his enthusiasm was infectious ... and so he passed on ... leaving a memory of a loyal friend and a gallant gentleman.

From *The Times*, T.H.W. writes:

Although I knew Reggie Tompson all his life, I had not the privilege of sharing his school days at Winchester, but as schoolboy and man he always lived up to the Winchester motto in its truest sense. At Merton, from his unfailing sense of humour, accompanied by a child-like laugh, he soon became known to all his friends as 'The Babe', and his simple, straightforward character endeared him to all of us. He was an invaluable man from every point of view in the college boat, and in 1898, his second year, he rowed No. 3 in the (at that time) famous seven-bumper, of which crew only four of us are left, and later got his Trials Cap.

I believe that he was destined for some other career than the Army and that it was the South African War which influenced him in 1900 to apply for a university commission. He was posted to a Battery in Newcastle, and it was there that he was renamed and thenceforward known as 'Tompo'. It was with the Aro Expedition of 1902 that he was awarded the D.S.O. for bringing in one of his badly wounded native soldiers, having twice to swim across a river under heavy fire to effect the rescue. So started his military career, and that brave act of a very young officer ... was typical of his unselfish, steadfast and modest character, never sparing himself but always out to help others, whether as a staff or regimental officer or as an individual, and always seeing the humorous side of a situation. Whether known officially with the prefix of his successive military ranks or as 'The Babe', 'Tompo' or just 'Reggie', he was, for want of a better word, as 'popular' with his superiors and his subordinates as he was with his equals. His last two appointments naturally meant his attendance at many regimental and semi-public dinners, and I only recently learnt that he was an excellent after-dinner speaker, and again it is typical of him that he attended his last dinner of this nature though a sick man, and soon after the end of his speech he collapsed, and so began his long and fatal illness.

Another correspondent recalls that the seven-bumper Merton Eight also competed in the Ladies Plate and Thames Cup at Henley. What Tompson's keenness and sunny nature meant to a crew only those who rowed with him can fully appreciate.

Of his association with the Parish and living of Woodstone in Huntingdonshire, where his father had been the Rector from 1871 to 1898 and his grandfather from 1829 to 1871, a local obituary records that:

From the time he followed his uncle (Major General W.D. Tompson) in the patronage of the living, he evinced the keenest interest not only in the family property but in the affairs of the church generally. Twice this year he addressed the congregation from the pulpit on matters of church finance and organisation, and he frequently attended meetings of the Parochial Church Council to discuss and advise on money matters. Mrs Tompson opened a garden fete three years ago and her husband has attended several, principally in the capacity of chairman in recent years.

Reggie is buried in the grounds of St Albans Abbey, where his brother-in-law Cuthbert was then the Dean. His stone tomb is finely embellished with sword and crest, but the lettering around the edge is weathered and barely decipherable to those who do not know of him. Nearby is buried another Gunner officer, Captain Jim Philippson, of 7 RHA, killed with the Parachute Regiment's Battle Group (3 PARA) in Afghanistan whilst Will Pike is also serving with it, in 2006.

Chapter Six

Willie Pike, Dunkirk, 1940

William Pike, generally called Willie in the Army, but always Bill or Billy by his mother and brothers, wins a scholarship to Marlborough College, where he is hungry and not especially happy in the aftermath of the First World War. He enters the RMA Woolwich in 1923, where he does well. His future father-in-law Reggie, then the Deputy Commandant, records in his assiduous notes on each cadet that Pike 'got into trouble over a supper party and two bottles of whisky in W House. To hospital with "nausea" as a result.' Like both his parents, he is quite short and thrives as a scrum-half on the rugby field. He is commissioned into the Royal Artillery and spends most of the decade 1927–37 in India, a country and people for which he develops a deep and abiding love. He becomes an excellent horseman, playing polo, point-to-pointing, hunting and pig sticking. He attends the last two-year course at the Army Staff College, Camberley in the late 1930s.

On 5 September 1939, two days after the declaration of war, and now aged thirty-four, he marries Josie (Jo).

During the night of May 9/10 1940, German forces 'sprang forward towards France', to use Winston Churchill's phrase, across the frontiers of Belgium, Holland and Luxembourg. On 15 May Willie travels to France to join the Artillery staff of the British III Corps, as GSO2 to the Commander of the Corps Artillery (CCRA), Brigadier Bill Duncan. At 7.30 am that morning, the French Prime Minister M. Reynaud telephones Churchill to announce, 'We are defeated. We have lost the battle.'

Willie keeps a private daily account of the days that follow, which he writes up on twenty-seven closely typed pages, as a kind of

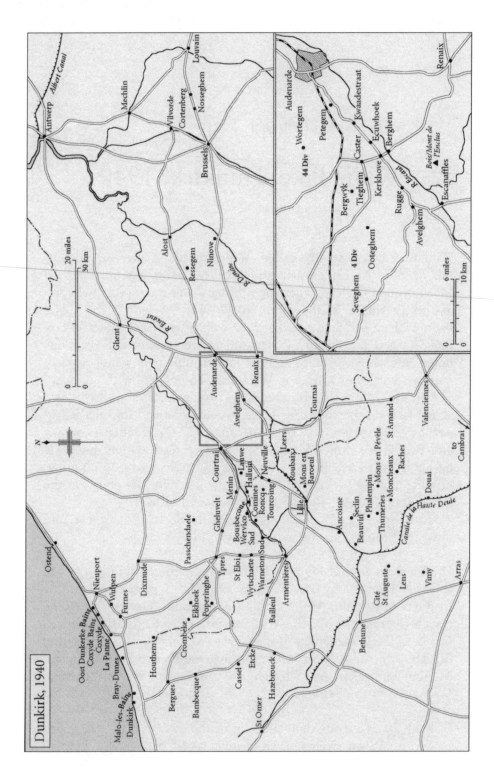

Dunkirk, 1940

20 miles
30 km

6 miles
10 km

N

Ostend
Oost Dunkerke Bains
Coxyde Bains
Coxyde
La Panne
Bray-Dunes
Malo-les-Bains
Dunkirk
Nieuport
Wulpen
Furnes
Bergues
Bambecque
Houthem
Crombeke
Eikhoek
Poperinghe
Cassel
Etcke
St Omer
Hazebrouck
Bailleul
Dixmude
Passchendaele
Ypres
St Eloi
Wytschaete
Warneton/Sud
Armentières
Gheluvelt
Menin
Bousbecque
Wervicq
Sud
Comines
Roncq
Tourcoing
Courtrai
Hallujn
Lanwe
Neuville
Lille
Roubaix
Leers
Mons en
Baroeul
Béthune
Cité
St Auguste
Ancoisne
Beauvin
Seclin
Lens
Vimy
Arras
Phalempin
Thumeries
Mons en Pevele
Moncheaux
Raches
St Amand
Valenciennes
to Cambrai
Douai
Canale de la Haute Deule
Tournai
Renaix
Avelghem
Audenarde
Ghent
R Escaut
R Dendre
Alost
Resegem
Ninove
Brussels
Mechlin
Vilvorde
Cortenberg
Nosseghem
Louvain
Antwerp
Albert Canal

Audenarde
44 Div
Wortegem
Petegem
Caster
Kwaadestraat
Ecuwhoek
Berghem
Renaix
Bois/Mont de
l'Enclus
Escanaffles
Rugge
Avelghem
Kerkhove
Tieghem
Bergwijk
Ooteghem
Seveghem
4 Div
R Escaut

'operational debrief note to self', presumably soon after the evacuation. These extracts capture the atmosphere of uncontrolled chaos that prevails:

Wednesday May 15th.

After a cup of tea we sailed down Southampton Water, past Ryde and anchored off Southsea, where I could see all the old familiar sights, including our flat on Clarence Parade [later bombed]. There was an odd collection on board including a very talkative fellow called Malcolm John who told me his life story, including the fact that he was very enamoured of a young lady in M.I.5 called Marguerite Lepper – I later discovered that Jo knew her [Jo was also working in MI5, along with almost every other nice-looking young woman with good legs and from 'the right kind of family', it seems!]. Unfortunately the lady in question did not share his affectionate regard. I don't think he was much of a fellow ... he asked me if I could pull some strings and get him a staff job which he said he would infinitely prefer to regimental soldiering.

Thursday May 16th.

Arrived safely at Le Havre. There was an air raid warning ... but no-one took any notice of it ... Bought a map [sic!] from the canteen ... The train pottered along ... but eventually arrived at Paris, where it disgorged its horde of gesticulating Frenchmen and screaming Frenchwomen ... Very sporting taxi driver landed us safely at Gare du Nord ... wished us the best of luck, shaking us warmly by the hand.

Tea at the Station Hotel, served by a pretty and very saucy maid, full of chat and smiles. Our train left at about 5.30 and we soon started to pass a stream of refugee trains coming in, with people packed in every conceivable form of carriage and open truck. There were also a lot of cars streaming along every main road, piled high with luggage. This was the main sign that there was a war on ... arrived in Arras at about 8pm. The blackout throughout the town was most indifferent ... but it is quite impossible to make a Frenchman black out.

Friday May 17.

Landed up in Bethune (Rear HQ 3rd Corps) where I discovered that Advanced HQ was at Roncq ... came across a last war veteran from the 60th Rifles called Sterns, who struck me as a bit odd. He spent the whole time between giving his clerks raspberries, in trying on and adjusting his web equipment and looking at himself in the long glass of the bedroom that was now his office ... [Eventually] we got to Roncq. The mess was in an old chateau, where I had dinner.

Saturday May 18th.

Our HQ was on the left of the road going up to Menin ... 3rd Corps staff in my opinion were never a team. I did not see enough of the Corps commander (Adam) to form an opinion of how he performed his difficult task but I am pretty sure that he might have been better served. The BGS (Watson) was capable but smug and I never really trusted him. The A/Q was capable but hairy heeled, untrustworthy, unpleasant and at the end distinctly windy ... Bill Duncan, my Brigadier, was the only one who never lost his head, never gave up hope, never allowed equipment to be needlessly destroyed, and was the last of them all to leave.

The situation at this time was that the other two Corps had advanced and were in touch with the Hun whilst 3rd Corps were in reserve on the Escaut preparing the position there which all three Corps were to hold when the other two came back. At the time we thought that this was to be the main line on which we were going to stop the Hun. Just after breakfast Bill Duncan told me that I was to go out and do a recce of the whole area and come back with a new layout for the artillery ... here I was to get an unrivalled opportunity to recce the whole front of the B.E.F. I was packed off in ten minutes without having had time to think of taking blankets or food with me. Driver Reeves, an old regular reservist, appeared with a two-seater shortly after, and we set off.

Dvr Reeves was in cracking form ... airing his abominable French [pot calling kettle black here!] ... main roads full of military columns and side roads much worse, packed with refugees on foot ... a pathetic sight. Managed to plan the new layout ... the Bois de l'Enclus particularly interesting as we got a view from an enemy point of view – a veritable gunner's paradise for O.Ps. We reached 44 Div about 5pm ... I was not impressed with 'Chops' Osborne, the Divisional Commander – a small, white haired, bad tempered little man, who spent the first half-hour cursing the GHQ staff ... now was not the time for recriminations when there was so much to be done to straighten out the muddle ... I then had to go off in the middle of the night to find 3rd Division at their new HQ. We set off in the moonlight ... Reeves still thoroughly enjoying himself, remarking that it was like Paul Revere's ride and would I please ensure that my loaded revolver was handy. No sign of 3 Div anywhere ... so we decided to settle down for the night. Reeves joined some soldiers in a barn whilst I slept in the car – we had no blankets and it was bitterly cold ... had to make the best of an anti-gas cape, which I found very cold comfort.

Sunday, May 19th.

Got up very early, stiff with cold from the hard floor ... no trace of anybody from 3 Div ... got back to Roncq for breakfast ... the worst news of the day was that our (RAF) Army Co-operation Squadron had been removed overnight ... we later learned that all the RAF had been sent home. Feelings ran very high that they should be removed at the very moment the real battle was about to start. Bill Duncan was livid.

1 and 2 Corps completed their withdrawal to the Escaut during the night and the bridges over the Escaut at Oudenarde and Berghem were blown in the early morning.

Monday, May 20th.

The Germans must have been following up fast as the Corps Medium Artillery opened fire on observed targets at 7am ... Also columns of German troops were reported ... unfortunately we had no reconnaissance aircraft and a glorious opportunity was missed.

Of our liaison officers, Stevens of 6 Heavy AA Regiment was the pick of the bunch. A small, inquisitive, very intelligent young man ... with 5 minutes training was twice as good an Intelligence officer as Barber-Lomax. The latter was ... very slow and could not stand up to the long hours and general racket. He had a stout heart but I had a lot of trouble to make him destroy unnecessary papers when we had to move quickly and often.

The ... Heavy Regiments were withdrawn early to the rear on orders of GHQ ... it was a frightful mistake that no one got these Regiments into action in the Dunkirk area and let them brass off their ammunition at something. 52 Heavy Regiment, however, later put up a very fine infantry effort near St Omer, where the Germans came up our back.

Tuesday May 21st.

The battle of the Escaut started in earnest today and from the point of view of a staff officer it was exactly reminiscent of a Staff College telephone battle except that the telephones were frightful and it took hours to get through to most people.

4 Div front remained pretty intact throughout the day, but 44 Div soon had a bulge, where the enemy crossed the river at Peteghem and extended the hole up towards the railway. I had several complaints about enemy aircraft flying unmolested over our front and spotting for their artillery – where were the fighters? Answer, gone home, and we had no heavy AA artillery forward and little light AA.

The pressure on the Belgians also increased during the day and Bill Duncan was a bit nervous about a possible tank attack breaking through there and on to our flank ... our L of C was already feeling the German breakthrough and we had no ammunition train coming up ... the Belgians were to take over 44 Div front ... 44 Div to withdraw into reserve ... They had put up a poorish show and ... had made little attempt to counter-attack and push the Bosche back.

From the stories coming about the breakthrough on the French front, it was now pretty obvious that we should have to withdraw ... A message [sent out] to all units about the possibility of withdrawal ... Chops Osborne went on to blame the abominable withdrawal of his Division on this message. This was preposterous, but feelings are still bitter.

Wednesday May 22nd.

I think yesterday we took the sting out of the Bosche attack and made them think a bit ... Some of the 44 Div artillery had already withdrawn without orders and had displayed a remarkable show of incompetence and wind up. 57 Field Regiment was the worst and this wretched party blew up guns and beat it for Passchendaele Church. They lost no fewer than 23 guns out of 24 ... Bill Duncan went out today and ... found guns which had been abandoned and was able to detail other regiments still in action to pull them out.

With a few exceptions, the Territorial regiments were ill-trained and incompetent – good material, but untrained, undisciplined and unfit for service. It was the same all through, right up to the final evacuation, where you got regular regiments full of heart ... whereas the Territorials came up as a rabble, downhearted, looking only for a ship and with no guns. In my opinion Kitchener had a flair of genius when he refused to have anything to do with them in the last war.

The night was fairly busy ... Chater-Jack rang up in the middle of the night and spun a long, tragic story of how the Bosche were forming up in the bulge on 44 Div front and of how desperate was the plight of the Division ... actually, the story was without foundation, and no German night attack materialised, nor for that matter a dawn one.

Thursday May 23rd.

Corps HQ moved back during the evening ... I went off early with the Brigadier and did a tour round the northern flank – Menin, Ypres, Gheluvelt and Passchendaele. The Belgians we met all seemed very calm but supremely self-confident! I think ... they had got to the stage where they really didn't care a damn. As soon as they were attacked they just withdrew without waiting to do anything so common as fight.

Friday May 24th.

A Despatch rider from 3 Survey Battery (Donovan) came back with very useful information given out imperturbably and without exaggeration ... This was in contrast to the Bombardier from 56 Medium Regiment who walked in and said '56 Medium Regiment is wiped out' ... he was told that even if it was true, he had no right to start alarm and despondency. He was then questioned closely and we discovered that it was mostly hearsay and that he himself really knew little.

It was today that they decided that things were really bad and that a selection of officers and NCOs per regiment and any that could be spared from the staffs should be sent home via Dunkirk ... 3 Corps was to get a new role. I forget the role but it changed quickly and never came off, but this was by now almost normal! ... There seemed to be some chance of a counter offensive at last. This was the one thing everyone was asking, 'When is the French counter-offensive coming off?' In discussion about the people to go home, the Corps Commander remarked, 'They are about the only people who will.' He was really talking to himself, but it was at that time the prevalent view ... What a lesson it proved to be – the British Army never knows when it is beaten and will always extract itself from the impossible.

I had my first bath since arrival and it proved to be the last before England. I had it in a tub of boiling water in the boiler house ... it was grand to be clean again.

Saturday May 25th.

Today started as a day of hope, as we were told that a counter-offensive by the French and British was being planned to close the gap which the Germans had made in the French line 30 miles to our south near Valenciennes and through which they were pouring all their tanks into our back areas ... The French were putting in five divisions and it was hoped that they would also put in an attack from the south on the other side of the gap ... It was a hastily organised affair and I doubt it would have succeeded, as the Germans had packed the flanks of the gap very strongly. But it never came off, due I think to the British and French refusing to agree to dates. This is rather speculation, but Gort said he could not do it for two days ... and the French wanted to do it earlier and refused to do it without British co-operation ... it was decided about this time to extricate the B.E.F. and embark as many as possible at Dunkirk.

There was a lot of bombing all round throughout the whole day ... That night, Corps HQ moved in a hurry to Lille, and we were treated to another bout of bombing, again without effect ... Our new HQ was a very temporary one.

Sunday May 26th.

Things were in a state of flux … We had managed to get some breakfast, including coffee and an omelette, from a café down the street where we had laid in a small stock of drink to take with us. This stock did us well and lasted us for a good many days to come when it was impossible to get any drinkable water.

The plan of withdrawal to Dunkirk was for 1 Corps to provide the rearguard with 2 Corps as flank guard on the east where the Belgians had defected and 3 Corps as flank guard on the west to stop the enemy who had broken through the French and were at our backs … It was a cleverly conceived plan though an extremely tricky operation: but it worked. Divisions as they withdrew from the line were to form up in a Corps Assembly area outside the Dunkirk perimeter; there, they were to cast aside and destroy all their equipment except a few vehicles and their carriers, guns, machine guns and rifles. Various Divisions manned the perimeter as they came back until the time came for them to embark … I am hazy about how the whole thing was planned, which was a brilliant effort considering the completely hopeless mess things were in now and with worse to come as the withdrawal continued.

Just before we left … Stevens spotted a nice looking motor bike outside the office. His own had crashed into a shell hole … so he asked if he might pinch it. I said 'Yes' … at that moment Black, from the R.E. staff, came scuttling out and mounted it in front of our eyes … As it turned out … Black ran into a shell hole doing 40 mph shortly after, completely smashed the bike and bust himself about a good deal.

Some of the villages were in a pitiful state as a result of the bombing. I think it was Neuve Eglise which was the worst: … There was hardly a house left standing and bodies were strewn about all over the place, including a number of horses. We reached Eecke just as it was getting dark and had to set about finding our own billets … Dunscombe used his finest tact to persuade the dear old lady of the house to take us in. Her previous soldier guests had broken a window and left without paying … she produced hot water and some coffee for us. Spent a good night on the floor of the kitchen and next morning set up an office in one of the other rooms.

Monday May 27th.

The enemy were still hammering away at our western flank, and various detachments of tanks with lorried infantry and guns had penetrated towards Hazebrouch and Cassell. During the morning we were suddenly shelled by tanks … astonishing how many people took charge at the same time … nobody quite knew whether they were coming or going ... fortunately neither the tanks nor the infantry pressed their attack home.

About midday we withdrew ... to the outskirts of Bambecque. The plan was ... to discard all unnecessary vehicles and equipment before moving into the perimeter, but (as a result) a lot of useful fighting equipment was abandoned. The good units refused to dump anything that was going to be useful, but the bad ones accepted it willingly and dumped everything they could ... Some senior officers ... kept their heads, refusing to allow units to throw away anything vital and keeping up spirits. Others ... completely lost their heads and went round quite early on, ordering units to throw away their equipment and beat it for Dunkirk.

We spent the afternoon burning all our papers and in cooking ourselves a meal which the scroungers had gone out to get. They found eggs and a little bread, the latter being a tremendous treat after days of nothing but bully beef and biscuits ... We also spent quite a bit of time watching the air fights over Dunkirk, usually at a great height ... we eventually got orders to move just after dark and we moved into our assembly area ... near the Bergues road. We collected by a farm where we sipped red wine and waited for a guide to show us our area ... There was also the immense blaze of the oil depots at Dunkirk which were alight. This blaze had been going on for some days and it continued until we left and possibly long after that. There was an enormous red glow in the sky and a terrific pall of black smoke over the whole horizon which looked like an immense black cloud. The only thing we never went short of was cigarettes! I was even presented with a box of good Turkish cigarettes just before I left Dunkirk.

Tuesday May 28th.

Before setting off for Dunkirk, I sorted out all my kit. We had been ordered to leave behind everything we could not carry. I kept the dressing case Jo had given me, the writing case B had given me, Jo's photograph and various other small things such as my alarm watch and Penel's handkerchief [Jo's younger sister, serving in the WRENS].

We left about 9am and took the Bergues road, passing a mass of abandoned transport en route. It was a miserable day, raining hard ... every bridge had an officer in charge to see that transport above the amount laid down was not brought in ... I did manage to get all our motor cycles in and they really were invaluable. We set up shop at a small farm at Notre Dame des Neiges, which would have been remarkably comfortable but for the presence of vast numbers of Frenchmen ... For sleeping, it was a case of choosing between the hard stone floor of the farm and the smell of dirty Frenchmen in the comfortable hay. We preferred the former!

It continued to pour with rain all day ... the whole country was being flooded by opening the sluice gates, and the fields slowly became complete swamps, with just the roads standing out high and dry. At this stage, it was generally considered that a very large part of the B.E.F. would not make it and the policy was therefore to get everyone possible away at the earliest possible moment.

The Brigadier returned and I was able to make him a present of Bertie Burton who had walked in to our HQ just before. I was sitting against my truck sipping the last of the red wine when Bertie just blew in. We had a great reunion and finished the wine before discussing business. We sent him out in his armoured O.P. to the area said to be occupied by the Bosche to see if he could shoot them up with his Regiment, which was now in action in the perimeter. They (the 16th) had come back with 24 guns out of 24, which showed what could be done.

One of the worst sights in Dunkirk when one arrived was the sight of all the heavy A.A. guns staring blankly to the sky with their muzzles fanned out. Some criminal idiot at G.H.Q. had got the wind up and ordered their destruction early on.

I went out in the evening with the Brigadier but we were short-circuited off our mission by the appalling traffic congestion up the main road east of us ... We did traffic control policemen for some hours ... Spent the night at the farm house on a very hard, cold floor and got up very stiff and cold and hardly refreshed!

Wednesday 29th May.

We started the day chiefly by organising the various bits of the regiments into groups. At about 10am I again met the odd captain of the Sherwood Foresters to whom I had talked the previous evening ... he was quite lost then ... and this time he was even dafter ... and I felt very sorry for his unfortunate company. He disliked intensely having to hold a sector and evidently had his eye on the beaches.

At about midday we were again shelled badly and ....I thought it best to select a new HQ. Just before we left we had another bad bout of shelling and took to the ditch until it was over ... I looked in to Corps HQ as we left and all the Brigadier General Staff (BGS), Watson could say was 'All control is lost'. It was the very worst time in the retreat with a vast amount of the fighting part of the B.E.F. still to come in and a stream of stragglers pouring down the main road. From the point of view of the Corps, he was right – control was lost – but not from the point of view of the Divisions, who were fighting their rearguard actions decentralised until they came back into the perimeter. It was the way he said it which sounded so bad.

Willie is separated from his car in the confusion and tries to find the new HQ location on foot.

After tramping over fields and lanes for about an hour, I failed to find it so had to return to the road ... a small party of sappers were making a hot brown stew and gave me a share, not only of this but of an excellent bottle of liqueur which was equal to the best meal at the Ritz. We watched the stragglers go by ... dirty, dishevelled, on foot, bicycles, a tandem, horse, cart and motor car ... but the main part of the B.E.F. was quite unbroken.

It was today that I caught my first sight of the beaches in the distance and they were packed with lines of men at the various embarkation places. The mole itself was, of course, the most important place, but they had rigged up a few jetties along the coast down to Bray made of lorries driven out into the sea and people walked along the top of them. There were also the other odd places where people waded and swam out to the smaller craft.

Thursday May 30th.

Watched Porter and his batman detaching a cow with difficulty from the herd and cornering it in a barn, where they proceeded to milk it. Unfortunately we had no tea to go with the milk. Our job over the next three days was almost entirely one of co-ordinating the various artillery units left, and visiting them. It was a very pleasant and interesting three days ... all the writing to be done could be accomplished with a pencil and a message pad.

Friday May 31st.

Corps HQ was now established in a house on the front at Bray, and that famous holiday resort presented a most unusual sight. The sea had a large number of ships of all descriptions and sizes ranging from destroyers to tiny sailing and rowing boats: there were also several wrecks with their funnels sticking out of the water. The beaches were covered with masses of sand holes which the troops had dug to protect themselves against bombs, and stretching out into the sea were several lines of lorries, which had been driven into the sea in a line, with duck boards on top to make improvised embarkation jetties. There were lines of troops at various points on the beach, some using the improvised jetties and some wading out to the small boats, whence they were transferred to ships. The remainder of the troops whose turn to embark had not yet come were located in the sand dunes behind the front. The front itself was stiff with troops, a mass of abandoned motor cars, and there were Anti Aircraft (AA) guns and AALMGs (AA Light Machine Guns) at various points along the front and on the beaches.

We took up residence on the top floor of our house, which was littered inside and outside in the garden with a mass of junk, paper and debris. There was of course no water or light. Next door to us was a dressing station where casualties from the beaches were brought in. In our front parlour was a dead Frenchman whom nobody would remove. He remained there till we left. Outside there were a number of last night's casualties waiting to be removed to a hospital ship and a few dead British soldiers who were later removed. I remember one particularly nice looking boy – a Gunner – and I wondered who he was.

A couple of Germans were brought in during the morning. Both were in civilian clothes. Both looked remarkably unpleasant: one was large, thick set and scoundrelly looking, the other small and evil looking, but an unwashed, unshaven appearance did not help them. They were told that if they could show where their uniforms were hidden, they would be treated as prisoners; otherwise they would be shot. Both, however, had guts ... They were taken off and I think failed to find their uniforms and were shot. I could not help feeling sorry for them ... Another batch of people, dressed up in British battledress, were caught by the Gordons trying to get into our lines at Bergues and quite rightly shot out of hand.

Met Johnny Johnston commanding 21 Anti Tank Regiment, who told me that he thought General Barker (1 Corps) was being removed by a soviet of divisional commanders headed by Alex [Major General Harold Alexander, commanding 1st Division, later Viscount Alexander of Tunis]. How they set about it I don't know ... anyway, Barker was recalled and Alex was given command of 1 Corps. I saw Barker that afternoon, sitting gloomily by a table.

We had a bad bombing attack later in the morning directed chiefly against the shipping. I saw one aircraft drop two colossal eggs on a destroyer which it hit with a blinding flash. There was a few moments pause and then the whole ship went up in a mass of smoke and flame ... when it cleared there was literally nothing to be seen. I saw Plushy Grant about this time, an embarkation staff officer, who said that Wednesday had been a bad day ... but on the whole they had not really pressed their attacks home and losses might have been much heavier ...

We got back late and were told that Corps HQ had moved to Omer les Bains a mile to the east of the town, which was maddening. After a trying journey in the dark, with a series of the most b..... minded French traffic control policemen, we made the map reference ... I nearly did shoot one who refused to let us across a main road ... he started to draw his revolver, but we let him have every French, British and Hindustani oath we could think of and he then wilted. When we got to Omer Bains, we found what we feared ... [no sign of

Corps HQ] ... so we had another trying journey back to Bray, with a mass of traffic coming the opposite way. Eventually, the expected occurred and we met a small car on the wrong side of the road, head on, driven by a subaltern who was fast asleep but who woke up in time to brake a bit. His car was badly smashed but no one was hurt ... We managed to make Bray, where we took our things back into the house we had left.

Saturday 1st June.

I must say the last days were quite easily the best. Everyone was cheerful, there was no despondency and discipline throughout was first-class. My impressions were confirmed by the naval officer in charge of evacuation at Dunkirk, who I met at Corps HQ. He told me that the navy had taken a very poor view of the first 'evacuees' who were an appalling, windy and undisciplined mob, but things got increasingly better and that they were full of admiration for the last ditchers.

In the evening Corps HQ moved to the fort near the Mole, and it was expected that we should get everyone clear that night. I had to issue orders that all guns were to be destroyed by, I think, 10pm and everyone was to be withdrawn and embarked that night. We picked our way through the streets of Dunkirk, which were in an awful mess, especially at one cross roads where an ammunition lorry had been blown up, and eventually found the fort which was a few hundred yards from the Mole. The fort was full of soldiers and sailors, both British and French ... It was here that we met Lang, commanding 14 Anti Tank Regiment, whom the Brigadier ordered to take his guns to certain places on the beaches and entrances to the town in an anti-tank role. Lang was very windy and difficult. He tried to oil out of the order and made all sorts of difficulties ... later a battery commander arrived and said that he had received the orders too late and that the guns had been blown up. I rather think that Lang got away with it.

Alex invited the Brigadier and myself to have supper with him and he gave us an excellent one, sitting in his car outside the fort.

It was a very dark night and a very noisy one. The Germans were shelling the place spasmodically and bombing it at regular intervals, but the most terrifying thing was the big French gun on the fort which went off with a deafening roar when you were least expecting it and had a premature over our heads about every third shot. In the meantime we joined the line on the Mole. There were two lines, one French and one British, in single file, and we moved slowly down the Mole, stopping at frequent intervals. The Mole stretched out a tremendous way into the sea and was high up out of the water, so the various shells landing around merely fell into the sea and exploded under us. Nothing but a direct hit could have hurt us. We kept together, clutching our few possessions, the Dial sights we had saved, and the Brigadier his precious wireless set. The troops were all very quiet but very steady, though some were nearly dropping from sleep. I remember clutching one man when, half asleep, he was lurching up to the front, and I just stopped him falling off the edge of the Mole.

Eventually, some ships loomed up in the distance and we all scrambled on board one of them. We stayed on deck some time, where I have a final picture of that enormous fire still burning sullenly in the distance, with a number of smaller fires in the city, occasional parachute flares lighting up the sky, and the distant noise of guns. Then we came below and were put into a cabin where we all fell fast asleep and were too tired to bother about any hazards of the trip home.

Sunday 2nd June.

When we woke up we were in Margate. We disembarked at about 7.30 and took a taxi to the Station, where we were given tea and sandwiches by the reception committee. The latter also presented us with picture postcards of Margate (1890 vintage) and took telegrams from us. I sent one off but, being Sunday, the Bentley Post Office did not deliver it till Monday. The train we went on went via London and the Brigadier announced his intention of getting off there to go to the War Office and report – a good piece of news for me, as I could go with him instead of being trundled off to some remote part of the world.

The train was due to stop for 20 minutes at one station en route, so I slipped out and tried to ring up Jo. It seemed to take a long time to get through and I got windy of the train going before its time. So I ran back and found my hunch was right and the train was steaming out. I just managed to jump on board in time. We got off at London and went straight to the War Office where we saw Otto Lund. The Brigadier had a furious argument with him about the R.A.F. [When we left] I went straight to Waterloo and caught a train for Bentley ... en route were two of the silliest and flightiest young wenches in England who talked about nothing but their Canadian boy friends at Aldershot.

At Bentley I cadged a lift from two sappers who were passing Bay Tree Cottage and landed up in the garden where Mrs T [Bridgy] and Penel fell into my arms. My wire had not arrived and I was a complete surprise. Mrs T rang up Uncle Henry (Montgomery Campbell) via the Flemings, who got on to Tony at the War office, who eventually got on to Jo, [at MI5] who came flying home and arrived just before supper.

Chapter Seven

Bridget Tompson, Bentley, Hampshire, 1940

After Reggie's death, Bridgy moves to Farnham and then in early 1940 to Bay Tree Cottage, Bentley, where she lives until her death in 1983, in her ninetieth year. Bay Tree Cottage becomes the family base throughout the War. Willie and Jo's three children, Melissa (1941) and then twins, Judy and Hew (1943), are all born there. In 1975, Bridget writes a short memory of the 'Dunkirk spring' of 1940 for the Parish magazine:

Each year, as May and June come round again, the memory of the spring and early summer of 1940 comes so forcibly to mind that it is interesting to make a small record of the happenings. We came to live in the village at this crucial moment of the Second World War, when the scant news of our Forces in France was anything but encouraging.

In those days, the A31 main road passing our house was fairly quiet and empty of traffic, except for much heavy army traffic going to the coast. As the days went on, and the news became increasingly alarming, the situation reversed: the army traffic returned going towards London, and our spirits sank lower. Then the news broke, and we heard of the retreat through France ending on the beaches of Dunkirk. Everyone knows the epic of the Dunkirk evacuation. In our small way we were instantly involved as trains loaded with our war-weary troops, some with their uniforms torn to shreds, came through Bentley station on their way to Bordon. Some of the trains went through Bentley without a stop. Our then head porter, Mr A.W. Smith, saw his brother-in-law waving frantically as he went through the station – he was a latecomer, and his family was most anxious for him, and this was his only means of letting them know of his safety. Other trains, again full of troops, had to stop at Bentley and wait for the single line to Bordon to clear.

It was then that Mrs Frank Joy (Mab), with her instant knowledge of what was needed, organised a canteen at Bentley station. The Porter's room was handed over to her use, a team of willing helpers was organised and their times of duty arranged. There was often quite a long wait at the station, and the thankful acceptance by our exhausted, hungry troops of the cups of tea, sandwiches, chocolates and cigarettes we offered was most moving. It is astonishing that such an efficient service was arranged so quickly, and functioned so efficiently in such restricted circumstances. And, too, it was a wonderful effort on the part of British Rail. Trains came back from Bordon, again loaded with troops, returning to their various units, and even in this short time they looked restored. The canteen eventually closed at the end of the first week in June.

Our own particular anxiety at this time (Willie Pike) arrived at the station when the rush was over, as he was with the last party to leave Dunkirk. He appeared at our house on a beautiful Sunday afternoon – early June at its best. The apparently dire situation, and our great anxiety for family and friends, no doubt accentuated our feelings, but the unforgettable beauty of that early summer and the lovely fields and river as seen from the steps outside Bentley station remain for ever in the memory of a newcomer. When waiting at the station between trains on a summer evening, some lines of Walter de la Mare always come to mind:

> How still it is; the signal light
> At set of sun shines palely green;
> A thrush sings; other sound there's none,
> Nor traveller to be seen –
> Where late there was a throng.

Looking back on those terrible years, it is a wonderful thing that these lines can still be quoted with Bentley Station in mind.

Chapter Eight

Hew Tompson, North Africa, 1942

The spelling of Hew seems to have come from the Dalrymple family, who spell it the same way. Colonel Samuel Dalrymple CB (a grandson of Sir Hew Dalrymple, Bart.) of the Madras Artillery is married to a Miss Margaret Hall, by the famous Colonel James Achilles Kirkpatrick, Resident at the Court in Hyderabad, at the Residency there in 1801. Mrs Sam Dalrymple dies at sea in 1809 on a homeward voyage from Madras with her husband and three daughters. One of these daughters, Eliza, marries the Reverend Mathew Carrier Tompson at North Berwick in 1829, and thus Dalrymple and Hew both enter the family 'short list' of names.

Hew Tompson is born in 1920, educated at Winchester, commissioned into the Royal Artillery and joins 11th (HAC) Regiment RHA, equipped with towed 25-pounder field guns, in time to sail with them on HMT *Samaria* via South Africa to the Western Desert, arriving in January 1942.

His mother Bridget Tompson and younger sister Penel are in Bentley Church when the telegram arrives that Sunday, 8 February 1942, at Bay Tree Cottage. Jo is there with her baby, Melissa, to receive it and breaks the news to them on their return from church: 'Deeply regret to inform you report received from Middle East that Lt H.F.C. Tompson RA, killed in action. The Army Council desire to offer you their sincere sympathy.'

These are bad times in the Desert Campaign, with the start of General Rommel's probing towards the Gazala Line, where the British are to be so disastrously outfought in May of this year. 11th HAC have an awful start to their war in the weeks following their

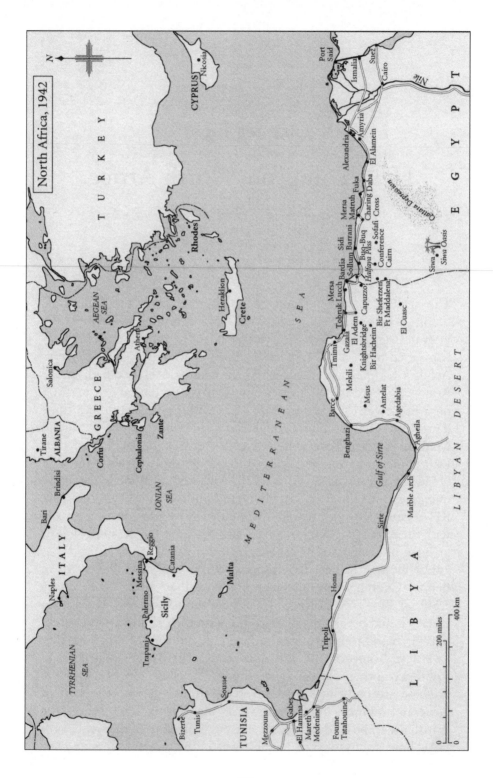

North Africa, 1942

arrival, and the Regimental History records how Hew is killed, somewhere south of Antelat in the Barce bulge, as follows:

Pressing north-eastwards up the ploughed-up, rutted track, E Battery had just reached an awkward defile when the ominous roar of Stukas was heard. Crews from the badly closed-up vehicles dived from their trucks to flatten in sand hollows while the Bofors guns dropped into action.

The tornado of sound – the staccato of the Bofors answering the crash of the falling bombs – was succeeded by a moment of silence broken only by the groans of the wounded and the furious swearing of the Bofors teams, both of whose guns had been put out of action; then another roar of planes as two enemy fighters swooped down spraying the valley with machine-gun fire.

A 3-tonner had joined the Battery as they entered the defile, carrying Lieut Hew Tompson and 2/Lieut B.H.S. Laskey and the crews of smashed B Echelon vehicles whom they had rescued. It was riddled with bullets. Tompson was badly hit. Laskey's driver, Gunner Hill, was killed. Every man in the lorry except Laskey was wounded [Laskey is killed in action later in the war], including Battery Sergeant Major (BSM) Hopson, a great loss to the unit; and there were several casualties among the Bofors detachments. A bomb had fallen within 15 feet of the Battery Commander and his crew, but they emerged untouched from the cloud of smoke and sand and splinters.

The wounded were loaded into vehicles; Major Benson picked up Hew Tompson who, however, died that night ... In the leaguer that night, the Battery snatched what sleep they could while the darkness was lit by green Verey lights from German leaguers all around, and occasional flashes in the distance followed by showers of sparks and a red glow as the Germans blew up a wrecked ammunition vehicle.

In one of Hew's last letters before leaving, written to his mother on 22 September 1941, from 'somewhere in the North of England', he writes:

My darling Mummeye, I don't suppose we shall, any of us, ever forget that famous day (and night) which I spent at home: it was lucky that we didn't realise at the time what agony it was going to be, or it would have spoilt a perfectly wonderful day, indeed worthy of my last day at home.

One expects and gets so much from one's parents that it is very difficult to sit down and thank you for anything in particular, when I realise that everything that I have had or done in the world has been given by you. And what a lot I've had; the best of everything in fact.

I do wish that it didn't take beastly departures to make us realise quite how much we do owe. Whatever you may hear from St Albans about the wonders of Aunt Rhoda [married to Cuthbert, Bridget's brother] and the rest of the 'exceptional parents' in our family, do please remember that as far as your children are concerned, they couldn't have asked for better parents and I shall be happy if I do half as well for my children as you have done for yours.

We left at 8.30, in fact I was only just in time as it was, I've never known such a miracle as brought that truck in the nick of time. Did that youth ever turn up? He's still got my money I hope.

We are living in the most appalling discomfort but I hope this won't last too long ... I doubt if I will get your letters for months but they will find me eventually.

P.S. This may never reach you but it's having a good try.

P.P.S. I haven't lost my luggage yet!

On 2 October, after three days at sea, he writes:

So far we have had no trouble except for an air raid warning this afternoon which, in the tradition of all I have ever witnessed, came to nothing! ... we are very comfortable, unlike the men who live in the most deplorable conditions like so many cattle, there being so many on board. They have nowhere to sit at all except on the decks which are terribly crowded and what's worse is the appalling stuffiness and smell, five decks down where they eat, sleep and somehow have their being. The conditions unfortunately encourage the attitude of 'Damn you Jack, I'm all right' except that damn isn't the word they use: this is a pity as it might be the same in real trouble, but I doubt it somehow as they are all in surprisingly high spirits ... Champagne is 7/6 per bottle! I think of you all and wish I could be with you again and bring some of the mass of butter with me ... We hear no news of any kind at all, wirelesses are not allowed.

Please don't be depressed. 'Sufficient unto the day is the evil thereof'!!! We must just live for the end.

On 16 November he writes:

We had the most incredible time in Durban where we stopped for a week ... whisked up by large cars and driven all over the place, given dinners, taken to all sorts of parties. They really are wonderfully kind to us ... I met an old Wykehamist wandering around the town one afternoon, a big man in sugar, he drove me all over his vast plantations ... We had a large Old Wykehamist dinner, people flocked in from miles around ... The English in Durban are rather

82

rich (2 shillings income tax) (and slightly common!) and I think slightly unpatriotic in their general attitude. They are terribly kind and I know very keen for us to win the war, but except for being very charming to us they do nothing whatever. If they were South Africans one could understand it but I am talking about the large number of (English) people who went there after Munich.

The Native is also treated in rather an odd way. He is just dirt and one is hardly allowed to ask him the way without going to prison!

And on 7 December:

I can't tell you how wonderfully they have behaved, the men in particular. Living honestly under unforgivable conditions and filthy food they have kept clean and happy, which 'makes you marvel'. I simply can't think why the Government let these shipping companies blatantly make money out of the troops ... the sailors themselves are very nice but below decks there is a set of stewards head, chief and ordinary, who are nothing but s——. I can't tell you how bloody they are to us all.

Will you tell Eggar that I met John (Eggar) who was at Winchester with me and we played a lot of Bridge together and is now I hope a lifelong friend; its maddening to me to think of all the people I knew and disliked when there, that I have met since and really liked; him for instance.

At about this time, the Signallers in Battery HQ present Hew with a certificate headed with the Regimental crest and signed by fourteen men, which reads:

We, Sir, the BHQ SIGNALLERS, would like you to know that each of us feels a sincere sense of gratitude for all your efforts to relieve the enforced monotony of our weeks at sea, and hereby record our appreciation.

After the news of Hew's death, Bridget writes to Willie, her son-in-law, who at this time is attached to US Army manoeuvres in Louisiana, following the American entry into the War after the Japanese attack on Pearl Harbour on 7 December 1941:

February 28th 1942.

I have written to so many people and still have a pile of letters before me that I feel I can never answer and must – and I have never written to you who are so far the most important person possible to whom I want to write. Thank you more than I can say for your cable, you don't know what it was to get that lovely loving message, impossible for me to try to explain, nor can I possibly begin to say anything about it at all, and therefore you are easy to write to, because I know you understand this and there are so many letters in which one has to say something and just can't, to almost complete strangers like the Headmaster of Winchester. There is something so utterly <u>stunning</u> about a loss such as ours ... perhaps it is merciful to feel like this though I never thought for one moment that Hew would get through, did you? Ever since we left the three and went to India they have been such a complete little partnership and I can't tell you how much I have admired the courage of both Jo and Penel ... <u>Please</u> take care of yourself – you don't know what it is to us to feel that we have you.

Jo also writes to her husband Willie about her brothers' death:

February 13th 1942.

Everything seems so futile and pointless to me and the misery of it is like a sort of load that one is always dragging about wherever one goes ... Mummy has been simply wonderful – but then she would be. Her courage is simply magnificent and when one thinks of all she has lost now ... I have an Air Mail letter card which Hew wrote me on the 5th January and was written to you too. I think I will keep it until you get home as I should hate it to get sunk or anything ... I must say he sounded terribly cheerful and ribald in it and one can only hope and trust and pray that the end was quick and clean. He complained of not having had one single letter from us though – none of them had heard anything from home at all since they arrived and I'm afraid he may still never have heard when he died, though we sent Airgraphs and everything.

Hew had not been especially successful at Winchester, his obituary written by his Housemaster in *The Wykehamist* recording that:

His Colonel wrote of him as 'always keen, cheerful and very efficient'. This would have been a great satisfaction to his father ... to whom Hew's inability to pass into the RMA Woolwich had been a disappointment. The fact was that he was a late developer and had no flair for mathematics: but he left as a Commoner Prefect, had some success at cricket and gymnastics and managed to pass into the RMC Sandhurst ... and from many letters it is clear that he 'found himself' on active service, having made many friends and won golden opinions during training at Larkhill, with 78th (Duke of Lancaster's Own Yeomanry) Medium Regiment and with the HAC.

His CO with 78th Medium Regiment wrote to Bridgy of his 'zeal and lightheartedness' as an instructor, going on to record:

> It was difficult to believe he was only 19, then a few moments later off parade it was suddenly apparent how delightfully young and boyish he really was ... In those days he came to my home frequently and like everybody else, my family, mother, wife and children all loved him. I do trust that your pride in the most delightful memory that he has left behind may be some comfort to you in your great sorrow.

Another wrote from the same Regiment that 'I expect you know how much we all loved him. Officers, NCOs and men – that is the only way to express it ... Your son was a big and very beautiful influence in our lives.'

Hew's Housemaster in Hoppers – where his father Reggie had been in Mr Turner's time – was Malcolm Robertson, a respected figure known universally as 'The Bobber', who writes a typically schoolmasterly though charming letter to Bridgy at Christmas time in 1942, enclosing a copy of *The Wykehamist* journal with its obituaries of those killed. His letter – wartime austerity biting hard, or his own natural economy? – is written on a half sheet of headed writing paper, on which he runs out of space and has to travel round the margins, the reader assisted with an arrow here and a link word there:

> My dear Mrs Tompson, This sad 'Xmas card' [*The Wykehamist* journal] (of which you no doubt already have a copy) brings you and the daughters our joint good wishes for as happy an Xmas and New Year as may be. I hope you will like the short account of Hew, but you will see, from the number alas! involved, that we had to condense; and we also agreed not to compete, as it were, in praise, and to try to make what we wrote ring true. There must be mistakes, and probable omissions which parents will regret: but they will all have fuller or more intimate letters or notices than can be printed in a supplement of this kind. One of the reasons that people always, I hope, trust my 'characters' of the living is that I always indicate any weakness as well as make the most of any strength. In writing of Hew, Henry Browne, Fred Hollins, even Bernard Pinney, I could not forget old anxieties or write as if they had never existed. But I think their friends will value the human touch in the restraint from adulation, which so easily rings false ... I thought you'd like Hew's father mentioned. I could never forget his love for the boy and his anxiety for him.

In his letter to Bridget, Hew's CO tells her how he is buried in the desert after dark, the Regimental Padre reading the service, the darkness lit by burning vehicles and green Very flares from German leaguers all around. A rough wooden cross with his name and personal details marks the place, he adds. Yet such is the mobile nature of the fighting in subsequent months, that Hew is now one of thousands with no known grave, whose names are inscribed within the arch of the El Alamein memorial. In November 1995, his nephew Hew parachutes into the desert with Major James Chiswell's Company of 2 PARA, during an exercise with American and Egyptian forces, and takes part in a Remembrance Day Service at the Alamein Memorial. He also talks on the *Today* programme by satellite link to John Humphrys about Hew, and the importance of remembrance.

On Remembrance Sunday in 2005, he talks about him in Bentley Church, where Bridgy and Penel were worshipping when the telegram came. He concludes:

'It is easy to ask, "What earthly good did the death of Hew Tompson and thousands like him do? What possible influence can their sacrifice have had on the outcome of the fighting and the war?" To which I would reply, "And what if they had not all been there, willing to lay down their lives for their friends? What then?"'

Hew's name faces that of his uncle, Frank Thicknesse, in the War Cloister at Winchester.

Chapter Nine

Willie Pike, Tunisia, 1943

In April 1942, now aged thirty-seven and a Lieutenant Colonel, Willie takes command of 77th (Highland) Field Regiment, Royal Artillery, equipped with towed 25-pounder field guns, training in Scotland for combined operations as part of the 4th Division. Besides Scotsmen, the Regiment includes many English and Welsh – not many from Ireland, I don't think – making for a strong cultural mix. In March 1943, they sail from Liverpool for North Africa as part of Operation Torch, the landings by First Army in Morocco and Algeria, following the breakthrough by Eighth Army at El Alamein in October 1942. The aim of the operation is to finally drive the Germans from North Africa, and specifically from Tunisia. Willie again keeps a private diary of operational notes that he writes up after the fighting, as he did at Dunkirk.

23rd March.

Arrived at Algiers disembarking on a hot day and marching with full equipment and small pack about 15 miles to Camps N and P where we were situated in two farms ... The march was a very tiresome one. The roads were hard and dusty; people's feet were soft after the voyage and packs were heavy. It was however very well carried out and practically no one failed to make the grade though there were a good many sore feet the next day. On the whole it was no bad thing as it started everyone with the idea that war is not a holiday.

24th March–1st April.

This period started off with the unwelcome news that one ship had been sunk and another long delayed with about a third of the Regiment's vehicles, guns and equipment aboard. The losses were at least equably spread out between RHQ and the Batteries ... the business of making good our deficiencies in sufficient time to move with the rest of the Division required a great deal of hard work. Fortunately we ran into a number of very good friends, chief of which was Alan Fernyhough who organised his ordnance minions and chased an efficient and willing team in magnificent fashion. The result ... was that we were able to move off with and take into action our full 24 guns.

2nd–5th April.

The Regt advanced from Algiers on 2nd April in two convoys, one fast and one slow, the fast group camping for the first night at El Achir, the slow group at Beni Mansour. Carriers and 150 men had to go by sea to make room for the vast quantities of petrol and ammunition we had to carry by road, and we did not see them till later. The advance continued with camps at El Bey and Souk Ahras for the fast group, the two groups reuniting on 5th April at Ghardimou on the Algerian-Tunisian frontier. An incident involving the death of two Arabs on the road ... was quickly closed with the aid of a very pretty and extremely charming Francaise who acted as interpreter with the French authorities.

The country through which we passed was mountainous and extremely beautiful. It was very cold at night but the days were

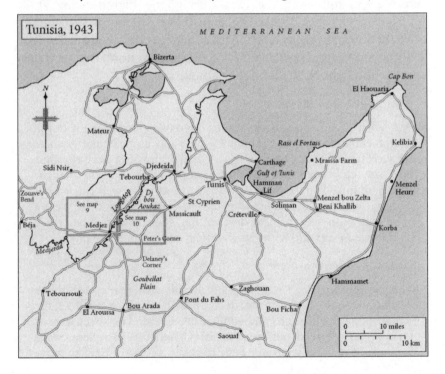

sunny and warm. The whole countryside was carpeted with spring flowers and the fields were a blaze of yellow and blue with splashes of white and red ... storks were nesting everywhere in houses and trees along the route. The locals ... lined the route asking for cigarettes, biscuits or sweets and offering oranges and eggs for sale. They did a roaring trade in both.

6th–7th April.

We took recce parties to see the gun area of 172 Field Regt, commanded by Cherub Graham who took the greatest pains and pleasure in showing us all around. But his 'bullshitting' was almost intolerable. Nor did we think much of his gun positions and digging.

8th April.

I reported to HQRA that evening and being the first artillery unit of the 4th Division to be ready, got orders to contact 78 Division and to come under their orders until the rest of 4 Division was ready. Ordered recce parties forward to meet me tomorrow at rd junc 327376.

9th April.

I went off at first light to find Brig. Wedderburn Maxwell, CRA of 78 Division, and found him having breakfast with Gen. Eveleigh (GOC 78 Div) at their HQ west of Oued Zarga. Brigadier very complimentary about the speed with which we had got ourselves up and ready for action.

Our gun area was the side of a ravine surrounded by hills ... 78 Division were in the process of finishing off an attack to capture the area Jebel Bech Chekaoiu (Pt 667), Jebel Rmel and Jebel Si Bel Mahdi. My initial deployment orders were disturbed by enemy fighters and bombers ... buzzing around but with little more than the nuisance value of angry wasps. Preparation of gun positions complete ... guns timing themselves to arrive at gun positions just as it was getting light.

10th April.

All Batteries got some shooting at withdrawing enemy ... enemy air very active, with a certain amount of machine gunning and dive bombing. Fortunately our area was protected by the Bofors of 49 LAA Regt ... who were magnificent shots and treated us during the next few days to the welcome sight of at least half a dozen Bosche aircraft in flames ... The main difficulty was to get a firm order from anyone ... HQRA 46 Division particularly difficult, pleasant but utterly vague with a CRA who spent most of his time reminiscing.

11th April.

RHQ was situated in a very pleasant gully with steep sides and a small stream which was very cool and handy for bathing. It had recently been a German position and was full of abandoned equipment, including mines, rifles, revolvers, machine guns, ammunition and a mass of other odds and ends. It was a comfortable position and when a couple of days later one shell arrived wounding very slightly Irvine and rather badly a driver of another regiment, it was made even more comfortable by the extreme willingness of everyone to dig. Spades flashed ... the only unfair part of this shell was that it smashed up my Z car, writing it off and damaging a lot of stuff inside with splinters. Fortunately neither I nor anyone else was inside it.

Although they can be tasked elsewhere, the primary role of Willie's Field Regiment and its guns is the artillery fire support of 12 Brigade, one of 4th Division's Brigades.

12th April.

12 Bde now consolidating and holding area Pt 667 (West Kents – RWK)–Jebel Rmel (Black Watch – BW) and Jebel Mahdi (Hampshires), Royal Fusiliers (RF) in reserve.

The day started with the Black Watch relieving their forward company with their reserve company by day instead of in the dark. The result of this foolish mistake was that both companies were caught in the open by heavy mortar, machine gun and artillery fire. Their positions in any case had not been well dug and these two factors were the main cause of our subsequent troubles, though in fairness ... the Jebel Rmel was a bare exposed feature in the middle of an open plain and an unenviable one to hold. Initially the main (enemy) fire seemed to come from behind (feature) 350 and Robin Fulton (Battery Commander – BC – whose Battery was supporting the BW), with Douglas Rankin (a Forward Observation Officer – FOO) at once came to the rescue of the Black Watch. It was a difficult shoot however in close proximity to our own troops and, in order to see [to observe and adjust the artillery supporting fire], it was necessary to work right forward amongst the foremost infantry. Robin went forward himself and immediately got the fire of his own Battery down onto feature 350 and behind it, thereby greatly assisting the infantry to readjust their positions. He had trouble with his set however and both line and remote control were cut more than once. On my way back (from seeing Pat Barclay, CO of the BW) ... Sergeant Pollard came back with the sad news that Robin and Douglas had been killed. Apparently Robin had had to call over Douglas in order to make use of his set and whilst they were together

90

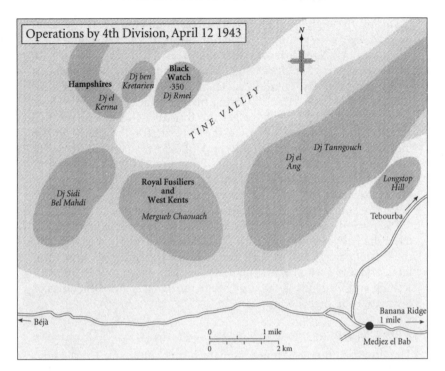

a shell fell within a few feet and killed them both instantly. Sgt Pollard himself was slightly in rear and had a very lucky escape being protected by the bodies of the other two in front of him. It was several days before we managed to recover their bodies which were left in no man's land but which we finally got back with a party at night led by Lance Bombardier Moore.

I sent for Ian Lang at once to replace Robin Fulton and Stirratt to replace Rankin. I also got up John Buckwell as a second Forward Observation Officer (FOO) on the Jebel Rmel feature. They did magnificent work [in support of the BW] but unfortunately Ian Lang and Sgt McNab were later wounded at the same time as Pat Barclay, the CO. Ian was badly but not dangerously wounded whereas McNab was very seriously injured and subsequently died of his wounds.

The Black Watch themselves had a severe grilling this day, suffering about sixty to seventy casualties including the CO and Adjutant, both wounded. They were forced off their forward positions and that evening put in an attack to retake them ... We put down a heavy concentration at 2100 but the attack was only carried out by one platoon (about 30 men) which lost half its strength in the attempt and failed to capture its objective – a platoon was lost on a feature this size and such a small sub-unit should never have been put in alone.

During the night Brigadier Callaghan, commanding 12 Brigade, ordered the BW to restore the situation by an attack at first light to be supported by a squadron of tanks and by us. His orders were vague and only sent by wireless which was working extremely badly in difficult atmospheric conditions. The BW themselves were in a state of considerable concern ... (fearing further attack). We had a most uncomfortable night trying to get the Brigadier's orders to the BW clarified and arranging our own fire support for the attack in the morning ... Just in time the tanks and infantry managed to marry up and the attack went in at first light. The fireworks were a fine sight, the artillery concentrations, the smoke, the tracer of the tanks and of the enemy with the usual number of rockets and flares. The Black Watch regained their original positions.

Such was the story of the 12th April and the night that followed – a day I shall always remember for the costliness of stupid mistakes and the loss of some great friends; the night for the futility of a platoon attack on a big feature, for the need for clear orders in person or in writing and the tendency to exaggerate the dangers and difficulties of a situation by night.

13th–19th April.

The situation in our area now remained much the same for the next week. The Bosche continued to be a nuisance to the Black Watch but we eventually got the measure of him by putting down on his positions ten times as many shells as he put down on ours. We gave him till the third round and then opened up [in response] ... [thus] the BW ended their days on this inhospitable feature in comparative safety if not in comfort. Our tanks ... did not show much evidence of wanting to go in for bold action ... they seemed to think too much of their difficulties and not enough of their possibilities.

It was about now that Brigadier Dick Hull [a future CIGS] took over command of 12 Brigade from Callaghan, who was a sick man and had been quite incapable of competing with the recent situations. It was sad losing him ... but the arrival of his successor certainly produced a very different atmosphere of efficiency in the Brigade. On the 17th Padre Broome buried Robin Fulton and Douglas Rankin on the Jebel Rmel. The LAD made crosses for them and for Fleming of the Black Watch who was buried beside them.

April 20th.

A hot but restful day. Later in the day I went off to join advance parties to new positions. As I drove to the new gun area in the dark there was a certain amount of shooting but I never guessed the trouble we were going to have later in the night ...

April 21st.

The enemy attacked us at an awkward moment. The Corps had warning of this attack early in the evening but it never got down to units who were taken completely by surprise. The attack was obviously a spoiling attack with the object of impeding our preparations for attack and it came in with tanks and infantry from the east ... There was heavy fighting in the whole of the Banana Ridge area and the hills to the south where they made some penetrations of our positions ...

Our own entry into the battle was in meeting a strong company sized patrol ... let in by the Gordon Highlanders who were as surprised as we were. The night or what was left of it is chiefly memorable for the large amount of tracer of both sides flying about, for the masses of light signals and for the occasional hand to hand encounters with the Bosche. The damage done in our wagon lines (WLs) amounted to Cpl Evans, Gunners Huggins, Booth and Graham killed, a few others lightly wounded and a dozen missing.

The day dawned with a fine old muddle to be straightened out. The man to do so in my opinion was the Brigadier commanding 2 Infantry Brigade but the latter thought otherwise. He decided his own HQ was too far forward, so beat it just before first light ... We did not see him again till the battle was over but this was perhaps just as well as I have seldom met a more useless man. The position had therefore to be straightened out and the battle fought by a soviet of COs consisting of Gibson (Loyals), Goldsmith (DCLI) and myself. Gibson was first class and I have seldom seen a better battalion. It was a tragedy when his battalion were cut up and himself killed some days later. Goldsmith was quite unperturbed but utterly wooden and seemed incapable of taking any positive action ...

In the early part of the morning however things did not seem to be in too bad a state ... The table land in front of us was full of Bosche tanks and trucks and we put down regimental concentrations [of artillery fire] over the whole area but there was so much shooting and so many fires from burning vehicles that it eventually became impossible to distinguish our shells from others ...

I went to see the Bedfords and Gordons later in the day, fixing up Artillery tasks for the rest of the day and the coming night. Eventually returned to an excellent supper which included delicious beans from the fields around us. A hectic day was followed by a peaceful night for which we were all remarkably glad.

April 22nd/23rd.

22nd was a quieter day... Orders for 4th Division attack. Phase 1 a night attack by the Royal Fusiliers (RF) ... One only had to look at the map to realise that this was an impossible task for one battalion even against light opposition. With heavy opposition ... it was ridiculous. It took four battalions of infantry, one battalion of tanks and a mass of artillery a week to capture and hold these objectives. Our intelligence was bad ... it was thought these places were lightly held and the bulk of the enemy had pulled out. Phase 2 was to be an attack by the BW with 12th Royal Tanks (12 RTR), followed by Phase 3, the capture by the West Kents and 12th Royal Tanks of the high ground south of Ksar Tyr. The night attack was to be followed by a pause of at least 6 hours for the sappers to clear mines and for the tanks and the artillery to move forward.

We thought this was the big attack but in fact it was not yet the big break through. I gathered afterwards that this and the other attacks ... along the line had two objects, to force the Bosche to use up his reserves and to find the best place for the real breakthrough ... Whatever the objects, it was a costly week we had in front of us.

April 24th.

The RF attack went in at midnight on 23rd/24th. They reached Oued Milah but then were held up by mines and wire. Maurice Brandon, the CO, was killed and they lost one entire company which was never seen again until some of it was recaptured in Tunis. This company

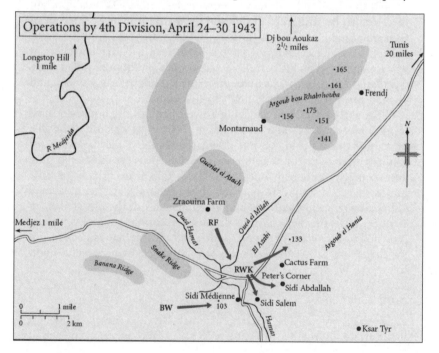

managed to get right on (we learned later), but was eventually caught in the meshes of Abdullah and Cactus.

With the failure of the RF to get beyond Oued Milah, the whole 4 Div plan fell to the ground … It was [then] decided that Medienne would be captured by a company of the BW supported by a squadron of 12 RTR and Divisional Artillery. At 1230 in went the BW company and the tanks under our concentration … As the company got to the top, I well remember Jack Harding saying to me 'What a waste of ammunition, there's not a Bosche in the place.' A few minutes later down came the inevitable mortar fire and in came the counter attack. There was some fierce hand to hand fighting and the BW had heavy casualties. The company was too weak and small to hope to hold such a big feature and at 1500 it was ordered to withdraw under a smoke screen which we provided. The tanks less those blown up by mines were also withdrawn. Had they been able to get right up the BW company might have done the trick but the tanks were held up short of the objective by the minefield and unable to help the infantry with the opposition on the reverse slope … A plot was then hatched to attack Medienne that night with the remainder of the BW … plus minelifting. A troop of Scorpions was produced … but it was all done at very short notice and everyone heaved a sigh of relief when it was cancelled.

April 25th.

It was decided during the day that the BW were to attack tonight and capture Medienne and Salem and that the RF were to capture Azabi. The BW went in at 2200 and the RF at 2310. The RF did not have much opposition but the BW had a bitter struggle with fierce hand to hand fighting. They went in with fixed bayonets and the pipes playing and took no prisoners. They had a lot to repay. They found however that Medienne was all they could achieve and made no attempt to get Salem, but they did get Medienne which was found to be a strong position.

It was during this night that I slipped up to our OP on Snake Ridge … to my horror I discovered that the very alert company of the DCLI up there knew nothing of the 12 Brigade attack and had been told themselves to expect attack from the very direction in which our own attacking troops were to go forward … a tragedy was thus narrowly averted.

April 26th.

Plans were laid today for an attack tonight … by two companies of the RWK on to Sidi Abdullah and Sidi Salem. The RWK attack went in at about 2230 and both companies ran into opposition … Salem was captured and consolidated but the Abdullah attack ran into much heavier opposition including flame throwers and were terribly cut about without achieving their objective. The squadron of Churchills went through the minefield gap at first light but suffered heavy losses through a combination of bad tactics, mines and cleverly sighted anti-tank guns ... During the night the BW had a heavy counter-attack ... it was beaten off, not however without a large bunch of stragglers coming back with panic stories. The main trouble with the BW ... is that they have lost so many officers and many NCOs are just not good enough to replace them in a crisis.

April 27th.

In the afternoon a company of the BW moved forward under cover of a smoke screen to occupy the Abdullah feature ... Got an intercepted wireless message from HQ 5 Jaeger Regt that Abdullah feature was to be recaptured regardless of cost ... At 1830 the counter attack came in. We dealt faithfully with the infantry but could not manage the tanks, which included Tigers – nor could our tanks or anti-tank guns who were not placed so as to be able to engage the Bosche tanks, who knew every inch of the ground and made full use of it. But a company is a very small unit especially on a vast feature like Abdullah and when faced with enemy tanks without supporting anti-tank fire. They were unable to face the music and their company commander was badly wounded. Someone on the spot gave the order to withdraw and back they came, pretty fast.

April 28th.

A relatively quiet day with plans for a double attack by RWK on Pt. 133 and RF on Cactus and Abdullah ... RWK advanced at 1905 and in a most successful attack captured their objective ... enemy counter attacked at 0400 the next morning but were beaten off after some fierce fighting.

April 29th.

At first light the RFs went in. The tanks got to Cactus Farm but unfortunately by-passed it instead of going through it and then made for Abdullah which they also reached. Bad bad tactics and the enemy anti-tank guns again took a heavy toll of tanks, and by the end of the day the whole area was a sorry sight littered as it was by our burning and knocked out tanks. Some of the RFs got into Cactus but the farm was never cleared and the situation was a most confused one with both sides in it and fighting bitterly at close quarters. RF also reported that they had got onto Abdullah ... other reports came back that we were not ... and the situation thoroughly obscure ... map reading of the RF put their position 1000 yards out and they were in fact that distance from Abdullah. Throughout the day heavy casualties were inflicted by both sides and a very hot sun made conditions most exhausting. During the afternoon the enemy counter attacked strongly with infantry and tanks ... It was eventually beaten off but although we had still probably got some people in Cactus and on Abdullah, the enemy was still more master of these features than we were. During the day a most unfortunate incident occurred. The company commander of the RWK on Pt 133 had been killed and a junior officer gave the order to withdraw without the knowledge of his battalion commander ... thus we lost an important feature. This and the by-passing of Cactus lost us the day.

Two companies of the DCLI were ordered to retake it tonight ... they started their attack at 2300 ... which gave them the chance to consolidate before daylight. The attack went in successfully and by first light they were established on Pt 133 ...

We shelled Cactus every five minutes during the night and at first light David Archer went in with the remaining company of the RWK. But to no avail. The Bosche light signals put up were the same as our own success light signals and in the confusion David was killed and his company failed – David a particular loss as a very fine and popular officer.

April 30th.

At first light we put down a series of smoke screens to help the DCLI get their transport up. They got a fair amount up but could not get enough ammunition forward. Thereafter they had some very heavy fighting and were shot up from all directions ... Eventually things reached such a state that they had insufficient ammunition and the Brigadier ordered their withdrawal. Without ammunition we (Gunners) were the only people who could cover them at all ... used immense quantities of ammunition and saved these two companies ... Kinnersley their CO told me afterwards that our guns had entirely saved them ... his men were full of praise and gratitude for their performance.

About this time we were told that we were to be pulled back and rested and reorganised for the big breakthrough attack which was to take place further north.

(There are a number of further apparent enemy counter-attack efforts through this day, none of which succeed and Willie records that 'the battle to all intents and purposes finished here.')

May 1st.

I was able to get round the troops and tell gun detachments and others how the battle had gone during the week. It had been a bitter week's fighting and Bosche prisoners captured after the fall of Tunis in many cases said that the Abdullah fighting had been the fiercest they had taken part in, including Russia ... There were doubtless good reasons for all the attacks which we put it. But to the participant in the battle, it was always a case of sending a boy on a man's errand. The lesson from the infantry's point of view was that the battalion and not the company is the tactical unit. A company, which is bound to suffer casualties in the attack, especially amongst its officers, is too small to capture, consolidate and hold features such as they were asked to do in this case. In almost every case a battalion could have captured and held each one of these features individually but their resources were whittled away the whole time by company attacks, which usually captured the objective only to be forced off it with heavy casualties. The tanks were the whole time handicapped by the presence of minefields and unlocated anti-tank guns, which prevented their getting right onto the objectives and helping to beat off counter-attacks ... in my opinion artillery fire on many occasions saved the day and prevented ugly situations from becoming disastrous.

On 1 May, Willie writes to his mother 'B', living in Bedford:

We have been having a very 'busy' time indeed lately but I have enjoyed it very much. We live rather like gypsies – entirely in the open and usually cooking and feeding in small detachments. My batman is first class and looks after me magnificently. He cooks very well, producing food and cups of tea at all times of day and night.

I can't remember when I last slept under a roof. There aren't many buildings about and what there are smell, have lousy (literally) people living near by or in them and are very popular as targets for bombs and shells. So we live in gullies and trenches instead which are cleaner and safer.

PS. Am writing this at an OP where I get a magnificent view of the Bosche lines. He's pretty quiet this morning but we see the odd bit of movement. Any more and we beat him up!

On 4 May he writes again:

All is well here and I am in extremely good health and heart. I get no news of the arrival of the twins [they had in fact arrived on 24 April] ... We've just finished a very bitter battle, with the Bosche fighting far too well. I don't fancy it is going to be a great deal longer before he is finished, but it is going to be a tough fight till it is finished. The trouble is that everyone is expecting an easy run through. I don't know why they should when the country is so difficult and favours defence and delaying tactics. The mud, thank heavens, has gone but has now been replaced by dust which is almost worse. One returns from any journey just like a snowman.

One of the things the Bosche is best at is concealing himself. One looks over an apparently utterly peaceful piece of country which might be a land of the dead. But as soon as one comes to attack it, one finds it bristling with men and weapons, magnificently dug in and defended. They've had a long time to prepare their present positions and have made good use of their time.

My acquired lilo is functioning very well so don't bother to send me another one. And the torch has been a Godsend. It is such a 100% efficient one. The Balaclava was very useful earlier in the hills but it is far too hot now for anything in that nature.

5th May.

Final orders for the attacks received. <u>Attack</u> is the big thing which is to be pushed right home regardless of casualties, with the watchword Tunis. In general the attack was to consist of an overwhelming force breaking through on a narrow front and thereafter literally sweeping the enemy off his feet by speed and numbers. 1 Div were to capture Bou Aoukaz on the left flank and 78 Div salient points on the right flank, on the same night. Previous to this main attack, 4 Div to attack on the right and 4 Indian Div to attack on the left, supported on a 3000 yard front by a mass of artillery and by tanks as soon as it was light. 6 and 7 Armoured Divs concentrated behind to go through the gap. Zero hour 0300 6th May.

It was an immense concentration of force and as events turned out so overwhelming that the plans as made were more than justified by the success they achieved ... The opposition encountered was a good deal less than it had been in the battles of the previous week.

6th May.

Spent the night at the 12 Bde forward command post and got an hour or so sleep before the barrage opened. It was a magnificent sight ... the fire of four Divisional Artillerys ... I went forward with Brigadier Hull in rear of the Black Watch just as it was getting light. A fair number of wounded were being brought back or were walking back and a fair number of prisoners but nothing very extensive.

From now on it is impossible to remember and relate the remaining details of the day. The other two battalions came up and final objectives were all reached before dark in a most successful day.

7th May.

By evening our armoured cars were reported in Tunis. Bizerta was said to have fallen to the Americans and the enemy were reported to be withdrawing for a last stand to cover his evacuation from the Cap Bon peninsula.

8th May.

The morning confirmed the good news that we were in Tunis and Bizerta and that the speed of our advance had cut the enemy in two ... I was told to take command on route C towards the neck of the Cap Bon peninsula ... our march was a slow one ... a complete jam of vehicles with 78th Division doing a victory march into Tunis going one way and thousands of prisoners coming out the other way ... Added to the party were the refugees returning to their homes. The prisoners were a magnificent sight and their numbers seemed staggering until we saw the even more amazing sights in the Cap Bon peninsula later on.

9th May.

Situation in our part of the world now was that 1st Armoured Division were trying to force the pass near Creteville without much success and 6th Armoured Division were attacking along the coast road through Hamman Lif with considerable success ... In fact 1st Armoured Div were remarkably slow this day and never forced the pass at all.

10th May.

The morning started extremely well with the arrival at last of my Selkirk car, with its lean-to, its '19' set [radio] and all its other appurtenances. Not much had been rifled from it ...

At this time the bold decision was made to push straight on in the moonlight to Korba – BW and 305 Bty in support to advance and capture Korba on the coast ... Beni Khallib was an amazing sight at this time with a congestion of vehicles, clapping native population, prisoners and French officials. The advance went according to plan, the only opposition being the odd sniper, though the route was lined with abandoned and burning vehicles. The BW reached Korba about 0300, taking the inhabitants both civil and military completely by surprise. They gained a rich harvest of sleeping prisoners and booty.

11 May.

The advance was more like a victory march than an operation of war...every hillside contained people waving the white flag ...Our

100

final objective was so full of prisoners that we could not get through and we had to skirt to the east of it to reach our positions for the night.

13th May.

News came that the campaign was over and that all the enemy had capitulated. Our chief impression of the end was that of immense surprise that the Bosche had so suddenly packed in after his magnificent fighting before the breakthrough. That they fight to the last round is untrue. Prisoners were all well fed, rested and well armed with plenty of ammunition.

The Regiment's casualties since landing on 23rd March amounted to 7 killed, 15 wounded (one of whom died of wounds) and 7 missing.

On the same day, Willie writes to his mother about the news of the twins arrival which he has now had, and tells her about their names. There is a possibly apocryphal story that they are in danger of being called Tunis and Bizerta until somebody sensible (Bridget?) puts a stop to it. He goes on to say:

All is very well here and we have finished polishing off the Cape Bon peninsula after a very exciting advance across the neck to cut them off, followed by a sort of victory march up the coast. Latter could hardly have been called a battle as neither Bosche nor Iti had much fight left in them, the two main difficulties being to collect the mass of prisoners and to prevent the troops all disappearing with the booty!! We ended the party by putting a gun into action on the northern beaches and shooting over open sights at the Bosche evacuating in open boats. As soon as we got near, every boat in turn put up the white flag and turned back towards the beach. We eventually got the whole lot in, and just before the navy roared in, which was very satisfactory.

And then, perhaps in deference to his brother, he adds: 'The Air has been terrific, and apart from a few mistakes when they dropped bombs on us ... no army could have had finer support from its air forces.'

In his personal memoir published in 1998, Eddie de Rothschild, famous amongst gardeners for his grounds at Exbury in Hampshire and at this time a subaltern in the Regiment, writes that Willie Pike was 'the finest commanding officer I encountered during my time in the Army. Before the war he had served in India – where, he used to reflect, "soldiering was so much more fun on a full establishment of men and horses" ... he was a brilliant, charming man and one who, to a junior officer such as myself, possessed the outstanding characteristic of a consistently even temper.'

Willie's award of the DSO is recorded in the Regimental War Diary on 29 May 1943. Early in 1944 he is posted to command an Officer Cadet Training Unit (OCTU) at Catterick Camp, North Yorkshire, an important role but a posting that he strongly regrets for the rest of his life, depriving him as it did not only of his command, with whom he would have fought in Sicily and the Italian campaign, but also of the chance for further operational service during the final phases of the war in Normandy and NW Europe. After VE day in 1945 Willie is earmarked for a role in the planned invasion of Malaya (Operation Zipper) in the continuing war against Japan, overtaken by the bombing of Hiroshima and Nagasaki, and Japan's surrender.

Among many others, the one-year-old Hew's godfather, Tommy Hussey, is killed on 9 June in Normandy, three days after the British 3rd Division lands on Sword Beach on D-Day. He is commanding 33rd Light Regiment RA in the Division – a Division that Hew will himself command in Bulford forty-eight years later. 33rd Light Regiment's War Diary records: 'Attack on Cambes. Royal Ulster Rifles (RUR) advanced from Le Mesnil supported by Divisional Artillery programme. Came under heavy mortar and shellfire. Casualties to Regiment heavy. CO killed by direct hit by mortar bomb on the carrier, remainder of crew uninjured.' His young widow Joyce eventually remarries, but when she dies in old age, her ashes are scattered on Tommy's grave in the Commonwealth War Cemetery at Douvre la Délivrande, just inland from Sword beach in Normandy. Reunited at last.

Throughout his life, Willie's links with 77th (Highland) Field Regiment's Old Comrades Association remain strong, through personal friendships and annual reunions, held alternately in Glasgow and Brighton – a good English-Scots compromise.

Chapter Ten

Cuthbert Thicknesse, St Albans and Hiroshima, 1945

Cuthbert, younger brother of Frank and older brother of Bridgie, is educated at Marlborough and Keble College, Oxford. He is highly intelligent, with a quick understanding of complex matters, but his degree results do not reflect this – he would excuse this by the magic word 'cricket'. After two years as a Curate in Hackney, he serves as a Forces Chaplain on the Western Front, until wounded at the Third Battle of Ypres, where he is tended by the same Medical Officer who later attends his dying brother Frank, and who in his letter to their father notes Cuthbert's 'coolness and grit'. The wound to his knee and thigh leaves him with constant pain and the need of a stick for the rest of his life. As Rector of Wigan from 1922 to 1936, where he is much loved and respected, his great achievement is the building of a new senior school, and the reconstruction of many church schools in the diocese, for which he raises £40,000 during the years of the Depression. Throughout his life, education remains his abiding passion. After the bombing of Hiroshima and Nagasaki in August 1945, and against the grain of national feeling, he refuses to hold a Service of Thanksgiving in St Albans Abbey.

Notes held in the Muniment Room at the Abbey, where he becomes the Dean in 1936, record that:

> His enormous energy and forthright ways hit the congregation like lightning – but it was life-giving lightning – once people got over the shock. On his second Sunday in St Albans he astonished the congregation by arriving to celebrate Holy Communion in Eucharistic vestments, not previously used in the Abbey. Many of the congregation left in a huff, but slowly they drifted back when they heard the talk of his fine sermons, his passion for music and his ability to

103

draw young people into church: the new 9.30 Holy Communion service which he introduced attracted many who had never been to church before. He revelled in plainsong, and sang every possible part of his services. During the 9.30 service he would march up and down the centre aisle of the nave singing lustily and thrusting hymn books into the hands of those not singing, telling them in a loud voice 'Sing!' His approach to his parishioners was friendly (St Albans is a Parish Church as well as an Abbey) and he mixed with the congregation: this was new. He endeared himself to the bellringers by waiting after the services to thank them for their work. During the Second World War the Firewatchers slept on camp beds under the organ loft until the siren sounded: he never failed to come in at 9pm and say prayers with them.

One of the most memorable features of his preaching career was his delight in public debate: he could certainly draw a crowd in the Abbey Orchard and at Speakers Corner in London, and hecklers were welcome. His action in refusing to allow a Service of Thanksgiving at the Abbey for victory over the Japanese after the explosion of the Atomic Bombs over Hiroshima and Nagasaki caused a national furore, and led to lively correspondence in the Church Times as well as the Hertfordshire Advertiser.

The Dean justifies himself thus, in his address to the Mayor and Corporation:

We may in all sincerity express our thanks to God for the cessation of warfare, for the victorious conclusion which has crowned the valour, the endurance, the patient sacrifice and steadfast unity of the peoples of the British Commonwealth of Nations and the King's Allies. We rightly rejoice with those whose loved ones are released from the cruel bondage and torture of prison camps, and from the separations and perils and anxieties of war: and we rejoice with their homes and friends in this day of happy release.

Let it not be supposed that any of us withhold our due sense of gratitude for this mighty deliverance and our immeasurable debts to those who have ventured life and all for our country, the cause of the United Nations, and our own security. This City, and the Abbey, which is its treasure, have been marvellously preserved through these long years of destruction.

The events of these last ten days have, however, given cause for deep searchings of heart for many people. The discovery of the power to use atomic force, described by the President of the United States of America as 'the basic power of the universe', has been employed for the first time in the destruction of the Japanese cities of Hiroshima and Nagasaki. The decision so to use the atomic bomb was made by the leaders of the democratic nations. We are all, therefore, though without our consent given, implicated in that act. It has, as it is asserted, brought the war to an abrupt end, and therefore shortened the agony of the world, but, as was said in a recent letter in The Times, posterity will condemn those who have first used it for this purpose, thereby creating the most dreadful precedent in the history of mankind.

This is not the time, nor have I the right, to debate the so vast moral issues involved in this matter: and it is a question upon which every man has a right to his own conscientious conviction. But I owe it to you, and the Council over which you preside, to give you this account of my reason for declining to hold a Service of Thanksgiving for victory in St Albans Abbey on this day. You will see that the Union Jack flies from its tower. I did not refuse permission for the Abbey bells to be rung this afternoon, though I understand that the Abbey Band (Bell Ringers), out of generous deference to my known wishes, did not avail themselves of that permission. You may have heard the bells ring. Those are public tokens of rejoicing which may express the feelings of the majority of the people in this City and of the Abbey congregation. I have, therefore, confined my symbolic protest to my own action, and to the matter in which my personal discretion and responsibility is undeniable. I do not hold a Service of Thanksgiving in St Albans Abbey today because I cannot honestly give thanks to God for an event brought about by a wrong use of force: by an act of wholesale indiscriminate massacre which is different in kind from all the acts of open warfare, however brutal and hideous hitherto. A greater power than the use of force, however vast, will be needed to enable humanity to restore what humanity has destroyed ... It is my duty to speak the truth to you as God shows it to me.

In another commentary, Jeanne Lindley writes:

Perhaps the climax of this, in many ways, conservative priest's life came when he, a staunch supporter of the war effort ... shut his Cathedral's doors, with the exception of the Chapel for private prayer, on a day of national celebration.

Taken by itself, this might have been mistaken for an outburst of frustration from a strong, authoritative and sometimes impetuous figure. What followed showed the prophet. First, he offered an explanation to the Mayor and City fathers on the evening of that day in which he had aligned himself with those (he optimistically estimated them at 50 per cent of the population) who are 'sick to death at this atrocious crime'. 'The atom,' he said 'was the basic element of the universe and the trusted leaders of our civilisation have chosen to use this power ... for the wanton destruction of two cities and half a million souls.' A Civic service was held in the Abbey on the following Sunday, at which the Dean preached. 'We use our God given powers to release a devastation we can neither understand nor control,' he said. Turning to those who argued that the ending of the war with Japan justified the means used, he asked in Jesus' words, 'What is a man profited if he shall gain the whole world and lose his own soul? Or what shall a man give in exchange for his soul? For the Son of Man shall come in the glory of his Father ... and then shall He reward every man according to his works.'

But Cuthbert Thicknesse did not leave it there, for he went out that Sunday afternoon at 4pm for one of his public 'Abbey Arguments', to face the heckling and questioning of the general public in the Abbey Orchard, and no punches were pulled. That evening, Bishop Philip Loyd backed his Dean quietly from the Abbey pulpit: the Mayor, himself a professing Christian, disagreed publicly from the Town Hall steps.

Meanwhile, Willie Pike, married to Cuthbert's niece Josie, takes a very different view from his new post at HQ 59 Army Group RA in HQ South East Asia Command, India, where they have all been bracing themselves for Operation Zipper, the planned invasion of Malaya in pursuit of military victory over the Japanese. On 22 August 1945 he writes to his mother, 'B':

Heaven knows what will happen to everybody and where we shall go. Still we ought to know soon and it looks as if the Japs are in fact going to pack in everywhere. I expect there'll be odd spots of trouble but that they won't continue to fight seriously anywhere. I must say it is an appalling anti-climax and everyone is very disappointed that things didn't go on for a bit longer ... We were all so much looking forward to having a crack at the Japs, that this has resulted in a terrible reaction. It is of course too obviously a good thing that fighting has stopped and lives are thereby saved, but our feelings are at least understandable. I'm not sure too, whether the way the end has come is altogether satisfactory. Japan doesn't sound like a defeated nation from her utterances. She will always feel and say (like the Germans after the last war) that her armies were undefeated and that it was all the atomic bomb ... One thing is sure, and that is that we are in for a more difficult time for a few years than ever we've had in the war. There'll be unrest, civil wars, strikes and riots all over the world. India will be in a turmoil and China is 100% snip for a civil war. Aren't I being cheerful?

Cuthbert's obituary in the *Church Times* of 4 July 1971 concludes:

He was the complete master of the business of every meeting over which he presided. He was sometimes a little impatient with the temporising timidity of those who begged to differ from him: but opposition fairly and squarely stated earned his respect. He could ride roughshod, but he was always most abjectly sorry when he caused hurt – although, as often as not, he needed to have his offence pointed out. Then he would go to any lengths to make amends.

He was never for a moment dull. He could be, and often was, infuriating. He had no small talk and no time for social conversational tittle-tattle. There can be no doubt that his time at St Albans marked the Abbey's greatest days since those of Abbot Thomas de la Mare in the 14th century. And in the latter part of his own days as Dean, he showed the marks of true greatness.

Chapter Eleven

Willie Pike, Korea, 1951–2

On 25 June 1950, North Korean forces attack South Korean positions south of the 38th Parallel. The UN Security Council, in the absence of the USSR, adopts a resolution calling for the withdrawal of North Korean forces to the Parallel, and calls on member nations to give aid in repelling aggression in Korea. Most people, including most soldiers, have to refer to an atlas to establish where exactly this obscure place called Korea is on the map. July and August see major North Korean advances, including the fall of the South Korean capital Seoul, with US forces in headlong retreat. On 29 August the British 27th Infantry Brigade arrives from Hong Kong, including in due course many Reservists from the Second World War, now compulsorily called up once again. On 15 September the US X Corps under the overall command of the American General Douglas Mac-Arthur, UN Supreme Commander, makes a dramatic and successful amphibious assault at Inchon, west of Seoul, enabling UN forces to break out of Pusan and push north, back towards the 38th Parallel. Seoul is retaken on 26 September, as UN forces sweep north and west, with the North Koreans in flight. Pyonyang, the North Korean capital, falls to the UN on 19 October. Chinese troops engage the UN forces less than 40 miles south of the Yalu River on 25 October, and halt the UN Eighth Army. As the impact of Chinese military involvement on UN fortunes deepens, with Pyonyang occupied by Chinese troops and the UN withdrawing once more across the 38th Parallel, President Truman declares a state of national emergency. In the spring of 1951, MacArthur is sacked by Truman after his criticism of his President's strategy of 'limited war' is made public. Less than two weeks later, the Chinese open their spring offensive, during which the Battle of the Imjin River and the famous stand of the Gloucestershire Regiment – the 'Glorious Glosters' – takes

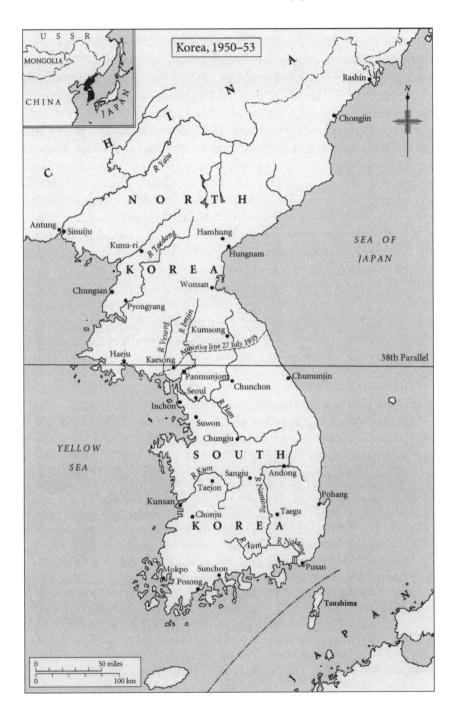

Korea, 1950–53

USSR
MONGOLIA
CHINA
JAPAN

C H I N A

Rashin

Chongjin

N

R Yalu

N O R T H

Antung
Sinuiju

Kunu-ri

R Taedong

Hamhung

Hungnam

SEA OF
JAPAN

K O R E A

Chungsan

Wonsan

Pyongyang

R Vesong

R Imjin

Kumsong

Armistice line 27 July 1953

Haeju
Kaesong

38th Parallel

Panmunjom

Chumunjin

Seoul

Chunchon

Inchon

R Han

Suwon

Chungju

YELLOW

SEA

S O U T H

R Kum
Sangju
Andong

R Naktong

Taejon

Pohang

Kunsan

Taegu

Chonju

K O R E A

R Yam
R Naktong

Mokpo
Sunchon
Pusan

Posong

J A P A N

Tsushima

0   50 miles
0   100 km

J A P A N

place. By the middle of June, the UN Eighth Army is in control of the vital Iron Triangle south of Pyonyang in central Korea, the heart of the communist supply and communications network. Against a background of protracted negotiations over such issues as prisoner exchange and demarcation lines, the fighting continues, much of it at a high intensity, for another two years until an armistice is finally signed at Panmunjom on 27 July 1953. From mid 1952 to the end of the war, for all the periodic surges of tactical activity and the ferocious struggles for hill numbers or map references, which costs thousands of lives on both sides, the strategic situation remains unchanged, in what increasingly becomes a battle of attrition, fought for concessions at the negotiating table in Panmunjom.

The British fight as part of the Commonwealth Division, made up of Australian, Canadian and New Zealand forces, and commanded by the British Major General Jim Cassels (a future CIGS). In June 1951 Willie becomes the Commander Royal Artillery (CRA) of the Division, in command of all the Gunner regiments found by these nations and providing the vital element of artillery fire support to the Division in the face of mass Chinese and North Korean attacks. On 8 June he writes to his mother, 'B', having arrived in Japan before flying to Korea to take over his new post:

I flew down here (to Hiroshima and Kure) today from Tokyo ... it was an awful air trip by US Combat Cargo Command – a bad pilot, a hard seat, parachute and Mae West on one the whole time, no window to look out of, no food, no drink, no reading matter and the plane full of Yankee soldiery, several of them smoking cigars! I did not need the advice I got on arrival, 'Never travel by US lines!' ... We are between Kure and Hiroshima (they practically run into each other). The former is practically completely rebuilt and shows few scars of war. I haven't seen Hiroshima yet but gather it has made a remarkable recovery from its atom bomb. The house where I am staying is run by Japanese girls who couldn't be sweeter or more efficient. The men are equally courteous and appear to bear no resentment against us. The Australians here who know them well confirm this. Our stock is a good deal higher than that of the Americans, as our behaviour has as usual been a great deal better. [Japan is used as a logistic base and leave centre for troops fighting in Korea.] The Americans strike one as a most virile nation who can't be kept down and just need guidance and the right leadership. Whatever one may think of MacArthur over the politics of Korea, he does seem to have done a fine job in putting the Japanese on their feet and giving them the right ideas. The Japanese have the greatest admiration and love for him and he has had a profound effect on the Emperor.

Regular letters to 'B' follow:

July 22nd. Korea.

We had quite a good move yesterday, 100 miles to Suwon and it kept fine, having rained all night. The roads were awful for the first 30 miles and then quite reasonable. We had one truck in the ditch but got it out all right. So we arrived eventually with all our vehicles (to the astonishment of the Americans who never do the trip from Pusan without a high % of write offs on their vehicles). It was a good effort, especially as many of our vehicles are merely reconditioned ones and often not too well reconditioned at that. We are now just north of Suwon, the usual smelly Korean city but of more interest than most as it is very old, with the old city wall and gates still standing. Our camp site [for his HQ, HQRA being a part of the Divisional HQ] is not very good as it is very wet but at least it has some fir trees, so that we get a little shade. The Cease Fire talks have been put into abeyance until 25th July, so we still don't know where we stand. At least it gives us time as a Div HQ to get ourselves ready. We shall be here for a few days, so hope to get a little washing of clothes done. It has been difficult to do any, moving each day, especially when it has been wet. You do need the sun to dry things. We seem to be on a civilian 'right of way' here! The locals, especially the children, are highly interested (especially in what they may be able to scrounge), and very inquisitive. You shove them along and back they come, just like trying to shoo off a lot of puppies ... The mud here is pretty awful and sticks to you like the clay of Tunisia.

To 'B':

August 9th.

We have just finished a slightly futile operation protecting the flank of the Division next door, who were doing a deep sally into our vast No Mans Land. We had to put on a small diversion. It all entailed crossing the Imjin which is in a pretty hearty state and a rather more difficult water obstacle at the moment than the Rhine. All went well until we were well over the river, when the heavens opened and the river gushed down. The bridges and ferries were all sent for six and there we were. Stuff had to be dropped by air and the floods abated fairly quickly, bridges and ferries re-erected and back we are. We bumped the Chinese in small numbers and killed a few of them but on the whole achieved mighty little for great effort. I went up in an Air OP [an Auster light aircraft] the day we were withdrawing and

111

we had a shoot or two but there was very little to be seen. What you do see, the moment we evacuate a position, is a mass of locals on the scrounge for anything left behind. One hill was covered with them and included an odd khaki figure (presumably Chinese) and it is very difficult to know what to do. Some of the Chinese certainly wear civilian clothes and one would be justified in brassing up the lot for their sakes. But one does not want to massacre these wretched locals ... if our troops are in any danger, you certainly brass them up but if not, as one chap said, you let fly if you are in a bad temper but otherwise let them be! ... Tomorrow I have a big day doing practice shooting with the Divisional artillery.

To 'B':

October 5th.

We have just been having quite a battle, which is almost over and very successfully on our bit of the front. The Yanks have not been quite so successful and have had quite a lot of casualties. Ours have not been too bad considering we have pushed the Chinks opposite us off some strong positions. We have killed and wounded a tremendous lot of them and taken quite a lot of prisoners. After two days tough fighting, we have got all our objectives. I think we shall find tomorrow that they have 'bugged out'. Late this evening, our Air OP saw them streaming north in groups and had one or two excellent shoots on them as they ran. We have fired a lot of ammunition off and given them a tremendous hammering with our artillery ... We had one very effective shoot to neutralise the top of a hill where we thought they would have an important OP. We got information later (through radio intercept) that in fact there was a Chinese OP there and that they had complained continuously to their commander for four hours that they could see nothing, that they were out of communication with their guns, that the guns were out of action, that the infantry were being overwhelmed and that finally they were knocked out themselves. It was very satisfactory confirmation that we had done what we were trying to do. Straight from the horse's mouth!

To 'B':

November 9th.

I'm terribly sorry for this gap on letters but I have been far too involved for the last 10/14 days to write any at all. The General (Cassels) went off, leaving me to command the Division until he returned two days ago. From the moment he left, problem after

1. A sketch of Captain Sydney Pike, aged twenty-four, made in 1899 when he is stationed in Gibraltar. (*Author's collection*)

2. Sydney Pike and Bessie Huddleston ('B') on their wedding day at Ely in April 1900. (*Author's collection*)

3 .The three Pike boys, Roy (centre), Billy (Willie) (left) and Geoff (Tom), in about 1917. They remain devoted to their mother, 'B', to whom they owe so much. (*Author's collection*)

4. Sydney Pike (centre, arms folded) with his Ordnance team in camp outside Bloemfontein in 1900. (*Author's collection*)

5. De Wet's Commando crossing the Orange River. (*Author's collection*)

De Wet's Commando crossing the
Orange River

6. The Merton College Boat Club, 1898. Reggie Tompson is sitting in the middle of the third row, without boater, guarding the cat. (*Author's collection*)

7. Reggie Tompson and two of his sisters, Winnie (left) and Irene, at their father's Rectory, St Mary's, Ipswich in 1897. (*Author's collection*)

8. Reggie and Bridgy on their honeymoon in Torquay, February 1915, during leave from France. (*Author's collection*)

9. A 75mm gun in action during the Aro Expedition in Nigeria (1902), in which Reggie distinguishes himself. (*National Army Museum*)

10. Wounded men at an Advanced Dressing Station, Western Front, where Reggie is wounded in October 1916. (*Imperial War Museum*)

11. HQ 7th Division in France, 1916. Reggie is second to the left of the GOC, Major General H.E. Watts. (*Author's collection*)

12. Bridget Thicknesse, who marries Reggie Tompson in 1915. Hers is the generation that lives through the agonies of two world wars. (*Authors collection*)

13. One of the 'lost generation'. Frank Thicknesse, who dies of wounds in October 1917 during the Battle of Passchendaele. (*Winchester College Collection*)

14. Cuthbert Thicknesse, Dean of St Albans, introduces his Verger, John Watkins, to Her Majesty the Queen in July 1952. Badly wounded as a Chaplain on the Western Front in 1917, Cuthbert uses a stick for the rest of his life. (*St Albans Abbey Collection*)

15. Pigsticking days in India. Members of the Muttra Tent Club, in 1936. Willie Pike is second from the right. (*Author's collection*)

16. Willie Pike (No. 21) at a point-to-point meeting in 1938 at Tweseldown near Aldershot. (*Author's collection*)

17. Off to France, 15 May 1940. Bridget Tompson with Willie and his wife, Josie at Bay Tree Cottage. (*Author's collection*)

18. Dunkirk. Filing out to sea to the ships. 'We kept together, clutching our few possessions,' writes Willie. (*Imperial War Museum*)

19. The beach at Dunkirk. 'I have a final picture of that enormous fire still burning sullenly in the distance,' Willie remembers. (*Imperial War Museum*)

20. Soldiers embarked off Dunkirk. 'Eventually, some ships loomed up ... and we all scrambled on board one of them,' Willie records. (*Imperial War Museum*)

21. Hew Tompson as a young Gunner officer. His Housemaster at Winchester wrote that he had 'found himself in the Army'. (*Author's collection*)

22. Fishing . . . (*Author's collection*)

23. . . . and a picnic near Winchester – 1936. Hew with his mother and younger sister, Penel, the picture taken by Jo. (*Author's collection*)

24. Hew at Bay Tree Cottage in 1941, shortly before leaving for North Africa, with his mother Bridget and Henry Montgomery Campbell. (*Author's collection*)

25. A 25-pounder gun in action in the Tunisian djebel, where Willie commands 77th Field Regiment in 1943. (*Imperial War Museum*)

26. A defensive position around the 38th Parallel in Korea, where Willie commands the Artillery Regiments of the Commonwealth Division in 1951–2. (*Author's collection*)

27. Korea, June 1951. Willie (right) with Lt Col Bailey, of 2 RCHA. Standing behind (L–R) are Major General Jim Cassels, GOC of the Commonwealth Division, Brigadier Rockingham (25th Canadian Brigade) and an ADC. (*Author's collection*)

28. Willie with Danny Kaye during his morale-raising visit to the troops in Korea, November 1951. (*Author's collection*)

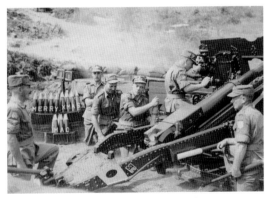

29. 2nd Royal Canadian Horse Artillery (2 RCHA), one of Willie's artillery regiments, wish Chairman Mao Tse Tung a Merry Christmas. (*Author's collection*)

30. A snap taken by Willie of 10 Platoon, D Company, 1st Royal Australian Regiment at Pt 188 on the Kansas line, Korea, August 1951. (*Author's collection*)

31. Willie Pike at a 77th Regiment reunion dinner in Brighton, May 1986. (*Author's collection*)

32. Hew Pike (right) with his platoon in the Radfan mountains, May 1964. Others are (L–R), Privates Tom Surgey, 'Fred' McFarlane and 'Ginge' Ross (in shadow). (*Author's collection*)

33. With much relief, soldiers of 3 PARA go ashore at Sand Bay, Port San Carlos on 21 May 1982. (*Tom Smith*)

34. Watched by local Falkland Islanders, the 3 PARA Battalion flag is raised by Alan Miller, the Port San Carlos Settlement Manager, 21 May 1982. (*Tom Smith*)

35. Soldiers of 3 PARA's Mortar platoon 'wash and shave' outside Estancia House after 3 PARA's arduous advance from Port San Carlos. (*Tom Smith*)

36. The western face of Mount Longdon, up which 3 PARA attacks and ammunition resupply is carried, and down which casualties are recovered. (*Graham Colbeck*)

37. The rocks of Mount Longdon, amongst which the soldiers of 3 PARA take the fight to the enemy. (*Graham Colbeck*)

38. Hew Pike at Estancia House shortly before the assault on Mount Longdon on the night of 11/12 June 1982. (*Max Hastings*)

39. 3 PARA soldiers under shellfire after the capture of Mount Longdon, 12 June. In the centre, a wounded Argentine soldier awaits evacuation. (*Tom Smith*)

40. Hew and Jean Pike leave 10 Downing Street after a dinner and reception given by the Prime Minister for military commanders, October 1982. (*Author's collection*)

41. Will Pike at the District Centre in Sangin, Helmand Province, early July 2006. (*Author's collection*)

42. 'A' Company 3 PARA negotiate a wall in Now Zad, 4 June 2006. (*Author's collection*)

43. 'A' Company advance to contact at the start of the operation in Now Zad, 4 June 2006. (*Author's collection*)

44. 'A' Company arriving in the early morning to occupy the District Centre at Sangin on 21 June 2006, watched from the walls by the locals. (*Author's collection*)

45. Entering Sangin. Will and CSM Turner (foreground) arrive in Sangin, with two signallers, and on the right, Captain Harvey Pynn, the Doctor. (*Author's collection*)

46. Chinook landing in the dust. 'Jumped off into the dust cloud ... and found myself completely alone somewhere near the river,' Will later records in his diary. (*Author's collection*)

47. The Shura on 22 June. Will is sitting near the tree trunk in front of the local man wearing a dark hat. (*Author's collection*)

48. Will Pike (right) and his Company Sergeant Major, Zac Leong. 'I will always remember the awful silence after the first blast ... and Zac Leong returning from his task covered in blood,' Will writes of the rocket attack on their base at Sangin. (*Author's collection*)

problem blew up, including a very heavy Chinese attack against us. We beat the latter off with great slaughter. We had about 250 casualties ourselves, but the Chinks must literally have had thousands. They just attacked in waves, quite regardless of casualties and were knocked over like ninepins. They overran the forward positions of two or three companies but we held them up, since when they have been fairly quiet. They have, however, packed up against us and we might have another party tonight. All sorts of other problems arose and I feel I earned my pay as a Divisional Commander! I also had Danny Kaye as my guest for two days. He gave a wonderful performance to the troops and luckily we got it in just before the attack: one day later and we would have had to cancel it. He is a most delightful man ... I am very fit indeed. Frosty nights and cold but sunny days with the air like champagne. Ye Gods, but the Yanks are a curious lot. I could tell you a lot but perhaps had better not on paper. If these Peace Talks fail over Kaesong, I think the fault will be at their door. They are complete amateurs at any sort of diplomacy.

In an aircraft between Korea and Japan, 10 November:

Am writing these notes in a special aircraft. Felt very important when it was sent until I remembered that the last special aircraft was to remove a Brigade commander who was getting the sack! The moment Jim Cassels left, things seemed to start to happen ... The Norfolks [an infantry battalion] were due to do a small operation to clear some ground but their company commanders felt it was too early as they were put together hurriedly as a battalion and were short of training. There were various comings and goings over this and other similar operations and one other big one by two other Divisions, all connecting up with the Peace Talks. Eventually, we were told to have things at 60 hours notice and limit our activity for the time being to active patrolling.

On Saturday 3rd November, Danny Kaye, an accompanist, two girls and a press photographer arrived with an escort of an American Air Corps Captain. They were all delightful bar the Captain. He was a real shocker and they all loathed him ... His main interest was (a) himself and his comforts, (b) the girls. Danny Kaye gave a show in the afternoon and was brilliant. He got a wonderful reception and was frightfully pleased with the audience who he said were far more appreciative and better behaved than the Americans. He himself went all over the Front and ended up with a pre-arranged film at a Canadian Dressing Station, the film to be used all over North America to gin people up as blood donors. They were perfect guests, apart from the US Captain loitering around the girls – without much success I'm glad to say. Danny Kaye talks seriously and intelligently with flashes of his terrific wit and sense of fun. I shall never now miss one of his films!

About midday Sunday 4th, things started to hot up. Shelling increased. There were increasing movements of Chinese troops reported, and agents who came in that afternoon gave some useful reports. About 4pm the shelling suddenly came on thick and fast, especially against the 28 Brigade front and particularly against the King's Own Scottish Borderers [KOSB, an infantry battalion]. The latter had the heaviest shelling for an hour that anyone has had so far in this war. They got pasted at the rate of 120 rounds a minute, I should say. Then to our surprise the attack came in at about 5pm (an hour before dark: they usually wait till dark.) A dozen or more tanks had shown up by this time and we got an hour's magnificent artillery shooting with observed fire plus several very quick and effective air strikes. We got three strikes within the hour against the tanks and most effective they were. Shortly afterwards, attacks developed against the Australians and the King's Shropshire Light Infantry [KSLI, an infantry battalion] and at dusk the Canadians were engaged by artillery and machine guns. They kept up what we always thought was and eventually turned out to be a pure diversion against the Canadians. The attack against the Australians was largely diversionary too, as it turned out. The attack against the KSLI by one Chinese Regiment [equivalent to a British Brigade] was hit terribly by our guns, who pretty well broke it up. It was never really strongly pressed home and it got nowhere. Next day, lots of bodies were found on the KSLI wire and there must have been even more a little further back, where our Defensive Fire (DF) targets caught them forming up.

The attack against the KOSB was far more serious. They put two Regiments [equating to two Brigades, since each Chinese regiment is made up of several battalions] against them, plus the heaviest weight of artillery. It was a pretty fierce battle which went on without a pause for nearly 6 hours. The Chinks eventually battered down our wire and swarmed onto the three forward company positions. One subaltern's story is typical. He killed 5 chinks with his own pistol at one time, one jumping into the trench as the first one was killed. The Bren gunner next to him let off three magazines in bursts at waves of enemy at ranges from 5 to 50 yards. They were just knocked down like ninepins. Eventually, however, sheer weight of numbers told and the place was swarming with Chinese. Some platoons just fought it out, one dying there to a man. The rest were ordered back, one company commander carrying a New Zealand FOO, wounded in both legs, on his back. We got the Battalion readjusted during the rest of the night and thank goodness did not have a Phase 2. I think we had given them far too bloody a nose for that, but it was an anxious night.

We had lost one important hill feature as a result and had to try to get it back next day. We put in the Leicesters [an infantry battalion – the old 17th Foot] to take it and they had a jolly good shot at it. But the Chinese had moved up fresh troops and had packed the place. We could only have got it with very heavy casualties and then might not have been able to hold it. The Leicesters are a new battalion in theatre, very good stuff but still green and it was their first action. They were my only reserve and I did not want them decimated. So I readjusted during the following night and decided that this particular piece of real estate did not justify the casualties. Besides, we are also very short of reinforcements. But it was a difficult decision ... Jim Cassels when he eventually got back, agreed 100% with all that I had done, which was very comforting. As it is, I am now on my way to brief the British Commander in Chief (CinC) Far East (General Sir Charles Keightley) ... because there are some pretty serious issues at stake ... they are not inside the Commonwealth Division, which really is a wonderful show.

Max Hastings, in his book on the Korean War, describes the KOSB action of that Sunday, in which Pte Bill Speakman wins the Victoria Cross:

On the night of Sunday 4th November, the Commonwealth Division suffered a characteristic surprise Chinese attack. The KOSB were manning their positions on Hill 355, seized from the Chinese during the October offensive. For three hours, an intense bombardment rained down upon their bunkers. Then, with the usual horn and bugle accompaniment, the Chinese infantrymen stormed through what remained of their protective barbed wire. The KOSB's mortars ran red-hot as they fired their counter bombardment, until the mortar platoon commander felt compelled to order his men to pour their precious beer ration down the tubes to cool them. Two platoons of B Company were driven from their positions. In the early hours of the morning, the Company runner, a vast, slow Cheshireman named Bill Speakman, with a fearsome record of disciplinary offences, clambered to his feet in Company HQ, stuffed his pouches, shirt and pockets with grenades, and strode purposefully out into the darkness. 'And where the hell do you think you're going?' demanded the Company Sergeant Major. 'Going to shift some of them bloody Chinks,' replied Speakman. He charged alone on to the ridge, grenading as he went, then returned for more ammunition. This time, others went with him. After repeated counter-attacks through the night, at first light the KOSB's positions were once more in British hands, at a cost of seven killed, eighty-seven wounded and forty-four missing ... Private Speakman, twice wounded, received the Victoria Cross. The story of his lonely action – and the legend of the alcoholic stimulus that played some part in it – passed into the history of the British Army. The battle? The battle was nothing, in the context of Korea; the kind of local action that units up and down the front found themselves compelled to fight at regular intervals through two years of positional war. If they won, they could pride themselves on a job well done. If they lost, the communists had gained another hill, and some other hapless unit would sooner or later have to pay the price for displacing them from it.

In a further letter to 'B', Willie writes:

We had another attack, against the Canadians this time, on Monday night. One battalion came in and got on to the wire of one of their forward companies but were beaten off and out with heavy losses. Then on Wednesday night, they staged a heavy attack by one regiment against the Australians. We caught it, however, perfectly with our artillery and knocked it for six to such good effect that the Australians were not unduly worried and the attack was never properly pressed home.

So you see I had quite an eventful stewardship for my nine days as Divisional Commander! It is a far heavier responsibility to be answering for someone else than when the real responsibility is entirely your own, so I was not sorry to see Jim Cassels back! So much for my first (and probably last!) battle as a Divisional Commander (acting, unpaid!).

On 16 November, he writes again to his mother, who has, not surprisingly, been reading the newspapers:

I agree with you about the accounts of the Korean fighting in The Times; it is remarkably dull reading. I have just been reading their account of our Nov 4th/5th battle; all I can say is that it certainly wasn't as dull as that here! Heartbreak Ridge belongs to the Americans on our right. We helped them at times with our guns but otherwise it was entirely American. They weren't too skilful and lost an awful lot of casualties. It was part of the same operation as we had, but they weren't as successful and got mixed up in a very expensive slogging match by the end of it. We are well over the Imjin now with our front line but our HQ is quite close to it. It turns north after our front, so further up belongs to the Chinese. I have just heard one quite amusing story of the attack on the KOSB. The OP officer and his party (New Zealanders) had their communications to the guns knocked out, were overrun by the Chinese and were having hand to hand fighting, throwing grenades etc. One of his signallers was hurling the most abusive language at the Chinese as he flung each grenade, until the young officer (a very gallant chap) nudged him and said quite seriously, 'Kindly moderate your language, Gunner Fitzsimmons.'

My kitten has settled down and taken charge of the caravan. Where it came from I really don't know. It is the first cat I have seen in Korea and just blew in.

To 'B':

20th November.

We are having a quiet night tonight for which we are all thankful as we have had a heavy attack on each of the three previous nights running. We've beaten them off each time but people are getting a bit tired in the front, especially as they have had pretty heavy shelling. They start their attacks about an hour before dark when the setting sun is in our eyes. It is now 9pm and nothing has happened so, touching wood, we may have a good night's rest for a change. We have done tremendous execution with the Divisional Artillery. It is impossible to estimate casualties, especially as they carry back their dead with local porters as soon as the party is over. However, we got a clue today as a patrol discovered a pile of about six hundred bodies laid out in the area they formed up in for one attack and which they have not yet removed. Very encouraging, one might say! These attacks have not been quite so heavy or so serious as the one on Nov 4/5th, but heavy enough to be quite nasty.

It is lovely weather here and one feels very fit. The days are really lovely and so bracing ... Tomorrow is supposed to be the day the Communists say Yes or No to the Peace Proposals. I wonder. Having dragged on since June, one is sceptical of anything ever being settled. The Yanks are almost as bad as the Chinese at arguing round and round the point and are no diplomatists in these sort of affairs. One thing strikes me more and more about Americans. They are very well educated on facts and statistics, but quite uneducated on the process of logical thought. They can't and don't ever appear to reason a problem out dispassionately or logically. I like them very much as people but I think little of their mental ability.

To 'B':

28th January 1952.

Don't take any notice of the Sunday Despatch and all this howl about winter clothing. We are perfectly all right and anyway the Korean winter is nothing like as bad as is made out. There were muddles in England over sizes of boots and Parka coats, due to their being rushed (due I think to a strike in the factory), but that and all the other things have been grossly exaggerated by the Press. All the Press want is a scare headline quite regardless of the truth. The only point where I agree with Aneurin Bevan is in sharing his low opinion of the Press. [Willie has this theory, somewhat tongue in cheek of course, that the Duffle coat is the badge of Communism, and Bevan did seem to wear one quite often when haranguing the crowds with his wonderful Welsh oratory in Trafalgar Square!] We knock their bunkers and digging about, raid them and so forth, but they are very persistent and soon repair them. The weather is quite reasonable at present, especially by day when it is very bracing. We had half a day after pheasants again recently and enjoyed ourselves.

Apart from a few reputable papers, they are the bottom and make themselves a darned nuisance out here. So there is nothing whatever to worry about, either me personally or the troops in general.

Things are still fairly quiet. The Chinese are busy digging opposite us and we don't quite know whether it is defensive or whether it is to help them launch an offensive.

To 'B':

February 22nd.

I left Divisional HQ yesterday by road as it was too windy to fly in a light aircraft and spent the night with a pal in Seoul. I had a pleasant evening with him including a hot bath (Korean type but still a hot bath!). It was a sort of square stone affair with a tin bottom with a fire underneath to heat the water. You had to squat on a rectangular stone and be careful not to put your feet on the metal floor. With a little juggling, you wedge yourself in and manage to get most of yourself under water without undue danger ... We had dinner with a French Canadian Psychiatrist there, who is a very nice chap and most amusing but very odd and badly in need of psychiatric treatment himself. We had breakfast served by very nice little Korean waitresses. They were prettily dressed ... very bright and efficient. How different to the poor women you see toiling in the countryside, working the fields or carrying loads of firewood on their backs, looking ragged and half starved.

We took off in the C in C's plane for an hour's flight to an island 100 odd miles off the south west coast. We had a fair day's shooting ... there were nine of us and we got 40 pheasants, woodcock and one quail. It was very stiff walking, with a lot of clambering over stone walls. It is typical Korean country except that it is divided by these stone walls. It is very like the west coast of Ireland and an old R.C. priest who joined us said it was exactly like his old home country in the west. He was a grand old boy and has been there for 18 years. I imagine life has scarcely changed in the last thousand or more years, women and children carting firewood on their backs, stocky little ponies pulling wooden carts and the most frightful roads.

To 'B':

May 21st.

What a mess the Americans are making over these POWs and the Armistice talks. They walked straight into it over the Brigadier-General Dodds episode. The man they sent to get him out and who made such an utter mess of things (Brigadier-General Coulson) was Chief of Staff of our Corps. He is a dull, dumb, dim-witted man, so it was no surprise to us that he put his foot in things. [Brig-Gen Dodds was the US Commandant of Koje-Do POW camp for the Communists, who were making maximum propaganda from the POW issue in the context of the Peace negotiations. Dodds had been taken hostage by the prisoners, and the concessions agreed to secure his release were widely seen as a further propaganda coup for the Communists.]

Willie has been awarded the CBE – Commander of the British Empire. In this letter, as well as in his assiduous attention to his mother through their very regular correspondence – she is always 'My darling B' – he acknowledges the great debt that the brothers owe to her:

October 20th.

Thank you for your congratulations which are the most welcome of any. I know that Geoff [Tom] agrees with me that anything we have achieved is entirely due to you and the wonderful upbringing you gave us. Whilst we may claim a little satisfaction from our successes, the bulk of the credit goes to you and no one else. My chief pleasure in collecting another gong is therefore that I know how pleased you are and how I haven't let down the most wonderful mother anyone could have had.

As a Major General, Willie goes on to become Chief of Staff, Far East Land Forces in Singapore and finally, as a Lieutenant General, Vice Chief of the Imperial General Staff (VCIGS) at the War Office in the early 1960s. He lives in Bentley until his death in 1993, much loved for his wisdom, compassion, humour and respect for his fellow men.

Chapter Twelve

Hew Pike, Radfan, May 1964

Hew and his twin sister Judy are born at Bay Tree Cottage, Bentley, Hampshire on 24 April 1943. Hew is educated at Winchester College and is in Turner's House (called 'Hoppers') like his grandfather Reggie and uncle, Hew. In January 1961 he enters the Royal Military Academy Sandhurst (RMAS), aged seventeen. When he returns to Sandhurst as the Commandant thirty-three years later, by which time the majority of cadets are graduates in their early twenties, he looks up his record and reports as a cadet, of which these are some extracts:

Charge Sheet: 'Making an improper remark to a Junior Under Officer'.

Charge Sheet: 'Making an improper remark to the Company Orderly Sergeant'.

'A cheerful young fellow. Unduly cheerful, perhaps, at times. He has a childish side to him.'

'I should guess that, as an officer, he might find a little more conformity judicious.'

'A cheerfully independent person. This ... used to take the form of minor indiscipline such as unpunctuality and even unauthorised absence from classes.'

'A bit of a rebel'.

'His work, once deciphered, is good.'

And from the historian John Keegan, then a young lecturer at Sandhurst: "His work is of a high standard. He writes with interest and fluency and has a wide range of interests ... He has a most attractive and easy manner.'

Hew joins The Parachute Regiment in 1963, and his early years of soldiering are spent with the 3rd Battalion (3 PARA) as a platoon commander, some of the time based in Bahrain.

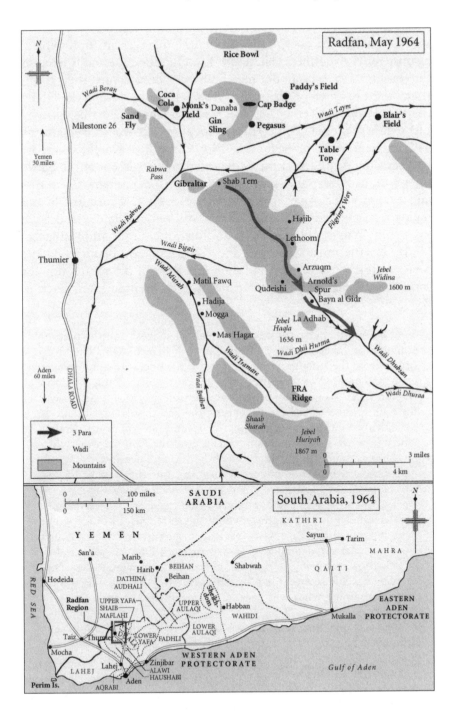

Radfan, May 1964

South Arabia, 1964

3 PARA is deployed from it base in Bahrain to Aden in May 1964, to take part in an operation in mountainous terrain 'up country' against rebel tribesmen. These are the Qutaibis, the main tribe of the Radfan area, who under new laws have been denied their traditional right to collect tolls from caravans travelling along the Dhala road towards the Yemen. 3 PARA is commanded at this time by Lieutenant Colonel Tony Farrar-Hockley, known universally as TFH, a veteran of the Second World War and of Korea, where he had been the Adjutant of the Gloucestershire Regiment at the Battle of the Imjin River, and subsequently a prisoner of the Chinese – and a mighty unco-operative prisoner, too. He is a formidable and highly respected commanding officer, still only thirty-seven despite his already remarkable record as a soldier of courage and resilience. He is also the most Christian and compassionate of men. By the time of Hew's patrol, the Battalion has been in the mountains for some weeks. Hew recalls this time in notes written later, back in Bahrain:

'And before the patrol moves out tonight, I suggest that the platoon commander takes a needle and thread to his shirt.' Thus ended my orders from the Commanding Officer, for the operation that I was to lead that night. We were near the village of Shab Tem, a remote Radfan jebel that was high, wild and barren. My task was to seize the high ground of the Hajib feature, the battalion's next bound in our advance along one of the ancient spice routes of South Arabia, where now we found only goat tracks. And the Colonel was right – my khaki flannel ('KF') shirt, which had long since lost its prickly newness, was now not merely well worn, but thoroughly ragged. Rocks, sweat and thorn trees had taken their toll over the past few weeks; and anyway, I rather enjoyed being ragged. I can't remember now whether I did do anything about the shirt, but if I did, I would have borrowed the necessary bits and pieces from Private 'Ginge' Ross, my platoon signaller, a Scotsman from Fife. He was a close friend, too, and being a better soldier than me, would have been carrying his 'housewife' (aka 'huzziff) – the tiny bundle issued to all ranks containing what was needed for darning socks and sewing on buttons.

This was the first real chance of action for the platoon since operations had started. The battalion had to be self-sufficient, and on previous moves forward we had been employed as 'fighting porters', carrying five-gallon jerry-cans of water and following up in reserve. It was May, and the humidity was high, even at night; so a lot of water was needed. The one 'Scout' light helicopter of 653 Squadron Army

Air Corps (AAC) supporting the battalion and flown by Major 'Mad Jake' Jackson, was performing a myriad of other tasks, whilst the big twin-rotor RAF Belvederes had proved too vulnerable to enemy ground fire, and were now being used only around the Brigade's airhead at Thumair.

I had left Sandhurst eighteen months before, and for me this was just what I had joined for – a 'North West Frontier' situation of sniping tribesmen, with the crack of bullets and spice of danger in the air, but with no threat from artillery or aircraft, and only an outside chance of catching a bullet. This was an adventure, and the best possible baptism of fire. Only we 'beastly British' had shells and fighters – 105mm Pack Howitzers, elderly 5.5 inch artillery pieces, and RAF Hawker Hunter ground attack aircraft. Yet even superb flying in the wadis, and great accuracy with rocket and cannon fire, could not dislodge the courageous 'Red Wolves', as the tribesmen came to be called, from their deep caves on rocky cliff-faces. It was from these positions, almost impossible to spot, that they sniped at us from astonishing distances with their ancient long-barrelled Martini-Henry rifles.

My qualifications for leading 3 Platoon into action were slender. At Sandhurst I had commanded several patrols – none very successfully. On the first occasion, I had given out some reasonable orders but had subsequently become totally lost in thick mist around Hawley Lake, near Camberley, and my Platoon Instructor, Captain Lennox Napier of the South Wales Borderers, had politely but firmly taken charge. He had won a Military Cross in Malaya, and I have always wondered at his forbearance that night. On my final Sandhurst patrol, during a test exercise in Cyprus, we had to ambush some 'terrorists' landing arms on the coast from a fishing smack. They landed their arms, and we watched them doing it, from concealed positions above the cove. But I remember no ambush.

The task this time was to seize the high ground including the village of Hajib, secure it for the battalion, and capture a prisoner. The prisoner was considered especially important, as intelligence on our enemy was almost non-existent. The Aden Government had little idea about who was leading the rebellion, orchestrated from Cairo and fostered by President Nasser's supporters over the border in the Yemen.

Four 'heavies' in the platoon were therefore grouped as the 'snatch party' for the prisoner. They were led by Corporal Paddy Rochford, a wonderful Southern Irish soldier, who had transferred to us from the 'Micks' – Irish Guards – after a tour in the Guards Parachute Company. Also in the party were to be Private 'Rommel' Hamilton, an Ulsterman who later joined the RUC and worked for Special Branch during the 'Troubles', Private Tich Freeman, a cynical but sharp and likeable young 'Scouser', and Private Roger Cole, an honest country boy from Lincolnshire, whom I had first met when I went to speak up for him in Spalding Magistrates Court. Had the Bench realised that my glowing testimonial was based entirely on hearsay, this being my first duty as the newly-arrived Platoon Commander, Cole might not have got off so lightly. But he was hugely likeable and an extremely keen soldier, who later did well with the SAS.

I issued the necessary orders to the platoon confidently enough, but it was hard to make much of a plan, because although we could see the Hajib feature away to the south-east, the map provided few clues to help us. Much of it was literally a blank white sheet with only grid lines on it. Even such detail as it did contain had been taken from an air photograph before being printed out as a kind of grey blur, and there were no contour lines. Worse still, we had no idea where the enemy would be, or in what numbers.

We all felt a certain tenseness, a feeling that this was an endeavour altogether more serious than usual. But the patrol set off that night with high hopes and plenty of confidence, just as we had done in training on similar nights along the Kyrenia Range in Cyprus, or from Al Khatt Dropping Zone (DZ) in the Trucial States (now the UAE) after insertion by parachute on airborne exercises. This was to be 3 Platoon's night; the battalion were to await our success, before the main body linked up with us. We had taken compass bearings onto our objective, and were reliant entirely on 'dead reckoning'. The night was moonlit, my navigation went well, and we made good progress. We moved in file down a long, wide wadi bed, not knowing when we might contact the enemy or walk into an ambush amongst the rocks that rose steeply on both sides. The night was humid and I vividly recall my head feeling peculiarly vulnerable. Helmets were too heavy and we wore our red berets throughout this campaign; very sticky and tight they were too, hence shoved into a smock pocket on every possible occasion, and certainly at night. At one point, one man who had cocked his 9mm sub-machine gun against orders, fired it by mistake. Our luck was in, as nobody was alerted, and the round went harmlessly into the ground. This same soldier had fired off a blank round when cleaning his weapon on an exercise some weeks before, and I had done nothing about it, beyond giving him an imperial rocket. We could have paid a heavy price for my earlier slackness – a casualty, the patrol compromised, our mission aborted.

We had been moving for several hours before we started to climb out of the wadi and up the steep cultivated terracing above a small village, now deserted, towards the high ground around Hajib. The terracing was awkward to climb even in fairly light order, as the wall at each succeeding level was a big stride up. We were, in any case, carrying considerable weights in ammunition and water alone. We also had rockets for the platoon's 3.5 inch rocket launcher, the tube broken into two parts and now muffled in Hessian cloth to stop it clanking. But we were a fit platoon and we had long since found our mountain legs, so we were still moving well as we fanned out, clear of the terraces, onto the rocky slopes above. By now we could make out a crest line ahead of us, and below it a small square fort, built of mud and stone, guarding the high ground. The time had come to deploy our snatch party, and they moved in to the fort as soon as the platoon had been deployed to cover the exits and escape routes. But it was empty, and there was no sign of recent occupation, only the distinctive musty, pungent smell of all such places, that form such a lasting memory of Arabia. The leading section now continued to climb towards the crest line, the snatchers following up with me, with the two other sections behind us to left and right. We began to lose interest in finding our prisoner, although there was another fort way up to our right at the summit of the feature, that could well be held by the enemy.

The shouts and shots came together. Excited Arab voices seemed to come from just over the crest line of rock, as if they were hiding in positions on the sheer cliff face that fell away beyond the summit. Their shots tended to confirm this, for they whistled harmlessly over our heads as if fired into the air as a nocturnal 'feu de joie'. However, this was the first time most of us had been 'under effective enemy fire', and we were going to make the most of it. The best thing to do seemed to be to rush the top of the ridgeline, so I shouted 'Charge!'

I noticed at once that there was some reluctance to respond to this order, and that I myself was advancing cautiously rather than heroically. When we did reach the top, not surprisingly, there was no sign of our enemy. They must have slipped away down one of the steep goat tracks well known to them, where in darkness we dared not follow in such unfamiliar and inhospitable country.

Meanwhile, our drills had taken hold, and covering fire from the platoon's three machine guns was now plastering the ridgeline as we advanced. This brought the Gunners into the act. We had a number of targets registered for the guns of Bull's Troop, as 'I' Battery of 7th Parachute Regiment, Royal Horse Artillery (7 RHA), were known. But there was a clear understanding that no targets would be engaged unless we called for fire on the radio. My excitement had put any such thoughts out of my mind, and anyway I had done little training in the art of 'calling for fire'. But the battery commander, Major David Drew, had heard our 'battle', and decided to fire the guns on his own initiative. His shells, however, landed not in front of us but behind us, on the slope up which we had just climbed. Bull's Troop must be stopped. A frantic and not particularly polite call on our A41 radio miraculously achieved this, and fortunately there were no casualties in the follow-up sections, despite the lethality of shellfire on such hard rocky terrain. Not surprisingly, the Gunners too were having problems with their map reading.

We now set off on a superb sequence of fire and movement by sections, up the Hajib feature to our right. We worked on the principle that since we didn't know where the enemy was, or when he might engage us, we would put down our own pre-emptive fire, to cover all movement. As a field firing exercise it was by far the best I had ever experienced, comparing favourably with anything we had done at Jebel Ali, our training camp in the desert between Dubai and Abu Dhabi, in the weeks before deploying to the Radfan. The 'prisoner' was entirely forgotten. The impressive, one-sided 'battle' that ensued would have made a splendid demonstration. All the principles of concentration of fire, keeping a foot on the ground, and skilful movement were applied, but at the summit of Hajib, we found another empty fort. While we settled down, triumphantly, to hold our newly-won objective, and to await the arrival of the Battalion, I wondered whether the tribesmen might try a counter-attack. The Radfanis did not seem keen on night fighting, and so I thought it unlikely. My final humiliation came when I challenged and then engaged with my rifle a scuffling sound outside our summit perimeter. It turned out to be a cow, obviously abandoned by villagers – and it escaped unscathed.

I have often dwelt, since that night, on what might have been the outcome if we had approached the ridge more cautiously, put out more cut off groups, reconnoitred more thoroughly, or pressed home our attack more swiftly? A group of prisoners, perhaps? A great coup for the platoon? In vain we sought blood stains, in the days that followed, in the area of our original contact. We had not disgraced ourselves, but nor had we covered ourselves with the distinction to which we aspired. I had never found the tactical command of the platoon easy, as there always seemed to be an awful lot to think about, and the whole business was so imprecise and untidy. Nor had I even done my young officers' course at the School of Infantry. But here I had had a marvellous chance, denied to most, and if I hadn't totally muffed it, I had failed to fully grab my opportunity. Probably the most important lesson for me was that the meticulous and careful preparation of a simple plan, in which every likely contingency is anticipated and rehearsed, greatly increases the chances of success. Then when things go wrong, people understand what is expected of them, will act on their own initiative, and will make things happen. That night in the Radfan taught me something about the crucial relationship between detailed planning and flexible execution. But it was not an easy task, in such unfamiliar terrain, and I comfort myself with the thought that many would probably have done no better.

We did not carry sleeping bags or blankets, only a roll of light hessian sackcloth which was used for shade and camouflage by day, and as a blanket against the cold by night. In these, we now wrapped ourselves and awaited the dawn. We were extremely tired, not so much from a long march and a steep climb, as from the release of tension, although what we had done barely qualified even as a skirmish..

When dawn came, I was joined by the Commanding Officer, TFH, who had moved up with the main body of the battalion. My debrief was short. 'Your movement and navigation have been commendable, old chap,' he began. My heart swelled. 'However,' he abruptly concluded, 'I am most vexed that you have failed to capture a prisoner.' Despite our wild, dramatic surroundings, his comments felt no different from the 'fatherly advice' I had frequently received from him back in Bahrain. It was all rather an anti-climax.

Vexatious too for the CO was the loss of his helicopter some days later, forced to land by enemy fire in the Wadi Dhubsan during the subsequent finale to this 'punitive expedition' against such brave and fiercely independent tribesmen. The Battalion had made a 3,000 foot descent into this huge tribal stronghold the previous night, and now found themselves under small arms fire from all sides. Supported by Hawker Hunter ground attack aircraft, brilliantly flown and very often firing their cannon from behind the attacking troops, one of the main hazards was the cascade of empty brass cannon cases falling from a great height and at terminal velocity, that clanged disconcertingly among the rocks around us. A hit on the head from one of those made a cricket ball the equivalent of a soft toy, and one man did indeed lose his scalp from a direct hit. Another hazard was certainly the sniping skills of the enemy, concealed high in their sangars in the rocks with their Martini Henrys. Some would move, so that each shot would hit the rocks or perhaps penetrate the thin trunk of a thorn tree from a different angle, leaving you in no doubt that you had been located and that a hit would follow once they'd got their eye in. We were quite glad to get out of that Wadi with few casualties two days later, the CO's Scout helicopter having been made airworthy once more by two skilful REME technicians, Corporals Bill Carcary and John Hustwith, working through the night in the darkness of the wadi bed. Ian Macleod, my great friend in the Battalion and the Intelligence Officer, had been on board the Scout with the CO when rounds started to rip through the cabin from below, one grazing Ian's forearm. He was later given a mild ticking off by TFH for daring to tell him that he thought he might have been wounded, although he refused to be 'casevaced' and was later awarded the Military Cross for his night patrolling and route proving activities throughout the operation.

And Private Jack Watson, one of the 'characters' in 3 Platoon, felt able to add an extra Battle Honour to the Platoon's recent history. 'Rye, Aviemore and the Hajib Feature' was now his war cry. And the less said about Rye and Aviemore the better!

Hew writes to his parents at one point:

I have now lost all sense of time but I think it is about Thursday 21 May. We are now very high up in the mountains and have been here about 10 days so far – we will probably be here for quite some time more. Have had one or two fairly exciting moments although 'exciting' isn't the word I'd have used at the time. The country is very wild and magnificent, with huge gorges about 1000ft or more deep. It is fairly rough going and very hot indeed. More news I can't give and I would guess that we are too far a climb for the average journalist to reach us! [Then, for his mother's benefit] Don't flap!

Those of the Battalion killed in action in this operation were Captain Barry Jewkes, an exceptional young officer attached to us from the Lancashire Fusiliers, when moving to give medical assistance to the badly wounded Sergeant Baxter, and Private Michael Davies, aged 21, from Filey in Yorkshire. Both lie in the Military Cemetery at Maalla in Aden. Among the handful of wounded was the gallant Arthur Shannon, the Regimental Sergeant Major, who led the Drums Platoon forward along the bed of the Wadi Dhubsan to 'rescue' his CO, ignoring the fire around him as if at the Battle of Waterloo.

Chapter Thirteen

Hew Pike, Falklands, 1982

From the autumn of 1969 onwards Hew is much committed to operations in Northern Ireland where he is Adjutant of 1 PARA in Belfast through the first winter of Army deployment (1969/70), a company commander in 3 PARA in Belfast in 1978 and commanding his Battalion, 3 PARA on the border in Co. Armagh and Co. Fermanagh through the winter of 1980/81. In 1982, while he is still in command of 3 PARA, Argentina occupies the Falkland Islands and 3 PARA are immediately earmarked to reinforce 3 Commando Brigade, Royal Marines.

In 1966 Hew marries Jean Matheson, the twin daughter of a RAMC Colonel, Donald Matheson, and his wife Eileen. By 1982, they have three children, Arabella (14), William (12) and Emma (9). As 3 PARA prepare to leave Southampton aboard the SS *Canberra* on Good Friday 1982, he writes to Jean:

> After my rather rushed letter earlier, I thought I would pen another to catch the helicopter tomorrow. It is now 10 pm so we have just sailed through that tremendous send off – really very emotional and unforgettable – perhaps the last time that a 'troopship' will sail in defence of what is left of the British Empire. Four hundred of us lined the ship with the Commandos. The 3 PARA wives contingent were marvellous, with that enormous banner. It's now a bit of an anticlimax, of course, but whatever happens now that will be remembered by us all and fills us with pride and confidence.
>
> Your letter was so good to get. I know how much this sudden turn of events has upset you all, but you must not worry and let's hope the whole thing is quickly resolved. When I used to ask Bobs [William] if he missed me he usually used to say 'No', but this time when I asked him if he would, it was an emphatic 'Yes' – and it really looked as if this year would be the settled one, when I would see lots of them. Well, it may still turn out that way after a bit – who knows? But I do

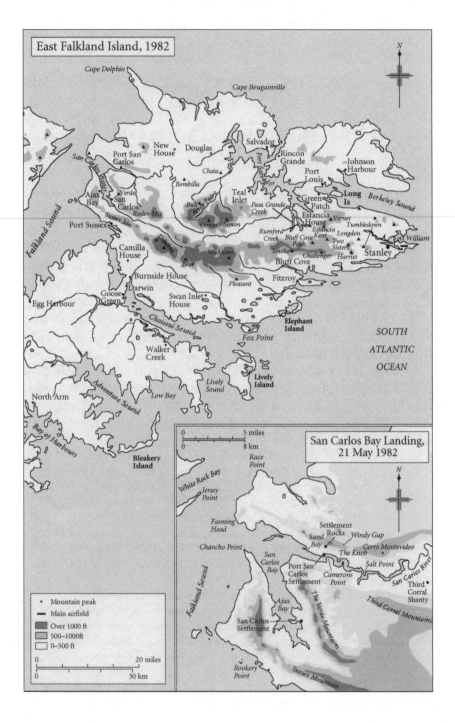

East Falkland Island, 1982

Cape Dolphin

Cape Bougainville

New House
Douglas
Salvador
Rincon Grande
Johnson Harbour
Port San Carlos
Chata
Port Louis
Bombilla
Teal Inlet
Green Patch
Long Is
Berkeley Sound
Ajax Bay
Verde
San Carlos
Rodeo Mts
Bull
Arroyo Pedro
Pasa Grande Creek
Estancia House
Vernet
Tumbledown
Port Sussex
Onion
Simon
Rumford Creek
Bluff Cove Peak
Kent
Longdon
Mt William
Camilla House
Usborne
Wickham
Smoko
Challenger
Two Sisters
Harriet
Stanley
Burnside House
Darwin
Blue
Bluff Cove
Goose Green
Pleasant
Fitzroy
Egg Harbour
Swan Inlet House
Choiseul Sound
Elephant Island
Fox Point
SOUTH
Walker Creek
ATLANTIC
OCEAN
Lively Island
Lively Sound
North Arm
Adventure Sound
Low Bay
Bay of Harbours
Bleakery Island

San Carlos Bay Landing,
21 May 1982

0   5 miles
0   8 km

Race Point
White Rock Bay
Jersey Point
Fanning Head
Settlement Rocks
Windy Gap
Sand Bay
Cerro Montevideo
Chancho Point
The Knob
San Carlos Bay
Salt Point
Port San Carlos Settlement
Camerons Point
San Carlos River
Third Corral Shanty
Ajax Bay
The Verde Mountains
Third Corral Mountains
Falkland Sound
San Carlos Settlement
Rookery Point
Sussex Mountains

▲ Mountain peak
— Main airfield
Over 1000 ft
500–1000 ft
0–500 ft

20 miles
0   30 km

Port Sussex

Falkland Sound

San Carlos River

Sussex Mts

know that they all need me, as well as you, and time goes by so fast. But I'm sure that their confidence and determination won't be affected, and that you will be marvellous with them … try to do as much as possible with them. I'm glad I fitted in that visit to the Imperial War Museum with William. I will write little notes to each of them now, these combined letters get a bit difficult! Anyway darling thank you for such a super letter and don't let things get you down. Of course I worry too – I feel that William needs me especially at the moment, which is agony, but we must be stoical. Do be especially careful with him – the girls are much less reliant on me, I feel.

PS. Yes, I saw you all at the window, I'm sorry the car turned the wrong way. Probably just as well! I'm sorry too that my goodbyes were rather short but it really would have been too tearful otherwise, I feel. Poor little William was almost in tears and you certainly were, and no doubt Beezee [Arabella] would have joined in! Anyway, God bless you all. [Emma is away skiing with her cousins.]

The CO's house is next door to Candahar Barracks in Tidworth, from where the Battalion depart. Jean writes on 8 April:

We watched you go from the landing window … I wonder if you saw us? Then we watched the fleet of coaches and lorries moving off. Then we went straight into Salisbury – I bought four bunches of daffodils to cheer up the house for Easter.

Hew writes on Easter Sunday, 11 April:

I will try to write often rather than at great length. We are now somewhere off Spain, I think, having come through the Bay of Biscay. Today was noticeably warmer, but it is now quite rough – but so far, no pills and not sea-sick! We are doing running (30 mins) and circuit training (30 mins) – exercises, sit-ups, fireman's lifts, press-ups and so forth, each day. Because there is so little space for fifteen hundred men to train in, the whole thing has to be very carefully programmed. The food is excellent. The soldiers are not too cramped and there are lots of washing machines and irons. Colonel Tom Seccombe (RM) is the Military Force Commander on Canberra and the deputy Brigade Commander, he is an excellent man, very relaxed and with a good sense of humour. We had a lot of telegrams from parents and families of soldiers, and quite a few from military people. Some of the waves are almost reaching my cabin window now. Last night after dinner with Denis Scott-Masson (the P&O Captain and an RN

Reservist), I joined the 'Doctor's Party' – the 'Canberra Medical Society' has been formed, by all the Surgeons and Doctors on board, organised by Commander Rick Jolly of the Royal Marines. The P&O surgeon and his staff are still on board; all quite interesting – we all feel that we are part of something really important.

A circular letter is sent round all the families, and we have this response from Mrs Bishop, wife of Lance Corporal S.D. Bishop, one of the Battalion's Physical Training Instructors (PTIs), who is quite moved when I show him the letter, and of course very proud of his wife:

'Utrinque Paratus'

To the Commanding Officer:

I was very surprised to receive a letter from you. I would like to personally thank you. As until times like these, you don't realise the people that do care about your feelings. I'd just like to say good luck to you all, and all come back safely, as we will be waiting cheerfully and patiently for you all.

Yours Sincerely, J.V. Bishop (Mrs)

To Jean:

14 April.

I have waited for a day or two, as no mail goes until we get to Freetown in Sierra Leone, where we take on stores and let off the Vosper Thorneycroft workmen who have been building the two helicopter flight decks on board ... Then on to Ascension Island which we should reach around 20/21 April. We will be there at least six days, practising various things. After that, things are pretty uncertain, as you may imagine. We are all fine, no more rough weather and there is certainly plenty to do. Sergeant Butters and his PT staff are improvising all sorts of things, and there is all the other training and briefing as well. Lots of meetings, too! We listen avidly to the BBC World Service, which comes through to every cabin from a central radio, and is our main source of information. Some antennae have been taken down to make way for the helicopter flight decks, so reception may be less good as we head south ... Some of the soldiers who have very recently got married are a bit unhappy about the whole thing. Naughten (MT) and Yeomans (C) for example – there are others. Worth a special interest at your end.

On 17 April, Hew's father Willie writes:

Don't forget that boldness, even audaciousness, and coming in unexpectedly always pays off. And if you get into a tight corner, remember the enemy also has grave difficulties, and that things are never as bad as they seem. It is the chap who holds out that extra bit longer who wins – and you have, I reckon, the best soldiers in the world in your British paratroopers.

To Jean:

19 April.

Well, we arrive at Ascension early tomorrow morning, and it will be interesting to see how many ships are assembled there. Certainly we will meet up with Brigade HQ. The ship's officers threw a drinks party on the bridge – beautiful with a warm evening breeze blowing – hard to imagine sometimes what we are possibly heading for. Certainly the weather will not be as kind as we sail further south, but at present it is lovely. There are lots of flying fish and dolphin, and a few birds. The RSM has just been running a football panel quiz, which was a great success. The cooks won it, headed by Cpl Arthur! [He is awarded a CinC Fleet's Commendation after the campaign for his bravery under fire as a stretcher bearer.] Today we also practised using the two helicopter decks. Getting the whole battalion out at the right time and place with all its equipment takes a little practice, but all went well. The press are getting very frustrated at how little they can report – I think the MOD are being rather heavy. I wonder how 2 PARA will fare – not as comfortably as us, I fear – but it means that we are all very fit and rearing to go. [2 PARA have now also reinforced 3 Commando Brigade and are sailing south on the *Norland*, a North Sea ferry.]

On 19 April, Jean writes:

The news continues to cheer and then immediately to depress! I think that we are all tempted to stop listening/watching – but how can we? I have always said that uncertainty is the worst thing, and it is, but one does begin to get used to living with suspense.

The ponies (Mandy and Bethan) were not popular this morning – a large gaping hole in the hedge by the water trough told me all I needed to know; I didn't even bother to look in the field but set out on a search with mounting panic. I searched most of Tidworth, finally discovering them down by The Ram! Doubly annoying however because there had been an extended interview with you on the Today

133

programme and I missed it despite having been listening from 6.30 to 8am, which is when I went out.

Hew writes on 21 April:

Everything is fine here, we are rather subject to security now for very good reasons, but as always with security there are inconsistencies and the whole thing is slightly absurd. The press are wild with frustration, as you may imagine. We have now linked up with Brigade HQ (embarked on HMS Fearless) again – what a good man the Brigadier is, what a relief! Mike Rose [commanding 22 SAS] I saw today too, and various other people – Mike is coming to dinner on Canberra tomorrow night, I hope. The weather is lovely here – very hot – and we all go ashore for a day or two of training and leg- stretch shortly. The whole affair is proceeding with an increasing feeling of inevitability about it, but everyone is highly confident and really wanting to see it through – I hope we do. Today, I flew over the assembled fleet by helicopter, en route to Fearless – an impressive sight! I am so proud of your marvellous reaction to the whole unexpected drama – and your letters are superb. My birthday looks like being spent on Ascension Island itself, field firing. I must list the places in the world where I have spent a birthday! [My 21st was also with 3 Para, at Jebel Ali, a training camp between Abu Dhabi and Dubai in the Trucial States, and in those days desert and jebel for miles in all directions.]

24 April. My Birthday.

A lot of people are beginning to wonder how slowly and indecisively the whole affair is going to drag on. It would be far better to get us in early, we are completely ready for it and I'm quite certain would win. But the whole performance is grinding on very slowly at present, and here we are, waiting. The midnight news is just starting – a lifeline – and the best source of information going. South Georgia retaken, which is great news and indicates that the situation must swing dramatically one way or the other – either surrender and withdrawal by the Argies, or an acceleration towards the retaking of the Falkland Islands. We are all in very good form and the only danger now is a long delay to proceedings, which will prove frustrating. Don't worry about it – I'm sure all these dramatic BBC reports make the prospects sound a lot more disturbing to you than they need to – we are well able to look after ourselves, I assure you. [We had been closely following the drama of the operation to retake South Georgia, which had so nearly gone terribly wrong and would have badly shaken confidence if it hadn't been pulled off.]

29 April.

It is now just midnight so I have switched on the News, and it all sounds pretty belligerent, with the Argentines now threatening to shoot down aircraft over the Falklands. But don't worry – we are brimming with confidence and just wish we could be allowed to get on with it – the longer the politicians wait, the more difficult the task ultimately becomes, so I do hope there isn't going to be a long delay. The sooner we get the job done, the sooner we will be home. But I don't think this will all be resolved quite as quickly as you think; security is becoming quite a factor so forgive me if I am not too specific.

5 May.

It may well be more difficult from tomorrow for me to get a regular letter to you. Please understand the reasons for this – and incidentally a useful defence if others complain of a lack of mail! I know it's much harder for you back there, detached and helpless, than for us here, involved and helpless! I'm sure you know, but 3 Commando Brigade at Plymouth run an information service, so if anyone wants to clear up queries or ask about anything (reasonable!), especially if they have been listening to the news and are worried, then the Rear Party (preferably) should ring up, by day or night.

On 14 May, Jean reports on the spring arrival of the Spotted Flycatchers:

The Flycatchers are here again ... I think they are using the old nest outside our bedroom window – I saw a bird just now with some nest material in its beak, sitting on the wire out there. I seem to have pinned my faith on them – like a lucky omen.

In another letter from Hew's 77-year-old father, he writes of the home front atmosphere:

We are bombarded continuously over the radio and TV. The BBC is very unpopular in that they give too much time to the Argentine point of view and the interviewers ask the most impossible and insensitive questions ... one which angers most is 'How many lives are worth the upholding of a principle and the removal of the Argentine control of the Islands?' They are under heavy attack in the House of Commons and in much of the Press. They must keep up their reputation (won during World War 2) for only telling the truth, but that is very different from being so impartial that you 'propagand' for the enemy, and undermine morale here.

It is a ticklish time and we await news avidly. I can't think that the UN is going to come up with a solution acceptable to both sides, though I think some sort of UN Trusteeship is probably the best answer, But the lesson of the Korean War must be relevant – aggression simply must not be allowed to pay. It has done so far too often since then, because the UN itself has no military power to stop it. Well, here's the best and I wonder what will have happened by the time you get this.

On 13 May, the day that the commander of 3 Commando Brigade, Brigadier Julian Thompson, issues his orders for the amphibious assault in San Carlos Bay, planned for 20 May, Hew writes to Jean:

Well, here we are, still on the high seas! I can't imagine when this letter may reach you, and somehow it takes the edge off writing if one has no idea of when it will get to you. But I do feel I need to write just as much, more if anything, as I suppose one feels that much more remote. The trouble with the Falklands is that they are so far away!! Anyway we are certainly now well clear of the sunbathing zone, and I hope we won't remain 'embarked' for too much longer. But security is now looming large so you should remind people not to discuss or speculate about future events, difficult as that is, I know. We are not allowed to brief the soldiers on what is planned at present, which is a bore, as life is getting fairly monotonous now, as you can imagine, and I don't want them to go off the boil. Eventually it is inevitable but I hope we will be let off the leash long before then. The mail is becoming more intermittent, however, and there's been none for a few days now, probably not as long as I think, but one loses track of day and date, quite honestly … The news does not sound too encouraging at the moment and I just don't know what sort of fight the Argies will put up, there are enough of them there. Try not to let all this waiting get you down. I'm sure the children with all their requirements, dates, plans etc are a great comfort to you, and provide such a vital role for you – they are utterly dependent on you, of course, and my trust in you is total … I think of you all constantly and please don't carry too heavy a burden of worry.

15 May.

Am sending a familygram as am not sure when these letters will ever get through – sorry the familygram is a bit brusque … we are definitely 'back to winter' –but have just heard that there may be a mail collection tomorrow morning. It all depends on the weather as it is taken off by helicopter and then put across by cable with a ship going north – both phases depending on a reasonably calm sea! I am certainly learning quite a lot about the RN! Incidentally, Mike

Layard is the RN Captain on Atlantic Conveyor. I haven't seen him yet, obviously, but had a message from him via someone else when I was on Fearless recently. Tom Seccombe had the three COs to dinner last night, which was a nice occasion. Also today I saw Chris Keeble, who came across from the Norland, and seemed fine; he stayed for lunch. It has got very rough tonight, on the first night out I'm sure I would have been sick, but now I'm fine. The Canberra really creaks and groans, like a great beast in pain, when it gets rough. Well, I hope next week will decide a few things – by the time you get this perhaps there will be news.

We have reached a plateau of training from which we cannot really advance until we go ashore, and I hope we do very soon. If the whole thing suddenly turns into a long political dialogue with military forces standing off, it will be very uncomfortable and very frustrating. And if we don't go in now, I really think I will have mass resignations on my hands! We are all very confident ... but I myself am as badly organised and ill-equipped as I am on most exercises! Anyway, there are plenty of people to look after me. And I have ensured that we are carrying a Union Jack and a Regimental Flag! The soldiers have been marvellous and I am so proud of them.

18 May.

We all sent familygrams but due to a rather petty sounding Treasury/ Financial regulation, that you have to have gone a specific length of time without mail before the cost of sending them is authorised, they never got sent and were all destroyed centrally. Ah well – so be it. Today is a beautiful day, and very calm – this morning like a mill pond, now a few white caps. I have seen Black-browed Albatross and Great Shearwaters, also a white type of Petrel or Fulmar that I can't identify. It is mid-afternoon and I'm listening to Radio newsreel 1815 GMT – we are four hours behind. We are now well advanced in terms of briefing and preparation, and everyone is going about their final preparations in a quiet but determined and confident way. The soldiers are all fine and in very good form, and longing to get on with it. It is rather like waiting for the Go/No Go Met decision before parachuting. But the main worry at the moment is the vulnerability of the Fleet to air attack, and it will be a great relief to everyone when this week is over, I think. Once we are ashore the threat to shipping is more easily countered by land-based air defence missiles (Rapier). I expect I will write again tomorrow as I feel an overwhelming need to do so. I think of you all so much, and long for the whole affair to be over, although of course I want us to have a great success first – I'm sure we will! I have been reading my 'Britain at Arms' anthology, and there have been some very topical and relevant bits which reflect exactly how I feel at present – it is a great comfort to read about past experiences, and to remember how many people have faced similar situations before, with calmness and courage.

I rather liked this extract from a letter by Marlborough to Sarah Churchill: 'My dearest soul I love you so well and have set my heart so entirely on ending my days in quiet with you, that you may be so far at ease as to be assured that I never venture myself but when I think the service of Queen and Country required it.' That is exactly how I feel, and I hope you don't mind me expressing it through someone else's words. This letter from Allenby to his wife, on his way to the Boer War, also hits a chord: 'I have too happy a life at home to make a really good soldier. I catch myself often half hoping that the war may be over by the time we arrive.' Well, I'm sure it will be over soon afterwards, and you can be sure that I intend to return to you all as soon as I possibly can! I feel you are carrying such a heavy burden while I am away, but on the other hand, I have supreme confidence in your ability to support this burden – I am so proud of you and I can't tell you what a difference it makes to know that your character and intelligence can win through in any situation. And although we are separated at present, our life over the past 15 years and our children are a marvellous comfort to me at this time, as I am sure they are to you as well. Incidentally, the Britain at Arms book has childrens' early scribbles on the back two blank pages, which is rather nice. I even have some of William's hankies with his name and school number on them, a lovely link with you all (WJM Pike 8).

Hew's notes recall the Battalion's sudden cross-decking from *Canberra* to the assault ship HMS *Intrepid*, sister ship to HMS *Fearless*, on 19 May:

As my Landing Craft rolled towards Intrepid, the spray breaking over the square bow, I felt relief that we seemed to have accomplished our unexpected redeployment without incident. It was almost dusk, and the scene around us was thrilling indeed. Here was a clutch of ships on which the Argentine air force must surely seek to inflict heavy and timely damage, if only they could first find them. If they could stall the amphibious operation at this critical moment, they might stop it permanently. At this stage, we were still beyond maximum range of land-based enemy aircraft, but the route towards Falkland Sound over the next thirty-six hours would take us within their radius of action. Everyone was aware of this, and we prayed for a foul passage, with high seas, low cloud, and poor visibility, despite the discomfort and sickness that would result. Our prayers were answered throughout the following day, and although there were a number of 'Red Alerts', the enemy never got through to us. The RN briefer at the Brigadier's Orders on Fearless a week before had sombrely described this final run in as 'the longest day'. The landing itself had been delayed closer to first light on the 21st, in order to give the Amphibious Task Group more darkness for the hazardous dash into Falkland Sound. This meant less darkness for the Marines and Paras establishing themselves ashore, but it was the right trade off. Sunk ships mean lost battalions, an incomplete bridgehead, and at worst, no landing at all.

HMS Hermes was to our left, as we made towards Intrepid's rear dock. Beyond Hermes, towards the horizon I could pick out the landing lights of a Sea Harrier, as it lined up for recovery onto her heaving deck. Such glimpses of the wider war were quite rare for us soldiers. We heard about the air and naval dimensions, but seldom saw them. The feeling of imminent action waxed strong in our minds, as we moved amongst the ships, 'somewhere in the South Atlantic'. So too did a feeling of loneliness, of insignificance, of expendability in this great enterprise.

Intrepid was overcrowded, but warmly hospitable. The soldiers lay head to toe along every corridor, around the engine room, in cabins given up for them by the ship's crew, anywhere there was a spot – even in cupboards. Now also, we rubbed shoulders for the first time with sudden catastrophe. There had already been losses of both aircraft and ships, but to us these had been news bulletins, no more. A Sea King helicopter carrying Special Forces soldiers also joining Intrepid for the landings ditched in the sea. It had suddenly lost power, probably from a bird-strike, and it sunk so quickly that only the crew and a few of the soldiers managed to get out. After moving to the area and dropping landing craft to search for survivors, Intrepid resumed her place in the convoy. There was a war to get on with, and nothing more could be done, beyond establishing who had been lost, and which next of kin now needed to be visited with the dreadful tidings. Some lines of WH Auden which I had learnt at school came to me as I dwelt on this incident:

> About suffering they were never wrong,
> The Old Masters: how well they understood
> Its human position; how it takes place
> While someone else is eating or opening a window
> Or just walking dully along;

> In Brueghel's Icarus, for instance: how everything turns away
> Quite leisurely from the disaster; the ploughman may
> Have heard the splash, the forsaken cry,
> But for him it was not an important failure; the sun shone
> As it had to on the white legs disappearing into the green
> Water; and the expensive delicate ship that must have seen
> Something amazing, a boy falling out of the sky,
> Had somewhere to get to and sailed calmly on.

21 May. Hew records the Battalion's landing in San Carlos Bay:

Somehow, we eventually extracted ourselves from the rabbit warren of Intrepid, onto the tank deck, and into our landing craft. 'B' Company had been the first to be loaded into the small LCVPs dangling from their davits on the upper decks, and these craft were now circling the ship in the dawn, waiting for the loading of the bigger LCUs in the rear dock to be completed. The move in formation could then begin across the line of departure and towards our beach. We eventually set off with one of the four LCUs still loading up 'C' Company, for I could wait no longer; it was a beautiful early morning, but perfect conditions for attacking aircraft, too. A complete formation of landing craft was not tactically critical, and it was now broad daylight. It was exciting to be starting in for the beach, rounding Chancho Point on a fine, calm dawn, passing the great white Canberra on our right, and watching the SBS putting down suppressive fire along the ridge to our left, towards Fanning Head over our left shoulders. It all looked reassuringly familiar from all our briefings. Duck and upland geese were taking off from the sunlit water – the first coastal or land birds we had seen since Ascension. It was a marvellous relief to be getting somewhere, at last, even if it was hard to relate what we were doing to anything other than some great, unopposed adventure, or to an exercise. This may have stemmed from a stubborn form of optimism, since the practicalities of the whole operation left us so extraordinarily vulnerable to enemy action. 'How could the enemy not have worked out that this was where we would land?' we had been asking ourselves. Yet he had not, and much credit for the safe landing of 3 Commando Brigade must go to the surveillance work of the SAS and SBS patrols in the weeks before 'D' Day, as well as to the careful judgement of Brigadier Julian Thompson and Commodore Michael Clapp, respectively Landing Force and Amphibious Force commanders.

As we neared Sand Bay, the feeling of vulnerability intensified. The four small LCVP with 'B' Company were supposed to be the first assaulting craft to hit the beach. But they proved slower than the bigger LCUs, and so 'A' Company, including my tactical headquarters, pressed on ahead of them; I told Mike Argue, commanding 'B' Company, that we would go in first. This was not to be, however, because as we neared the beach, the LCUs bellied about twenty yards offshore, and then backed off to find a better approach. One of the crewmen tested the water depth with a long boat-hook, and it was clear that we would have been swimming, or more likely sinking under the weight of our ammunition, if we had tried to disembark. The crew could find no better approach, and rode helplessly offshore, whilst the shallower-drafted LCVPs moved past us and disgorged

'B' Company ashore, as originally planned. Their only problem was a ramp on one LCVP that would not lower, even with a multitude of anxious paratroopers' boots against it. Its embarked compliment somehow scrambled over the side, nonetheless, in their eagerness to get ashore, the empty LCVPs then reversing alongside the LCUs for further, unplanned 'cross-decking' operations, twenty metres out from our landfall. The later LCUs carrying 'C' Company and our recce vehicles, nosed in just along the shoreline to the left of the beach, where the water was deeper, though the rocky bank formed a steeper and more awkward exit.

It had not been quite as we had all probably imagined it would be, with dreams of a heroic 'storming ashore', but we were safely on East Falkland, thankfully unopposed, with nothing worse to show for it than wet feet. It was a good feeling, rather like landing by parachute on a moorland dropping zone in a still, peaceful dawn somewhere in Wales or Scotland, after a long, noisy, bumpy, smelly, low-level approach in a C130 Hercules. The sudden contrast in atmosphere and the intense feeling of relief were both familiar. So too were the excited cries of wading birds, which now filled the air, protesting at this strange invasion.

There was no sign of the enemy, and the SBS patrol on the beach had detected no activity in Port San Carlos Settlement. In fact, forty or so Argentines had apparently been based in the Settlement for some days, and the locals later told us that they had been resupplied by helicopter the day before. I discovered after the campaign that the SBS patrol had been forced to withdraw in the critical few days leading up to 'D' Day, for fear of compromising the landing area. They had been reinserted too late to detect the movement of troops into the Settlement, but were confident that the coast was clear and didn't tell me about the gap in their surveillance. There were therefore no clues to the enemy presence as we moved up the long, gentle rise from the beach, and then over the crest and downhill towards the scattered homesteads sheltering below Settlement Rocks. As we advanced, a Sea King helicopter, carrying an under-slung load and escorted by Gazelles to each flank, fitted with SNEB rocket pods, flew up the Bay to our right, and turned over the Settlement, which we had still not reached, let alone reported clear of enemy. I was horrified, even though I still thought that the Settlement was probably safe. Suddenly, the Sea King plunged to ground-hugging height, and clattered back noisily over our heads and out to sea again, having cut its underslung load. The two Gazelles were less fortunate. Both were brought down and destroyed by small arms fire from the enemy force withdrawing East towards a feature called The Knob. One helicopter came down in the water just off the woolshed jetty. The other crashed into a shallow gully about a kilometre further east, between the settlement and The Knob. Three of the four crewmen in these aircraft were killed. The only survivor, Sergeant Eddie Candlish, managed with great courage to swim ashore with his mortally wounded comrade, Ken Francis, still under fire from Argentine soldiers around the jetty before they made good their escape into the 'camp', as the locals called the countryside. Ken Francis died from his injuries a short while later, in the Bunkhouse near the jetty, which was to become our Regimental Aid Post. I arrived there as his body was being carried out and loaded onto a local Land- Rover. As I moved back towards the Settlement Manager's house, a slow- flying ground attack Pucara whined over the Settlement from the East, spraying the area with rocket and machine gun fire. Doubtless like many others, I had already 'pondered' as I splashed ashore, that whatever the outcome of the war, a page of history had turned for the Falkland Islanders. Now I threw myself behind a large pile of peat, suddenly realising that in all this madness, the enemy seemed to be just as determined to make a fight of it as we were. It could be a long, bitter war, I thought. The excitement of the voyage south, and the eager anticipation of combat, vanished in those early minutes of noise, violence, indignity and death.

George Brown, the MTO, attended the funeral of the three air-crewmen at the aft end of 'D' Deck, on Canberra, later that day. Experienced soldier though he was, he told me that night that he could not control his tears, even for men whom he had not known. That Auden poem came to me again, for the accidents of war are no more than the accidents of life in more concentrated form, and in a greater madness:

> How, when the aged are reverently, passionately waiting
> For the miraculous birth, there always must be
> Children who did not specially want it to happen, skating
> On a pond at the edge of the wood.

Jean writes from home on 22 May:

The first news of it [the lost helicopters and crewmen] for me came from Graham Farrell [The Regimental Colonel of the Parachute Regiment] when he telephoned to tell me that the helicopters were not 3 Para. Thank God he told me that before I heard it on the news – it was devastating even so. Ever since then we have been glued to the TV and radio. Not much news is getting through yet except that a beach head has been established ... by far and away the best report came from Robert Fox at midnight as he reported 'going in with the Paras' – we heard it all happening. So you must be on the Island and I am thankful that you are no longer on one of the ships – not that we know anything for certain.

I know there is still so much to be done, but everyone here is so proud of what has been achieved already. We saw a picture of Paras raising the Union Jack and another of someone who could have been the RSM [It was! Laurie Ashbridge] talking to some elated looking Islanders. We have all been shaken by the tragic helicopter losses. When it was first reported it was not made clear that next of kin had been informed, so when they said it was soldiers, a lot of unnecessary distress was caused to a lot of people. They really must get this right.

On the 25th, she writes:

We are getting reports now of the conditions in which you are existing ... The Navy seem to be bearing the brunt of it at the moment. Brian Hanrahan's reports are brilliant, very descriptive and absolutely to the point – not so Michael Nicholson who can't resist reference to his own heroics and gets carried away and melo-dramatic. But top of my list is Robert Fox. I went down to the families office yesterday, where there was almost a feeling of elation. I can't bear the thought that we might tempt providence, so I did remind them all that there is still a long way to go.

The logistic realities of life become clear at the first Brigade 'O' Group held since the landing, on Tuesday, 25 May. Hew writes:

The Brigadier had regularly seen and talked with his commanders individually during the hectic first few days ashore, but this was the first occasion on which we had all gathered together. It was a rare event in this war – there were to be only a handful more of such assemblies before we re-captured Port Stanley. I flew by Gazelle from Port San Carlos, skimming low over the calm water of the bay, round Chancho Point, where we had experienced our fraught dis-embarkation from Intrepid, and south-east down San Carlos water, to Brigade Headquarters near the San Carlos Settlement. The folds in the ground afforded little concealment in such open terrain, but the tracked Volvo 'BV's of the Headquarters were as neatly tucked away as they could be, with their small penthouse tents attached to the back of each vehicle. It was into one of these that we all squeezed. There were mugs of soup and packets of hard-tack biscuits neatly arranged on the small table around which we sat – for this was more of a conference than a formal orders session. Such attention to detail, and the careful organisation that lent an air of calm and efficiency to proceedings, was typical of the style of John Chester, the Brigade Major (we had been fellow students on the 1975 Army Staff College course at Camberley) and particularly helpful when things didn't seem to be going too well. Now the news was certainly gloomy.

143

There was no intention of developing operations further, until the off-loading of ships was more advanced, and for the moment recce tasks for SAS, SBS and patrols by the Royal Marines Mountain and Arctic Warfare (M and AW) Cadre had the first call on helicopter resources. Insertions were planned onto Mount Kent, Mount Rosalie and towards Salvador Water, but they were being hampered by bad weather. There was also a lack of Passive Night Goggles (PNG) – only recently introduced into service, in small numbers – and a shortage of crews trained to use them. The raid planned on Darwin, to be carried out by 2 PARA from Sussex Mountain, the most southerly battalion position and thus closest, was postponed indefinitely. There was concern about how much the enemy knew, and about his reinforcement of the area. More importantly, there was the question of logistic support, and of recovery to the bridgehead after the raid. There was, for example, apprehension about the Scorpions and Scimitars not merely getting bogged down in unsuitable terrain, but finding themselves out of fuel, stuck embarrassingly and highly vulnerably in the middle of nowhere. The meeting broke up with little doubt in any of our minds that we had some more waiting to do – perhaps even until 5 Brigade arrived. [5 Infantry Brigade, comprising Battalions of the Scots Guards, Welsh Guards and 7th Gurkhas, are sailing south in the QE2 to reinforce 3 Commando Brigade.] Things were terribly uncertain, and a clear concept for the development of operations towards Stanley seemed not yet to have emerged. Yet we all knew we must look East, for Stanley was our objective, and a concept based on raids therefore appeared to most of us to be a wasteful use of resources, and one unlikely to greatly advance our cause, even if it achieved a degree of moral ascendancy. It seemed unwise to squander the Brigade in this way, and unnecessary to wait for 5 Brigade. All the Commanding Officers felt this same impatience, spared as we were of the pressures placed on our Brigade Commander.

H Jones, commanding 2 PARA, was particularly frustrated, since it was his raid that was now postponed, whilst the rest of us had 'nothing planned', as it were. It is a feature of military life, one of its great joys as well as sadnesses, that you often don't know where and when you are next going to see a friend. There now seemed no immediate prospect of battle, and we therefore climbed into different helicopters after the briefest of farewells, as H stooped to pick up the badge that had fallen out of my beret. I had first met him when he had joined 3 PARA seventeen years before, to be greeted with the unwelcome news that he was to return with the Battalion to British Guiana [now Guyana] from where he had only recently returned with his own Regiment, the Devon and Dorsets. Now, we had parted for the last time.

I flew back to Windy Gap after the meeting, and walked round our positions, chatting to the soldiers, and updating them as best I could.

The situation the following morning is well summarized in the letter Hew writes to Jean:

It is just after first light, 7.45 am. So as it gets dark at about 5 pm the night is quite long – it is the equivalent of late autumn here, of course. Yesterday was much like previous days, fortunately dry and sunny but with a cold south-west wind. I walked around 'A' Company positions down in this valley, then had to go off to a Brigade 'O' group, the first time COs had all met up since the landings. We are really waiting to get on top of the air situation before making any further moves. Please guard this information carefully – I know you will – as it is somewhat sensitive. Then I walked around 'B' Company's positions up on the ridge to our north – much higher up, windier and pretty exposed. They have built up well with peat and rock, as you can't dig down very far before hitting water and/or rocks. There is a Cara-Cara Eagle – I think that's what it is – living in Settlement Rocks. The news yesterday, as on most days, was mixed. We think we accounted for as many as ten aircraft, but may have lost a Destroyer and, even worse, the Atlantic Conveyor, with a lot of helicopters and Harriers aboard. The news is not clear yet, but this is a terrible blow if it is true. The Argies certainly seem to know what to go for. I have just been given a mess-tin of porridge, into which I put a little bran! They make it here for us and we have it in our ration packs anyway. The RSM, Lance Corporals Begg, Bunkle and Offa are my team (the three Lance Corporals are signallers) and they also do my food and brews for me. I couldn't cope with doing it myself, there just isn't time. Heaven knows when you will get this letter – we still have sacks of incoming mail waiting somewhere in the system, I am told. There is fair chaos on the shipping side of things, they are having a hell of a time. I beg you not to worry unduly, we are all together which is a great comfort, and everyone is working well. From tonight a platoon at a time from 'B' and 'C' Companies will come down into the woolsheds by the jetty for a dry night.

Hew records in his notes:

Then, in the early evening of the 26th, we received a written order to advance East to capture Teal Inlet. No time scale was outlined, but it was clear that we were expected to move after 45 Commando, and behind them, to Douglas Settlement, and thence pass through them towards Teal Inlet. This struck me as being needlessly laborious and not a very good plan. I talked to Alan Miller, the settlement manager, about the best route to Teal. It was not, as I expected, via Douglas, but on a much more direct line, south of Bombilla Hill and skirting north of Bull Mountain. Alan pencilled out the route on a large scale map; he had often done it by motorbike. I put the proposal to the Brigade Commander, who quickly accepted it, and that night our battle procedure got under way. Platoons were pulled in and rested as far as possible. Rations were issued, radio batteries charged. The following morning at about 0730 hours, the Brigadier arrived and we quickly went over the plan in Alan Miller's dining room, with tea provided by his housekeeper Vi Heathman, a lovely, down to earth and sensible soul, who seemed to be greatly enjoying herself, and relishing all the military disruption. At times, it was hard to believe that we were in a farmhouse in the South Atlantic, and not on an exercise in some remote corner of the British Isles. Our Gunner CO, Mike Holroyd-Smith of 29 Commando Regiment was with the Brigadier. He judged that we would take three to five days to make Teal Inlet; I wagered that we would be much faster than that. We agreed a series of nicknames for report lines covering Company routes, and then the Brigadier left. The Company Commanders came in, and were quickly briefed, the priority being to get cracking. We would meet up, once we had assessed a realistic rate of progress, at one of the designated report lines. By 1030, after frenzied activity during which many people probably didn't quite know what was happening, we were on the move. Several were hovering on the jetty to be given last minute shouted instructions, as the small group forming my Tac HQ climbed into Rigid Raiders before bouncing over the smooth calm of the San Carlos River. We landed a couple of kilometres upstream on the right hand bank, in a small gully. The Rigid Raiders then went back to ferry 'A' Company up to the same landing point. Meanwhile, 'B' and 'C' Companies started to move along the ridge line through Gregorio Rocks and Cerro Montevideo, crossing the Port San Carlos river upstream from us. Pat Butler's Patrol Company had already deployed two patrols to secure this crossing point. The Mortars with their heavy weapons and ammunition were following up on two tractors and trailers provided by Alan Miller, driven by his son Philip and a friend from Teal Inlet, Dave Thorsen. We were on our way.

I had found it a disconcerting trip up-river, for the whole process of leaving had been somewhat fraught. But no-one else seemed at all concerned, and Laurie Ashbridge, the RSM, was thoroughly enjoying his first trip in a Rigid Raider. The atmosphere of a rather exciting and unusual exercise kept coming to mind, as I watched how others reacted. We were certainly all pleased and relieved to be on the move. The Battalion's confidence was as strong as ever, and few seemed to wonder how difficult our move might be, how long we would be on

146

the march, or what might lie ahead. It was pointless at this stage to try to work out how far we should aim to move in a day, or in a night. We would learn this by experience; it had always been the way the Battalion had played it. My own upbringing in 3 PARA took me back to marches along the Kyrenia Range, in Northern Cyprus, and to the Radfan campaign in South Arabia. As evening drew on, we could see Third Corral Shanty, a lonely dilapidated shack in the middle of nowhere away to our left, and soon we again hit the winding Port San Carlos river line. A small Grebe was pushing upstream, impervious to the war and to how much was at stake, just like those fat grey farm cats we had left back in the Settlement. We tucked ourselves into a sandbank and had a brew. Then, deciding to postpone wet feet as long as possible, we took off our boots, rolled up our trousers, and forded the freezing river. It was worth it – though most of 'B' Company, when they arrived a short time later, just plunged through. They had already done one crossing, below Cerro Montevideo, and so had nothing to lose.

Once it was dark, we set out with few illusions, on one of the worst night marches I can remember. Our only real aids to navigation were the fence lines, for we could take no bearing to our north on Bombilla Hill in the dark, and the terrain was otherwise pretty featureless. The going varied from bloody to bearable, but we struggled on, hour after hour, resting occasionally for a short time to relieve the aching weight of equipment. For some time we stumbled needlessly across rivers of rock on the northern shoulders of Bull Mountain, having strayed too far to the south east. Many soldiers had been out on patrol during the last few nights at Port San Carlos, so were already wet and tired when we started. Signallers, medics, machine gunners and men in the MILAN detachments were carrying especially heavy loads, and although some weapons could be passed around each group, many loads were more personal and could not be swapped so readily. Every MILAN operator carrying a firing post, for instance, had devised a different method of doing so – one that suited his build and gait. Those with medical or signals equipment had to carry Bergens, but this was avoided where possible. Belt order alone placed a heavy enough strain on the back, with so much ammunition stuffed into pouches as well as into the generous, baggy pockets of windproof smocks. Even when really well fitted, wet pouches tended to rub increasingly painfully against upper thighs, and the yoke supporting all the weight on the belt pressed heavily between the shoulders. My signallers were bearing up well, but grew tired as the hours of stumbling and discomfort continued. A certain numbness overcame the pain after a time, but after each stop the aches tended to return.

It was very dark, and so it was hard to tell how people outside one's immediate group were getting on; but as long as each small group was holding together as a team, well trained and led, we would win through. As the night wore on, there was distant noise and the occasional flash in the sky to our south; 2 PARA must have made contact with the enemy on their advance towards Darwin Hill. It was hard to imagine that we would meet much in the midst of this desolate terrain, but Teal Inlet itself might be a different matter.

To our great relief, we finally hit the fence line running south-east from Bull Mountain to Bombilla, at about 6 am on the following morning – Friday. We had only lost one man, with a badly twisted ligament, and he had been left with two soldiers for protection, somewhere on Bull Mountain, in the middle of the night. This casualty was finally lifted out by helicopter later that day, but his escorts somehow got forgotten. They spent the next three days on an involuntary survival exercise, feeling no doubt like the small change of war. Now, we basha'd up along the fence line in pouring rain until dawn, wet, tired, but encouraged by our progress. As soon as it was light, we pressed on again, along the ridge line, and down into the Arroy Pedro River Valley. It was a clear morning, and we were much relieved to get tucked in the valley, to rest and brew up where we felt safer from air attack and from prying eyes on hilltops. By the end of the short day, all three Companies had rallied in the same general area, though sensibly dispersed. All had coped well with their advance, despite a number of exposure cases and one incident in which a soldier accidentally shot himself through the shoulder as he fell in the long tussock grass. Now we were ready to move quickly over the last few kilometres to surround and secure Teal Inlet in darkness.

The night advance had been exhausting, but it had helped many of us to settle down a bit. We were becoming more seasoned, overcoming that early hesitancy and feeling more familiar with our environment. Teamwork was developing, and there was more wry humour. Each section commander was becoming a shepherd to his tight little group of soldiers, bonding them closer, cajoling and encouraging them almost like children. Making himself comfortable in the field, whatever the conditions, had always been a matter of pride and individual resourcefulness to the parachute soldier. The stronger men in each group were also emerging, giving a particular character to a section or patrol, and helping in this bonding process. 'I wonder how old I'll be when this is over,' remarked Corporal Duggan to his men, over a brew of tea.

Tucked away in the folds of the Arroy Pedro River valley, we could no longer catch the sounds of battle towards Darwin Hill to our south, as we had occasionally during the night. But battle there had been, throughout the day, and towards evening Julian James, the Mortar officer, walked over to my little group, sheltering against a tussock bank above the river. He had spent the day hauling forward mortar ammunition on the tractors and trailers from Port San Carlos Settlement, and his platoon were now ready to support us, as we moved into Teal Inlet during the night. At this late stage of the day, we had still heard few details of 2 PARA's battle on either the Brigade net or from my own Main Headquarters back at Port San Carlos. Julian seemed to have heard more on his Mortar Fire Control frequency and after outlining his news of the battle, he added, 'You won't like this, but Colonel H, David Wood and a number of others have been killed.' He did not know numbers, or other names. But the impression was of fifteen or twenty killed, many by Pucara air attack. 'H' had apparently been killed assaulting a machine gun position in a bunker. I imagined something concrete and permanent, which he had been trying to clear of enemy.

The news seemed at once inevitable, yet scarcely believable. Months later Peter Dennison told me that I had been visibly shaken by what I had been told, and I am not surprised. I wondered, as I looked out over seemingly peaceful moorland and hillside, whether any war could justify this casual loss of life. I felt most keenly not for 'H' himself, good friend though he had been, but for Sara and his boys. I thought of them, and then of my own wife and children. It was easier for us than for them. We were actors in the drama, who could not escape our duty; they were helpless spectators.

Now, although we were shocked and could ponder on this awful blow within ourselves, grief would have to wait. 'The individual shrinks to nothing. He has no right of an opinion. Only the Regiment matters,' writes Lord Moran of his experiences as a Regimental Medical Officer (RMO) during the First World War. Small wonder, in this all pervading atmosphere of uncertainty and loneliness, that comradeship grew even tighter. It was the stuff of survival.

On 30 May, Jean writes from home:

I heard yesterday at the girls' Commem [at Sherborne School] that poor H had gone and I was overwhelmed by a feeling of awful deep sadness, not just for him and Sara, but for everyone involved in this terrible affair. The waste, the tragedy of it and the endless suffering that it will bring to so many people.

Hew's notes continue:

The day had been wet, but the weather cleared towards evening, and that night, as our sister Battalion lay up around Darwin Hill, awaiting the final outcome of things at Goose Green, we moved on Teal Inlet. There had been reports of wounded enemy in the Settlement, but we found none, and there was no resistance. Our approach route had crossed one particularly awkward, deep stream and one of my signallers, Corporal 'Taff' Offa, fell in. He was completely immersed and his gasps of agony were fearful. The night was cold, clear and frosty and if we had not been able to get him to shelter in the Settlement later that night, he would have been in real trouble.

The Settlement was entirely blacked out when we arrived, and some of us were greeted in Spanish as we knocked on doors in the early hours of the morning. I went to find the Settlement Manager, Mr Barton. He and his wife were living and sleeping (under the table) in their kitchen, and I was offered tea and small round cakes, freshly baked and absolutely delicious. Even in these circumstances, in a barricaded kitchen reminiscent of the London blitz, I began to be embarrassed by my greed as I gobbled down my sixth or seventh cake. I told them about the casualties in 2 PARA, and of the CO's death, and reassured them that we had come to stay – this was more than just a visiting patrol, which is what they had evidently come to expect from the Argentines. I added that they must expect a fairly rapid build up of Headquarters and logistic units, since Teal Inlet was so critical to future plans, and that this in turn meant a serious enemy air threat. Digging was therefore just as necessary for them, as for us. Mrs Barton told me that she had originally believed that they should all leave the Falkland Islands, in the face of Argentine invasion, rather than be the cause of young men dying in a war for their recapture. But now she had changed her mind, and saw the necessity of recapture, of standing by people, principles and the right to self-determination. She was an intelligent, thoughtful woman, who had lived at Teal Inlet for many years, and was clearly devoted to the place. Like the families at Port San Carlos, she treated with derision any question of evacuation. All the settlements we had either occupied or heard about – Port San Carlos, Teal Inlet, Douglas, Darwin and Goose Green – had been badly treated by their so called liberators, who had failed to respect any privacy, possessions, or the right to free movement and communication. The Islanders also wisely assessed that they were now far safer in and around their houses, where they could take their own precautions against an air attack, than floating helplessly out at sea as evacuees.

For the remainder of the night, all three companies took advantage of whatever shelter they could find, in the wool sheds by the jetty and the outbuildings around the Settlement. We maintained local security, but there was obviously no immediate threat, and we were exhausted. My little party ended up on the wooden floor of a small workshop, and were mercifully sheltered from the heavy hailstorm that came on in the early morning. It was comforting to be inside, but we had no sleeping bags, and I shivered through what remained of the night in the green quilted trousers and jacket that we all carried, and could zip into. My 'karrimat' was also a great bonus, and I slept a bit, after changing my socks and smoking a Hamlet cigar. I had got into the habit of having one after dark each night, and certainly felt I deserved one now, after the liberation of Teal Inlet. Amongst that huddle of weary men on the workshop floor, I reflected that the scene might have made a marvellous addition to that famous line in Hamlet TV advertisements. Later on in the war, when all my cigars were gone, I would resort, like almost everyone, to cigarettes. They were a great comfort – as was the fat King Edward cigar that I was given by a generous Max Hastings on one occasion towards the end of the affair.

At first light, we got busy with our defensive positions all round the Settlement. Most of the soldiers were proving predictably resilient, though some had awful blisters. I hoped that we would get the day or two of respite they would need to fully recover. Our Doctor, John Burgess, had flown in to join us with the RAP, and was now doing brisk business based in the Settlement's bunkhouse, whilst Norman Menzies, the Battalion's wonderful, ever optimistic and 'fix anything' Quartermaster was setting himself up in the tiny schoolroom. I walked round our positions, chatting and giving the soldiers news that had by now reached us of the large scale surrenders at Goose Green. This provided a great boost to spirits and confidence, for the enemy had now been broken in battle. If 2 PARA could do it, so could the rest of us – though the casualty figures seemed like a gauntlet thrown down to those of us still to be blooded. For news of three hundred Argentines thought to be based at Estancia House, protected by minefields, reached us that evening too, with orders to advance and capture the area. It seemed that we were to be further tested even sooner than we expected, and I found myself balancing fatigue against tactical imperatives. I would have liked a longer pause, before tackling what sounded like quite a tough nut, but would not admit that to the Brigadier. We would have another night at Teal, and move off in the morning. We awoke to snow, and saddled up for Estancia, now accompanied by Mark Coreth's four Blues and Royals recce cars – two Scorpions and two Scimitar, that had closed up to us, after a remarkable drive over exceptionally difficult going. Initiative had triumphed over doubts about both terrain and fuel supplies. One of his cars was now positioned incongruously alongside a neat, green painted clapper-board house occupied by a family who had only recently emigrated from Northampton. With young children, a cow and some goats, they had selected these remote islands as a haven of peace in a wicked world, but now had a Scorpion light tank parked in their back garden. Teal Inlet was later to be the location of our Field Surgical Team (FST) during the mountain battles, and this tranquil, beautiful place was also to be the temporary burial place for most of the 3 PARA soldiers killed in action.

We had now been joined by Terry Peck and Vernon Steen, two Falkland Islanders of stalwart character who had escaped across country from Port Stanley, using motor bikes. We discussed likely enemy positions and minefields around Estancia. Terry thought most of the tracks would be mined, and he had heard that the people there had been warned to keep sheep out of certain areas. He thought there might be two or three hundred enemy deployed there, and I put him with Pat Butler in the Patrol Company, where we could best use his knowledge as a guide. A former policeman, and allegedly on the Argentine 'black list', he was a hard man who would not have taken kindly to being left out of things. Vernon Steen was equally courageous, with a manner suggesting quiet but single-minded determination.

By early evening we had reached the substantial bridge north of Lower Malo House – one of the only bridges I ever saw on East Falkland – and the Patrol Company pressed on ahead with Terry Peck, to look more closely at Estancia. This night move proved to be a second 'epic march', with navigation made more difficult by having to skirt Pasa Grande and Rumford creeks. We tended to move too directly eastwards, thus hitting creeks too far north and having to make southerly detours to find a way across. Progress was slow, but we eventually reached the gate and fence line at Rumford Creek, extremely tired, in the early hours of the following morning. We basha'd up against a bank on the edge of the creek, very conscious that we would be dominated in daylight by any observers in the Smoko Mountain area to our south. The Companies were still moving independently, at their own pace. It was the best and safest way in this terrain, but all were pressing on splendidly. We rested up in our creek until first light, and woke to snow again, although it quickly thawed. I was again glad of my quilted trousers and jacket, and my karrimat, for I could not have slept without them. After porridge made from rolled oats, and a good brew of tea, we pressed on to make contact with Pat Butler and his patrols in Long Creek. The weather was fine, and the Battalion now seemed to have settled very much into its stride, moving well and making the best use of tractors, sledges and the CVRs, to haul forward mortar ammunition and MILAN missiles. By the end of the day we were all set to occupy Estancia that night, and Pat Butler reported that his patrols had found no minefields and no enemy. There was perhaps a tinge of disappointment mixed with my relief; it seemed obvious that sooner or later we were going to have to fight, and I thought that we might all be less tense once we had a battle under our belts. At the same time, this further stay of execution was not unwelcome, for we were all pretty tired. It felt rather like a parachute jump called off by bad weather – for the time being one could relax, although the commitment to the task remained, to be honoured another day.

The investment of Estancia thus turned out to be a similar operation to Teal Inlet. We had gained splendid views of this little farmstead from the hills east of Teal Inlet – as clear as if it was only a few hundred yards away. All went without incident, and my Tac HQ spent the rest of that night in one of the corrugated barns adjacent to the house, before moving across the brook, and up to Mount Estancia at first light. We set up Tac HQ in the rocks on its eastern summit, and on that clear Tuesday morning we had our first view of Port Stanley, the bay and the lighthouse at Volunteer Point beyond. It all seemed oddly familiar, from maps and photographs – as if from a different life. The feature obscuring Stanley to the right seemed at first glance to be Mount Tumbledown. But closer inspection of the map confirmed it as Mount Longdon, and it soon became clear, after talking to the Brigadier, that its capture was a likely task for us. We now made ourselves comfortable in a round-walled sangar covered in ponchos, and when the Brigadier next visited by helicopter, he said 'Well done!' Such an accolade was not given lightly, I had come to learn. I was pleased and encouraged by it; for the Battalion had indeed done well.

It was on this mountain top that I received Hughie Henderson's 'bluey':

'Sir,' it read. 'Although many years have passed since I had the good fortune to serve under your command in the Radfan (3 Platoon, "A" Company), the memories are still fresh in my mind. Now, after years of civilian boredom, it once again makes me feel proud to see 3 PARA off to active service.

I find it very hard to write this letter, Sir, because I never was the type to put pen to paper. The main reason for my writing is to wish you all the best of luck. In other words, keep the old tradition up and give 'em some bloody hammer. I am still in touch with a lot of the old ex-Paras and to be honest, we're dead jealous.

You may be a hell of a long way from home, but we're behind you all the way and sorry that we're not there with you. Good Luck, 3 PARA.

Best Wishes, Hugh S Henderson.

PS. If Dougie Saunders is still serving, tell him to make sure he keeps his head down. He still owes me ten rupees. HSH.'

Most of the soldiers now on these windswept mountains would only have been about two years old in 1964, and some would not even have been born. For a Battalion is composed mainly of very young men. Three of those killed in action with 3 PARA in the Falklands were not even eighteen. But the 'old tradition' as Hughie Henderson had put it, was there all right. The same attitude of mind that had carried us deep into the Wadi Dhubsan in South Arabia would carry us across East Falkland. As the Battalion Commander, I knew this – and drew strength from it. And when I sometimes pondered how this attitude of mind could pass so silently, yet so powerfully, from one generation of men to another, there could only be one answer. It must be through their training. The attitude of far, fast and without question, is bred by a certain approach to training, and by the consistency of that approach. It is an approach that generates high morale, confidence, and success.

The liberation of Estancia led to the arrival of numerous tractors, trailers and land rovers, from outlying settlements. These were to prove invaluable in our preparation for the assault against Mount Longdon, the drivers all doing magnificently under the direction of Roger Patton, the Battalion Second in Command, terrier-like in his energy and determination. They were led by Trudi Morrison, a colourful and courageous Falkland islander in her mid-30s, living somewhere near Green Patch with parents and grandmother – she had once been married, I was told, but was currently single, and revelling in her 'macho' role. Men, she seemed firmly to believe, were best defined as 'people in need of a woman's leadership'. From the top of Mount Estancia, I watched the little fleet driving in along the valley to the north from Green Patch Settlement.

Hew's own feelings during these waiting days are best illustrated in his letters home to Jean:

On a Mountain above Estancia House.

Sorry no writing for so long but has not been possible – we have walked a long way since I last wrote! From where we are now, we can see Stanley clearly and the airfield – although we have just moved position so can't actually see it now. The weather is pretty bloody – wet and windy, even snow twice, but it could be worse and it's amazing what one can get used to. My team are marvellous cooks, so we are as comfortable as we can be under the circumstances. The RSM is really great to have around – he organises our home in the rocks whenever we move. I expect you know as much (or more) than I do about the military situation so I won't go into all that – I am so sad about 'H' and feel so much for Sara and his children – but I fear we are all at risk till this is over. We are static at present before the next big move forward, which is giving people a chance to recover from a very rapid and remarkable advance – 3 PARA certainly holds the record for having marched further, faster than any other battalion, across East Falkland. It is hellish country to cross, especially at night, but we have almost done it now so may as well finish it off on foot, too. Helicopters are mainly used for lifting artillery and ammunition. The weather has been very misty and cloudy lately which has slowed the build-up. The quilted clothing is really good – you can carry it in your poncho roll and do without a sleeping bag for a night or two, as you have to travel as light as possible or it becomes too exhausting. Feet are the main problem, as it is so wet. I have got lots of pairs of socks drying out in my sleeping bag at the moment. My feet have been fine all the time. I am smoking, I am afraid. First Hamlets, and now they have run out, cigarettes. I have got one book, the yellow one, Britain at Arms, which I dip into occasionally. The nights are long – fourteen hours of darkness – so we don't go short on sleep. The Brigadier comes most days by helicopter to chat about what is happening, we are really waiting for 5 Brigade to get sorted out before we go on. A bore, as we'd like to get on and finish it off. Not long now though, I hope. The Argies are definitely on a loser and if only they'd throw in the towel, we could all come home. But it shouldn't be too long and I assure you I shall not take needless risks. I think of you all so much and love you all so dearly, darling, I know what it must be like, always waiting for news and being so much at the mercy of events – but I know you have the character and courage to live through this difficult time and keep the family together. I so long to be back with you and I shall value our life together as never before when this is over. One takes so much for granted – although I have always had at the back of my mind the knowledge that the unforeseen might occur and have savoured and relished our life together and joy of our children, quite consciously – though I know I have sometimes been awful. My darling, I love you more than I can possibly express and I pray as I know you do, for us all to be together again. Please pray – I'm sure it helps us all.

8th June.

Have had a lot of mail, up to 17th May, plus letters from Marty Stratton, Buck Kernan and even a former member of my old platoon, Hughie Henderson from Manchester. It was lovely to get all your letters and news. I won't repeat it all here but I am so pleased that the weather in May was so gorgeous and that the children are all so well and on good form. It is such a merciful reassurance and comfort to know that all is 'normal' at your end in this very abnormal situation and I just go on praying that you continue to be well and that you are all looking after yourselves. We are all fine still, the arrival of 5 Brigade and a Divisional Commander has slowed things down somewhat, but hopefully for the long term good of all. So we have been static for almost a week now after our historic hike across this island and are now waiting to be launched forward again. The weather continues variable – today and yesterday clear and sunny and dry and not at all cold, but high winds, cloud and rain at night. Everyone is surviving the elements remarkably well and we are trying to get platoons down to Estancia House for a night in a barn occasionally, in rotation. We continue to consume a monotonous but high calorie diet – the Arctic Ration Pack – better than the Ration Pack GS that William gets from me. It includes rice, apple flakes, beef/mutton/chicken depending on the type, lots of hot drinks, including chocolate, lots of sweets, etc., so we are all quite healthy! In fact I feel extremely well and am even managing to take my bran. I have a small supply.

The pack also contains rolled oats which make excellent porridge, so that's what I have each morning, like Emma! There is a great deal of helicopter activity each day, bringing gun ammunition forward and not too much enemy air I'm pleased to say. I am writing this letter in the CP – a shed at Estancia House – so I'm afraid it is a bit disjointed. The people here (the Heathman family) are being marvellous, as they have been everywhere – incredibly tolerant of the complete take-over but then I suppose they owe us something! I went back to Teal Inlet – which we liberated before coming on here, for Brigade Orders. I saw John Waters there, he was the Brigadier in Northern Ireland and is now Deputy Divisional Commander, still suffering with his back and hoicked out of London to come here – and of course David Chaundler is now also here but 2 PARA are part of 5 Brigade again so I haven't seen him. It is a great comfort having people I know well around me, it makes the whole thing bearable and almost like another exercise! There are women and children here who take the whole thing in their stride. Sorry the letters are so intermittent now, but it is just a case of taking the chance when it comes. I will hope to write as often as possible, perhaps soon it will be easy again and soon I'll be back so I won't have to.

9th June.

Well, here I am, I have brought my small Tac down from the hills to this house, where our main HQ is based as it is easier to co-ordinate our next move from here. Also it's a damn site more comfortable! I am in a tent and am sitting by an iron stove (burning peat) in an outhouse which is our CP. Roger Patton is cooking his supper on the stove – I have had mine in my tent, cooked by the RSM and Lance

Corporal Begg. We also got papers today taking us up to the day before we came ashore. Don't worry about who does or does not get mentioned by BBC/Press – it's all so much over-dramatised bullshit anyway and highly inaccurate frequently. But the news does give you a fair picture of what is happening. Today was a fine sunny day again, with a frost this morning and only one hailstorm. Last night was very clear with a full moon. I had William's last letter too by the way, I hope his cricket is going OK, I'm afraid the poor little chap hasn't had much of a chance compared to most of them. I never seem to be there to practise with him before the summer term starts. But he has an excellent eye and as with everything, is such a little keenie – and his leg shots are excellent. I do hope little Emmie is fine, too. We should soon, I hope, have a clear idea of how long this whole thing is going to take to resolve. Some of the soldiers are taking pot shots at geese and duck here. They are very slow flying and large static targets. The place has an enormous population of geese, everywhere you go they get up in large groups, honking and whistling noisily – it is I suppose quite good scenery for water colours, pale green hills, grey rocks and sky – very monotonous with very long fields of view – miles and miles – which doesn't always help us.

11 June.

I am writing in the middle of the day – it has been a fine but very cold morning, like a sharp, clear, sunny winter's day at home – and so I am warming my toes in front of the oven in the Ops Room shed. Not much news since my last letter, really, but by the time you get this, I do hope the whole thing will be wrapped up – at least on East Falkland, after which I can't see much point in their continuing to hold out on West Falkland. Yesterday we had a Brigade 'O' Group and I saw David Chaundler. Johnny Rickett, CO of the Welsh Guards was also there, they have had a pretty awful start I'm afraid – so unnecessary, too, like so many of the losses we have had. David was in good form, after a hell of a journey to get here, and it was nice to see him. Of all the situations in which to meet up, this one would seem as almost as unlikely as any that one could dream of. Everyone is in good form, surviving the weather but I don't think that we can do so indefinitely so we really must get on with it. Feet are the main problem, of course, and our boots are hardly ideal for these conditions. I think of you all constantly, and all that we have done together, and of all that we will do when I get back! You are always in my thoughts and I do love you all so very, very much. You are my whole life, as you well know. Nothing else matters to me in the final analysis as our life together and we will all appreciate it as never before after this. It is a relief that everyone basically seems to

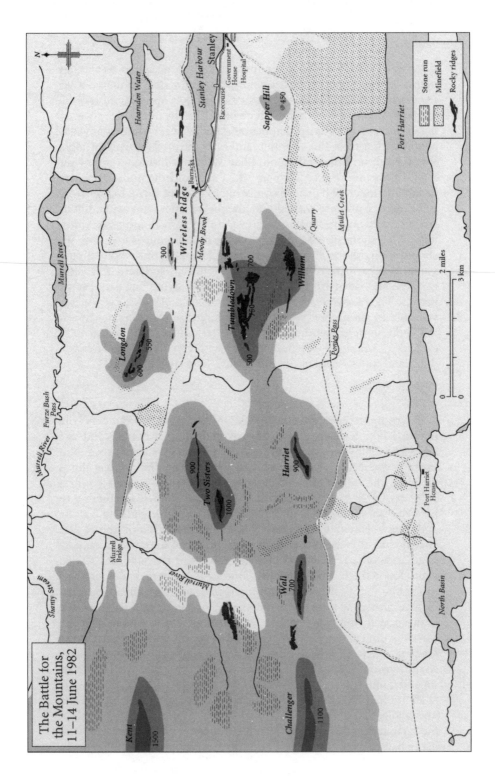

The Battle for the Mountains, 11–14 June 1982

Stone run
Minefield
Rocky ridges

N

Murrell River
Shanty Stream
Kent
1500
Murrell Bridge
Murrell River
Furze Bush Pass
Murrell River
Two Sisters
900
1000
Challenger
1100
Wall
700
Harriet
900
London
600
550
Tumbledown
750
500
William
700
Fenies Pass
Quarry
Mullet Creek
Port Harriet House
North Basin
Port Harriet
Sapper Hill
450
Wireless Ridge
300
Moody Brook
Barracks
Racecourse
Government House
Hospital
Stanley Harbour
Stanley
Hearnden Water

2 miles
3 km
0
0

158

get on well, and the Brigadier is splendid, so straight-forward and philosophical. We are not sure what 5 Brigade are up to but we seem to be just getting on with it without them. I do hope you are all fine, and happy – do try not to worry, as it will do no good as you well know. It is such a comfort to me to think of you leading a normal, happy life at home, to which I so long to return. Last night I had Upland Goose for supper, cooked by the RSM, shot by Corporal Phillips – quite a few have been sniped now! I am feeling very fit and well and my feet have given me a lot less trouble than on most exercises – no blisters and I have managed to keep them quite dry by changing socks whenever we stop. Sorry for such a mundane letter, but I thought that I would get this one off as it might be a bit more difficult as we close with Stanley! We don't really know what sort of a fight they will make of it now, but rather hope they will see the writing on the wall and see discretion as the better part of valour – we'll see – anyway we had a comfortable night here in a tent last night before getting on the move again.

Meanwhile, Hew records in his notes:

The advance and battle for Mount Longdon followed. It is the hardest thing in the world to write about the chaos, confusion, and terrible nature of a battle. In a sense, all you can do is to tell your personal story, whether you are a young soldier in a Fire Section or the CO. We had made the best plan we could, constrained as we were by the range of our own artillery and the uncertainties that lay along the Moody Valley between Mount Longdon and Tumbledown Mountain, especially the probability of mines. As it turned out, we advanced from the West (about a three hour night approach march) across the stream running south from Furze Bush Pass, and straight through an unmarked enemy minefield, which accounted for two serious casualties, Cpl Brian Milne and LCpl 'Shirley' Bassey. In essence we planned for B Company to attack up or around the western slopes to secure the western summit, for A Company to secure the ridge of moorland to the north of Longdon with a view to further exploitation, and for C Company to be held back in reserve along the low ground of the Murrell River, ready to be committed wherever a problem arose and to exploit success, we hoped onto Wireless Ridge. This was very much the spirit of the Brigade plan of which we were part; a silent night attack, exploiting surprise but with artillery immediately on call to engage pre-planned targets. The three battalions, 3 PARA onto Mount Longdon, 45 Commando onto Two Sisters and 42 Commando onto Mount Harriet, with 2 PARA in reserve, were all under instructions to exploit and get on as far east as possible. Ourselves onto Wireless Ridge, Four Five onto Tumble-down Mountain and Four Two onto Mount William. In the event, overcome as we all were by the physical and mental demands of fighting through many hours of darkness, none of us felt able to exploit beyond our primary objectives. Moreover, until our artillery batteries could be flown forward, their ability to support us onto these subsequent objectives was very limited, whilst the Frigates supporting us with their 4.2inch guns – in our case, HMS Avenger – needed to get further east well before first light.

The fighting was conducted in the most awkward and difficult terrain: huge slices of ice covered granite outcrop, rising like great fins from the steep, grassy hillside, provided great advantages to the defender. By the time I had moved up with my little party of signallers to the foot of the mountain behind B Company, their leading elements had already fought their way through sniper and MG fire to the western summit. But here, despite our own close support artillery fire, they came under further and devastating fire from enemy positions that dominated this crest line from further east, and the Company started to sustain many casualties. I came across Jonathon Shaw, one of B Company's platoon commanders, trying to rally and regroup, but clearly shocked by this 'ambush of fire' that his soldiers were doing their best to overcome. As we pushed on over the top ourselves, doing our best to exploit the protection of the rocks, we passed Sgt Gray and young Pte 'Baz' Barratt, both wounded and lying under groundsheets muttering encouragement to each other. We veered over to our right as I tried to link up with the Company commander, Mike Argue, and then shifted left again, to find our-selves in a bowl with great rocks on its eastern side, that afforded a measure of protection from ground fire. By now the artillery and mortar fire of both sides had intensified, and as the rocks around us rang to this harsh and deafening noise, we went firm in what cover we could find at the front end of the bowl, where I could try to exercise at least a degree of control in the confusion of so much close-quarter fighting. Mike and his soldiers were having a terrible time, as they attempted to get round the flanks of well prepared enemy positions that dominated the little tracks and approaches running below the spine of the summit ridgeline. The southern slopes were impossibly dangerous as artillery fire plastered them from positions around Port Stanley, the northern approaches the only option, but well covered by enemy direct fire weapons. Typical of so many firefights is the account given by Cpl Ian Bailey of the gallantry of his little team and of Sergeant Ian McKay:

'Shortly after Mr Bickerdike, the Platoon commander, was shot and wounded, Sgt McKay and I had a talk and decided the aim was to get across to the next cover, which was 30 to 35 metres away.

There were some Argentine positions there but we didn't know the exact location. He shouted out to the other corporals in the platoon commanding fire teams, to give covering fire, three machine guns together, then we set off with three other soldiers. As we were moving across the open ground, two of them, Neil Grose and Jason Burt, were killed by rifle and MG fire almost at once; the other soldier got across and into cover. We grenaded the first position and went past it without stopping, just firing into it, and that's when I got shot from one of the other positions which was about 10ft away. I got hit in the hip and went down. Sgt McKay was still going on to the next position but there was no one else with him. The last I saw him, he was just running on, running towards the remaining positions in that group. I was lying on my back and I listened to men calling to each other. They were trying to find out what was happening but, when they called out to Sgt McKay, there was no reply. I got shot again soon after that, by bullets in the neck and the hand.'

Our MILAN teams were also doing sterling work against positions further in depth, but often necessarily from exposed 'forward slope' positions. In one awful moment, over my right shoulder, one shell from an enemy 105mm Recoilless Rifle killed a complete three man crew – Cpl Ginge McCarthy, Pte Peter Hedicker and Pte Geordie West. As I discussed the situation with Mike, three enemy corpses lying close to us in the moonlight, we concluded that his company could not continue to batter themselves in this way against such stubborn opposition, and I then talked to David Collett about what he thought he could do from the north. He had already had three of his own soldiers killed by enemy fire that dominated his positions from the rocks, but we agreed that he should now try to pull back and approach on the same axis as B Company, then passing through them and continuing to press the attack home. All this took many hours – many hours in which the constant shelling and fire fights instilled in me a growing feeling of helplessness, yet a conviction that with our magnificent soldiers we must and would prevail. So as the darkness began to give way to the dawn, with David's men still crawling forward 'on the belly' as he put it, taking out one position after another in a systematic process of attrition, resistance was broken, and the opposing forces starting to melt away in what remained of the darkness. The mountain was ours.

But at what a cost. By this time I was well onto the forward slope, overlooking Wireless Ridge, taking advantage of a well built enemy bunker which contained brandy, a great round cheese, letters and all the paraphernalia of daily life in a defensive position that had been occupied for many weeks. There was human excrement everywhere, too – hygiene discipline had been non-existent – and just outside our new bunker was yet another dead Argentine soldier, one of his feet separated from its leg. The shambles of the battlefield was beyond all imagination – corpses starting to give off that sickly-sweet, distinctive odour of death, clothing, bloody shell dressings, discarded boots, belts of ammunition, ration boxes, field cookers, and life's detritus spread all over the hillside. Adding to the depressing scene was the confirmation of our own casualties through this ghastly night battle – 17 dead and 40 wounded, some very seriously. Amongst the dead were some of our youngest and most recently trained soldiers, like Ptes Grose, Burt and Scrivens, as well as some of the great characters of the Battalion, like Cpl Doch Murdoch, and Sgt Ian McKay. For two days and nights thereafter we continued to endure pretty constant shelling and mortaring, the latter in some ways the most lethal as there was no warning whistle before the awful moment of impact. In these days, despite our best efforts to pull back as far as possible from the exposed forward slopes of the mountain, we lost six more good men, including Cpl Stewart McLaughlin, a scouser and brave as a lion, who with Pte Craig Jones was killed by mortar fire as Jones was helping him, already badly wounded, down the reverse slope of the mountain. Also killed in this dreadful period of shelling were young Dickie Absolon, who had grown up in New Zealand and had been one of our most daring patrol scouts as we advanced, and LCpl Peter Higgs, who had been one of our supporting drivers in Belfast and had then transferred to the Regiment. Both young NCOs of great quality and promise. There was a deep sense of grief in the Battalion at our losses, all such good men, with their lives still before them.

Personal memories came to mind, even in these frightful circumstances. Playing squash with the delightful, bright and highly promising Ian McKay, who had also been a battalion footballer, but who had had worries over a persistent knee injury. The bachelor "Doch" Murdoch's exotic holidays in Thailand, with which he used to regale us, in his lovely Renfrew lilt. Stewart McLaughlin, the embodiment of the passionate professional soldier, looking always to teach his young soldiers new tricks, exuding enthusiasm and physical energy. Having a beer or two with Ginge McCarthy, a big, gentle man full of wry humour and intelligence. Chatting with 'Fester', as Anthony Greenwood was always called – such a friendly and likeable figure, who had once driven with me around some very dodgy roads near the Northern Ireland border in the most clapped out car in the MT park. And the young Kiwi, dark haired Dickie Absolon, cruising over a Dropping Zone (DZ) on Salisbury Plain on his beloved Army patrol bike, utterly contented with his soldiering life. These and other good men were now gone. Caroline Dodsworth, Mark's widow, would put up a memorial to him in Palace Barracks, Holywood, across the waters of Belfast Lough from her home in Carrickfergus, where they had met, so that they could go on chatting to each other. Michelle Lovett, the slim, quiet yet fiercely determined widow of Chris, killed as a medic going forward selflessly to help others, would want to know exactly how he had died. The physical challenges of 'casevac' were, for sure, amongst the toughest, and faced with great bravery by the battalion's mechanics, drivers, clerks and cooks, as well as the medics themselves, struggling under fire through the darkness over those turf slopes and around huge icy boulders to reach the wounded. And after that, the grim task of accounting for the dead, and preparing them for their journey back to Teal Inlet, overland by BV and then by helicopter when clear of the shelling. The task of caring for the dead fell primarily to the medical team in the RAP, led by our two doctors, John Burgess and Mike von Berteli and by their Colour Sergeant, Brian Faulkner. The poor Padre, the strong and gentle Derek Heaver, rendered too a last service to these men, many of whom he had known so well and spoken with so often, as he safe-guarded their personal effects and ministered to them. No wonder the Duke of Wellington is reputed to have remarked that there is nothing so melancholy as a battle won – unless it be a battle lost.

On the 14th of June the enemy surrendered and we found our-selves, to our disbelief but enormous relief, in Port Stanley. It had been a terrible time, but we had prevailed.

On the same day, Jean writes from home:

What prophets of doom Sergeant Major Carter and I have become ... any 3 PARA wife seeing us on the patch [married quarters] bolts inside like a scared rabbit in the hopes of shutting out the bad news. The only pleasant aspect is those whose wounds are minor; slowly the wife realises that it's all over for her and that he will be coming home. How strange it felt yesterday listening to the details of the casualties coming in – and yet not daring to listen ... surely success cannot be far away now? ... We are all being wonderfully patient here though, and everyone continues to be quite marvellous – stoical. I shall never forget how some of the girls bore up to the news that we had to tell them yesterday and on Saturday. Even poor Mrs Dodsworth – five minutes later she was smiling and showing us pictures of him with his much loved dogs in Ireland.

On 16 June Hew writes to Jean:

Well, here we are! If you look at The Times of Saturday, 22nd May, page two, there is a picture of Stanley – I am in a bungalow in the bottom half of that picture! We arrived in the afternoon of 14th June, and the sudden collapse was as unexpected as it was marvellous. Never have I been so utterly relieved and elated – even that morning after first light, artillery was still raining in on our position on Mount Longdon, and I was that morning giving out orders for an attack that night (14/15 June) on Moody Brook Camp – we would have taken it, but only at still more loss. A hailstorm was falling, and I was becoming quite concerned at the closing winter and how long the battle would continue, with more casualties in worsening weather, freezing, snowy, wet. That we would succeed I had no doubt, it was the cost that was concerning me so much.

But I have not even described to you our magnificent attack on Mount Longdon, which was certainly one of the decisive defeats which persuaded the Argies to pack up. I'm sorry I didn't write as soon as we arrived, but I have been sitting in this bungalow writing to Next of Kin and drafting citations and still have not finished, and I do want to get them cracked now, while we pause to discover what happens next. We finally assaulted Mount Longdon on night 11/12 June, and I suppose it was as fine a feat of arms as 3 PARA has ever undertaken, surpassing anything since World War 2 and I reckon at least the equal of any World War 2 battles fought by this battalion. We lost twenty-two dead, plus one 9 Squadron RE attached, and we have forty-eight wounded, some terribly badly. But I do hope and pray that no more will die. Tomorrow I am flying to the Uganda to visit them all, so shall know more then. The battalion fought superbly against very large numbers, all night, from 9pm to 7am, when it got light – and the resistance was very fierce as it was a key position which they had to retain. Having had two months to prepare their bunkers and defences, it would have been impregnable if we had been defending it. 'B' and Support Companies took most casualties, 'A' Company quite a few, and 'C' Company were kept in reserve and really got away unscathed. You will presumably know the casualty list by now, so I won't go through it. What a cost, and such good people lost, most terribly young – but what a merciful relief that it now seems to be over. The sun came out and it was a fine, crisp afternoon, quite firm going underfoot, as we almost ran into Stanley, down the moorland – to be greeted by scenes of destruction and shambles. Later on I went out to the airfield in an Arg. Mercedes Land-rover, and we came back with five – we just booted them out and made them walk – mostly senior officers; I also rolled up Menendez's planning map in Government House and walked out with it, with numerous Argie staff officers watching agog! The map covers the whole route we took, and shows us in red (ie enemy) near Estancia – so a historic piece of booty! But the shambles on the airfield was also astonishing, with miserable columns of Args making their way out there. The greatest shambles of all, however, was on our position on Mount Longdon as the grey, misty wet dawn came up after our battle. I have never seen such an appalling scene of death and destruction – the artillery fire of both sides onto the Mountain – ours till we'd got it, and then theirs when we had – caused havoc, and all the 3 PARA soldiers went in with bayonets in the end. To see these soldiers moving through the misty dawn, with bayonets fixed, after they had finally secured their objectives after an all night battle, was a sight I shall never forget. They were magnificent, and incredibly brave. I am so terribly sad at the people we lost though – I will continue on a second letter as although the future is very unclear, I at least want to write to you about it.

On 17 June Jean writes:

John Carruthers [the Families Officer] got up at the Wives Club yesterday and read out the long and very sad list and it was one of the most awful times – lots of wives were in tears and all looked stunned and grey. I don't think any of them had had any idea of just how high the cost had been. I was particularly saddened too because I had to stand up and say what a gruelling task the Families Office had had, with our top preoccupation being coping with the bereaved and those with wounded husbands – because a growing complaint had started amongst other wives that they had not been told of the losses. So I told them that rather than thinking that, they should be considering what they could do to help. Anyway, we are organising ourselves very well and I pray we shall support those in need in every way we can.

On 18 June, Hew writes to Jean:

Yesterday, I flew to the SS Uganda in Grantham Sound, to see our casualties – they are being marvellous, so brave, and all will live – but five have lost limbs, you will know who, I expect – all have sent telegrams and most have spoken on the Marisat telephone to their families – one lost eye, two can't speak at present. Saw Richard Bethell from Scots Guards there – he is OK. The organisation on board is marvellous – quite superb – I even had a Gin and Tonic and sat down to lunch with the RN Commander on board! Such civilisation. Then, en route back, we landed at Port San Carlos to change helicopters, so saw a few of the people there whom we first liberated – then on to Teal Inlet where twenty-one of our twenty-three dead are buried – Corporal Hope and Private Absolon are at Red Beach, San Carlos Bay as they died after reaching hospital there. They all have crosses and marked graves, on a nice patch, overlooking

165

the sea – but it wasn't fenced and there was a calf blundering over one of the crosses – we've fixed that. Anyway, it looks as if all bodies may come home now. I hope so, although what a thankless task. We held a Memorial Service in Stanley Cathedral this morning. Brigadier Julian Thompson came, and I made a short address, we had three hymns (incredibly slow playing organist), prayers, a lesson (RSM) and Corporal Steggles read the names of the dead, Corporal Black some prayers. It was absolutely the right thing to do although of course we will have a full one with families in Aldershot Garrison Church on return. [It was in fact held as the central event at an open air parade that October in the Aldershot Town Football Ground, in the presence of the Prince of Wales, our Colonel-in-Chief.]

On 18 June, Jean writes:

With each passing day things are getting easier. Yesterday we could tell three wives that their husbands were off the VSI list. Mrs Sinclair, Mrs Kelly and Mrs Rehill, and I can't tell you what a joy it is to be the conveyor of good news after all that has gone before. We were very concerned about Mrs Rehill – she is so near to having her baby that we didn't say just how bad he was, and now it is a relief to know he is improving and will be well.

On 18 June, the Battalion holds a Service in Stanley Cathedral. In Hew's address, he begins by reading out signals from HM The Queen and HRH The Prince of Wales:

I send my warmest congratulations to you and all under your command for the splendid way in which you have achieved the liberation of the Falkland Islands. Britain is very proud of the way you have served your country.

Elizabeth R.

I have just heard the news of the 3rd Battalion's gallant action and wanted to send you all my deepest sympathy for the losses you have sustained amongst your friends and colleagues. I am sure you will not have time for such things, but my very best wishes go to all those who were wounded in the operation. It is only too clear that despite appalling conditions of the most testing kind the 3rd Battalion has lived up to the extraordinary, courageous traditions of The Parachute Regiment and has given us all reason to be intensely proud of what you are doing so far from home. My thoughts and prayers are constantly with you for whatever you have to do next and I can only say that it is the greatest privilege to be associated with such a magnificent Regiment.

Charles. Colonel in Chief.

Then he continues:

The Prime Minister has described the recapture of the Falkland Islands as boldly planned, bravely executed and brilliantly accomplished.

As a passage of arms, your part in this operation must rank on a scale more hazardous and demanding than any of the campaigns since 1945 in which the Battalion has taken part.

The enemy has been powerful, and often boldly dominant, in the air. He has been highly skilled, and heavily armed, with artillery and mortars. The best of his infantry, such as those of 7 Regiment, whom we fought on Mount Longdon, have held ground with fierce determination in the face of our attacks. The ground that you have covered has been arduous and exhausting by day. By night it would have quickly defeated the will of lesser men. The climate has been increasingly foul and inhospitable, frequently proving to be the greatest potential enemy of all. Yet through your resilience, your resourcefulness, your determination, your practical application of your training, and above all your abundant good humour, your have not just survived these conditions. You have shrugged them off – and you have continued to advance eastwards with a resolution which the enemy can neither have expected nor understood. Finally, you have closed with him, with an aggression and a fighting spirit that has made his defeat swift and inevitable.

It is now known that the enemy assumed that we must have been moved eastwards by support helicopter, such was the manner of our advance. In fact, as you will all remember for the rest of your lives, the Battalion marched, without air or ground transport, from Port San Carlos to Stanley. Many patrols covered certain stretches of this trackless, boggy terrain repeatedly. You probably rarely felt like victors or heroes during those hours of marching, mostly in darkness. But this Battalion has always been proud of its ability to march far and fast, and you have now demonstrated this capacity superbly. In the final battle for Mount Longdon great bravery and skill were displayed, mostly by very young men encountering battle conditions totally outside their previous experience. It is this same courage, pride and unbeatable spirit that I witnessed yesterday, when visiting our wounded on the Uganda. Two cannot, at present, speak, one has lost an eye, five have lost arms or legs; all suffer pain.

It is the friends and comrades killed and wounded since we landed at Port San Carlos, exactly four weeks ago, whom we are gathered here to pray for, and to remember. We shall do so again, in Aldershot, on our return, with our families and friends – and theirs.

Some days later, Hew receives this letter from Major John Evans, enclosing an order of service:

It has been my honour and privilege to visit the family of the late Lance Corporal Peter Higgs, who was killed on Mount Longdon. Although it is very sad to meet the family of one of the soldiers in our Regiment under those circumstances, it was with a deep sense of pride that I went to represent you, the Battalion and the Regiment. You may have seen some of the English newspapers and so you will know that, as a nation, we are at a loss for words to express our admiration for the way you, and the 2nd Battalion, have acquitted yourselves down in the Falklands. All of us left back here in the UK have been grieved by the loss of life experienced by the Battalions, and hope that the little we are able to do, to share in the sorrow of the bereaved families, will somehow set your minds at ease until your return.

Today WO1 [RSM] Wilsher and I went to a memorial service for Lance Corporal Higgs. He was born in the very small village of Kingston Winslow near Ashbury in Wiltshire. The service was held in the Ashbury Village Parish Church (St. Mary's) and was conducted by the local Vicar, the Rev. Derek Blunsdon. The Tidworth Senior Chaplain to the Forces (Rev. J.P. Clarke) was in attendance and said the Airborne Prayer as part of the service.

In his address, the Vicar mentioned that Peter Higgs had been baptised as a baby in the Font at the back of the Church, had sung in the Choir, and had been a familiar figure to the worshippers of the Village. It was obvious that he was well known and liked, as the Church was completely filled (approx 300) and most were visibly moved by the event. There was also a group of eight members of the Parachute Regiment Association from Swindon; they had taken the trouble to find out for themselves if there was to be an Act of Remembrance for Lance Corporal Higgs. It was good to see them there representing the Regiment 'past', as I was there to represent the Regiment 'present'. They were upright of bearing, well turned out and obviously very proud of the tradition and heritage to which Lance Corporal Higgs and his friends in the Third Battalion have given so much.

In the church itself (a charming building and so typical of parish churches in the countryside), a large wooden crucifix had been laid on trestles in the choir before the altar. At its head a lighted candle. A silent and poignant symbol of sacrifice.

Roll of Honour 3 PARA.

Richard Absalon MM
Gerald Bull
Jason Burt
Jonathan Crow
Mark Dodsworth
Anthony Greenwood
Neil Grose
Peter Hedicker
Peter Higgs
Stephen Hope
Timothy Jenkins
Craig Jones
Stewart Laing
Christopher Lovett
Keith McCarthy
Ian McKay VC
Stewart McLaughlin
James Murdoch
David Scott
Ian Scrivens
Alexander Shaw (REME attached)
Philip West
Scott Wilson (RE attached)

On 19 June, Jean writes:

It is hard to talk to people who seem to think that now that the surrender has happened, we can get out the bunting and shrug off the whole thing. In Tidworth, we are still counting the cost in human terms, and I feel bruised and battered by what has happened and what I have had to do and what I have seen here. I suppose one will come to terms with it soon, but it is impossible to rejoice. There is nothing 'glad' about war.

Chapter Fourteen

Will Pike, Helmand Province, Afghanistan, 2006

Will Pike is educated at Milton Abbey School in Dorset and joins the Parachute Regiment from RMA Sandhurst in May 1992, aged twenty-two. He serves on operations in Northern Ireland, where he receives a GOC's Commendation, and in Macedonia. Following in the footsteps of his forebear William Tompson of the 17th Foot, in 2002 he deploys to Kabul with 2 PARA, as part of the peace-keeping force following the defeat and fall of the Taliban regime. By the time Will returns to Afghanistan in April 2006 now aged thirty-six, this time to Helmand Province as a company commander in 3 PARA, peacekeeping is about to give way to serious fighting, notwithstanding the optimistic comments on the military outlook by the then Defence Secretary, John Reid. Like his great-grandfather Reggie, Will is an assiduous diary writer, as he experiences the difficult early weeks of the British deployment in Helmand and the re-emergence of the Taliban as a power in the land. In July 1999 he had married Alison Thomas (Al) at her home village of Aldbourne in Wiltshire. By 2006 they have three daughters, Amelia (6), Imogen (Imme, 4) and Clemmie (1). After a work-up exercise in Oman, Will records the deployment into Helmand Province:

Sat 15 April.

Am now sitting in a C17 transport aircraft with about 30 other members of the battalion, including the CO [Lieutenant Colonel Stuart Tootal], as well as a dismantled Chinook helicopter. Left Brize Norton at 7am and are now en route for Turkey and after a short stop, on into Kandahar. This has been the most extraordinary and in many respects saddening build up to a deployment. At its core the problem seems to have stemmed at the strategic level. First, the UK

170

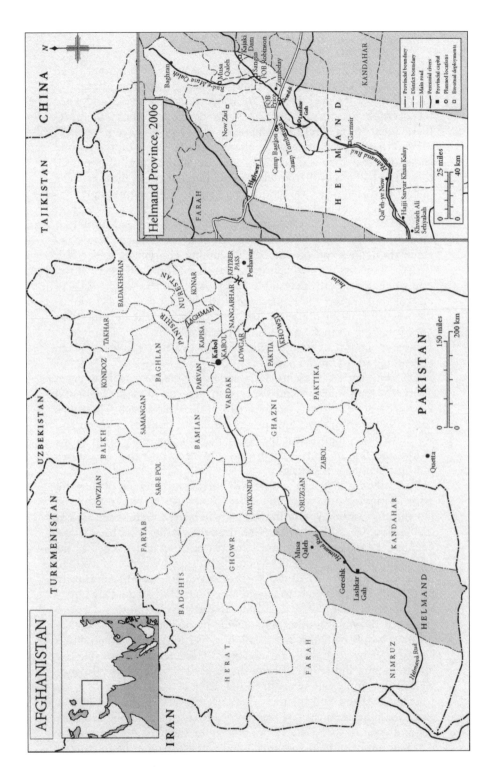

171

waited till January to formally declare that we would commit, even though it was clear a year ago that there was no credible alternative to committal. [Hence] the rush at the operational level. Second, once the decision was made and the plans developed, those at PJHQ [Permanent Joint HQ, Northwood] and higher have resolutely refused to allow the plans to be altered despite events on the ground suggesting that they should be – for example the [need to organise] the arrival of the full battlegroup within days not months! The impact of this higher level ignorance of sound military principles has evidence in moral and physical areas – huge uncertainty and constant changes of plan, so . . . the soldiers feel f***ed about and think that much less of the chain of command. Physically we have yet to see, let alone train on some of our battle winning equipment – Tac Sat, ICOM Scanners, etc – which is disgraceful. Moreover we have run foul of that perfectly detestable British staff officer who seems to mistrust/not respect the requests of field commanders and demands thorough formal justifications for everything, so that he can either put off having to make a decision or probably just say No anyway. This is an ugly trait in the military psyche which would make an interesting Staff College paper.

The tour itself represents a significant challenge and is without doubt the most demanding tour of my career to date. Helmand Province is, to an extent, virgin territory, there have been few troops here, it is Pashtun, the major poppy producer, borders Pakistan and will have some support for the Taliban, with sanctuary areas in the North and South, and with an easy run back into their madrasas [mosque schools] in Pakistan.

My Company is first in and we will operate initially out of Gereshk prior to moving out, when the other Companies arrive, to form the Operations Company. Our initial task will be to dominate the area of the Bastion, Gereshk, Lashkar Gah triangle – rather a lot for a single Company! Despite this we are likely to be stretched further as far as Sangin (north of Gereshk) where there is a confluence of Taliban influence, Narco traffic, and so forth – they don't much like authority up there! So we are likely to have a lot on our plates from Day One – the threat is high, from roadside Improvised Explosive Devices (IEDs) to full-on ambushes and suicide bombers. Of all, the IED is the most worrying and scares us all; however it can be countered to a large degree by good drills and alertness. The suicide bomber one can do little about but try to identify the signs. The ambush is OK since we can just apply our strength to defeating it.

Leaving Alison and the girls gets harder every time and I hate it and hate doing it to them. I feel physically sick from about 12 hours out and want to spend the 12 hours hugging them all close but know that will not help them very much and will make more of an issue of going away. I left the house at 1.30am which was easier since all were asleep and there is no great parting. The process reminds me how much I love them all and owe them so much, especially Alison who is so strong and pragmatic.

Sun 16 April.

We arrived late last night into Kandahar. All very quiet. Today was a rather strange day – little is actually confirmed and the CO has yet to have clear direction from above, which makes trying to plan rather problematic. Sangin is high on list of desires and I expect to deploy up there with the Company on about May 15 following a spell in Gereshk. It is rather cheeky up there with Taliban and Narco/ Tribal dynamics. We go on a recce the day after tomorrow. Comms [communications] system is woeful. It is staggering that with all the problems over Iraq we still cannot get this right. Not nearly enough Tac Sat sets or networked terminals – and all commercially available. Spoke to Al this evening. Hugh and Sally [Thomas – Alison's parents] are there this w/e, which is comforting to have the initial hurdle of separation and the Easter w/e softened a little. Girls are well.

Mon 17 April.

Another slightly curious day, a lot of briefings etc – mostly centred on the Sangin area where there is something of a fixation – and a distraction from focussing effort in the central area around Lashkar Gah – Sangin certainly important with a melting pot of narco/tribal/ Taliban currents playing up, all well mixed up by the US ODA activity which is deeply unhelpful and irresponsible. US pressure building for a series of ambitious offensive options towards mid/end May. Talking about defeating the Taliban insurgency – cloud cuckoo land – with what is a two week, temporary offensive with no lasting effect. Too many parallels with the books I am reading on Indo-China! [The French defeat by General Giap and the Viet Minh in the early 1950s.]

Tues 18 April.

A busy day. Left early by CH47 (Chinook) with CO's recce party to Camp Bastion, Gereshk then Sangin. Rather a whistle stop on the first two but had four hours in the last, which was very useful. Snatched half an hour with the Company at Bastion who also arrived there this morning. Annoying to be mal-located but will join them at Bastion shortly.

Wed 19 April.

A day of planning and backbriefs. Key aspect remains 'Sangin Effect' though we are keen that this should not overly detract from the

Battlegroup's (BG's) main effort in the triangle of Bastion-Gereshk-Lashkar Gah, i.e. the centre of Helmand governance. Sangin ... has little or no central government authority ... Thus I think I will be there from about 15 May but instead of occupying the Forward Operating Base (FOB) Robinson there, we will approach the task differently – i.e. a mobile Company Group operating with 'dynamic unpredictability' in the whole area – appearing, delivering effect and then moving somewhere else.

Spoke to Al this evening – all well and girls back at school. Clemmie walking now with hands in the air.

Thurs 20 April, Camp Bastion.

This morning Commander Helmand Task Force (TF) (Col Charlie Knaggs) briefed Brigadier Ed Butler (commanding 16 Air Assault Brigade and our 'peacetime' Brigade Commander) on his concept of ops for Helmand. CO gave his piece and I my rough concept for how we might do business in the Sangin area. Had to leave the meeting early to catch a C130 to fly to Bastion where I arrived about lunchtime. Something of a dustbowl, very talcum-powdery dust which gets everywhere – interesting for aircraft trying to land. Blokes living in basic tents and without much kit but all in good spirits – spoke to them all about what we are likely to be up to over the next few weeks – Gereshk and Sangin.

Fri 21 April.

A rather unproductive day – we have very little kit and so are unable to do a great deal, though we can crack on with such things as medical training, which is key. Some of the air freight arrived today so now I have my battle box and we have the .50 HMGs and sniper rifles etc. Established a briefing room which is good and was able to give the blokes a good feel for some of the dynamics. Very dusty today with something of a sandstorm in early afternoon, everything covered in a fine layer of dust and tent nearly blew away.

Wrote to Al and the girls tonight.

On Easter Day, Hew writes from home in Bentley:

You will now be settling down and getting into your stride, and you will also realise that you are constantly in our thoughts as you go about your business. No doubt there will be difficulties and frustrations – in a sense, all military operations are a 'complex of difficulties', but they are there to be resolved, overcome or just lived with, and I can't think of an organisation better equipped or trained to cope with this environment than a parachute battalion. Remember, too, that today's challenges and sometimes disappointments become tomorrow's reminiscences/humour/legend and the comradeship that all your young soldiers are forging will last them a lifetime of reunions and 'war stories'. I suspect that in your situation, rather as in Ireland, caution and even cunning, certainly unpredictability and thoughtfulness will be at a premium. The impulsive will be vulnerable, and I guess that as ever the fundamentals of battlefield discipline will very much apply, 'the skills of survival'.

Will's diary continues:

Sat 22 April.

Another rather chaotic day in the dust. CO arrived early this morning by C130 ... he gave me orders for the 1st Phase in Gereshk to last until 10 May when either B or C Company will take over. Gave the blokes a verbal brief for the move tomorrow – 40 into Gereshk to be followed by the remainder on 24th. Still no Gunners or Engineers, though.

Sun 23 April.

Alison's birthday. Flew into FOB Price at Gereshk this morning with 40 of the Company Group (Coy Gp). Gereshk is an important town since it sits at the junction of Highway 1 and the Helmand River. It is also the home of Governor Daoud and the last major urban centre before the Taliban/Narco dominated areas to the north, especially Sangin. Its proximity to Highway 1 – the principal Main Supply Route (MSR) – means that it is a magnet for the IED attack, especially as it has one of the few crossings over the canal and Helmand River ... there is almost certainly a Taliban IED cell operating within the town.

Spoke to Al this evening, as a scorpion was edging my way – despatched with a rock. Rather miserable to be by herself – one is increasingly aware of the burden that we put our families under ... bought her a necklace, earrings and belt which she liked, which is good.

Mon 24 April. FOB Price, Gereshk.

Remainder of Coy Gp flew in today and now the camp is bursting at the seams – rather a lot of hangers-on which we will thin out. A frustrating day in many respects as we grapple with the problem of bringing this place under some sort of control ... Task has appeared, to send a patrol down to Lashkar Gah which is a bit of a bore since I don't think we will be properly balanced and equipped, so to send a patrol a reasonable distance from here without being properly squared away is not all that helpful. Had a bit of a scare on the guard this evening which we thought might be a suspect device – an empty cardboard box as it turns out, but good for drills practice none the less. Had good e-bluey from Al this evening.

Tues 25 April. FOB Price, Gereshk.

Another rather frustrating day but at least a little light at the end of the tunnel in that the Ops Room is coming together. Had a letter from Daddy today with a quite excellent passage within it which accurately describes my feelings – despite him having no idea of the state of things here. It is a depressingly familiar situation and feels like climbing the Eiger! Had O Group tonight – blokes all set – now just need all our kit/comms etc.

Wed 26 April. FOB Price, Gereshk.

At least things are moving a bit on the procedural and physical side and am gaining more confidence in our ability to exercise real control over the battle space. Mortars adjusted their illuminating targets tonight – all went well – though they started a fire in a wadi – home grown drug eradication programme! US ODA seem to have got rid of their 'pet' monkey which sadly prevents my plans for vengeance!! [Will had been bitten by the monkey on the recce in March, which led to a course of rabies vaccinations and much amusement around the Battalion and medical chain.]

Thurs 27 April. FOB Price, Gereshk.

E mails from Al today, girls well. Talk this evening on the new tourniquets and quick clot and field dressings – all good stuff and might need them!

Fri 28 April. FOB Price, Gereshk.

A better day today and making progress on the ops side and some of our kit arrived, albeit in a parlous state and missing some things. CO and Battalion Tactical HQ (Tac HQ) arrived as did my Gunner troop, which brings welcome numbers and support. Long chat to CO over the issues here [there is much difficulty with the US Special Forces elements with whom they share the base, and questions of where operational responsibility lies]. Bit of an issue over ballistic protection for the vehicles, not enough to go round, manufacturer cannot make them fast enough, all of which comes back to the delayed announcement of the deployment and thus no activation of budgets – and no kit! Senior military should say 'Minister, if you delay the decision we cannot get this kit which means soldiers dying unnecessarily.' So allow early purchase despite no political announcement, since we need the kit anyway. Feel that we are badly let down.

Sat 29 April. FOB Price, Gereshk.

Amelia's birthday. Woke up thinking about Amelia, Al and the girls. First patrol today. Support helicopter (SH) lift into Gereshk. SH pilots typically awkward – stated 'we don't do dummy drops'. Wrong answer, and indicated their inability to see the tactical requirements. Patrol went very well but very hot indeed. Bustling Afghan bazaar selling all sorts of stuff – meat hanging outside, donkeys, carts, rickshaws, stench, open sewers etc. Scoped hospital and police station and then wound our way to the west, initially through tight feudal streets and then more open desert fringes, then back in. Hard work for signallers and Electronic Counter Measure (ECM) carriers and we will try to mitigate this by more helicopters and more vehicle pick ups etc. Spoke to Amelia and Al this evening, all well and enjoying her birthday.

In a letter home, he writes:

Gereshk is an important little place, astride the only river and road in the south, used for the movement of supplies, opium and insurgents. The place is awash with opium and cannabis-opium in about 90% of the fields that follow the Helmand river ... The foot patrols we do are the best but also the hardest, as the heat takes a merry toll with all the kit we must carry – water is a key resource. The camp is becoming more established day by day and is pretty comfortable.'

Will goes on in his diary:

Sun 30 April. FOB Price, Gereshk.

A day marked by comms difficulties. We have Bowman Secure HF and Tacsat, however both are relatively new to the blokes and so we are not yet skilled in their use. Added to which the HF is not at its best in arid conditions and the Tacsat needs to be pointed in the right bearing and elevation. Problems this morning when Rob Mosetti was out with his Fire Support Group (FSG) to do some .50 HMG zeroing – couldn't get comms at all – very frustrating and a feeling of being powerless to react should they run into trouble. Reports of a Taliban meeting in the town and the targeting of us with a motorbike suicide bomb. Not sure how credible this is – we can do various things to offset the threat, one of which is actually attracting people, although we know the Taliban will not want to inflict many Afghan casualties – but this is no guarantee. Patrols platoon is overwatch to the south of town and they will move into the District Administrative compound at 0745 to secure it prior to the arrival by vehicle of 2 Platoon, myself and the CO, snipers on the roof with Forward Air Controller (FAC), and Rob Mosetti's FSG screening to the north of town. CO to conduct meeting with District Administrator and then we will be off. Afghan National Army (ANA) ambushed with IED about 12 kms down route, between one and four killed and a few wounded. Were brought here for treatment – rather grizzly, especially the four bodies laid side by side by the clinic and our accommodation. Out early tomorrow.

On 30 April, Hew writes:

You sound to be having a typically trying time, as in the early stages of any major deployment, when there is much uncertainty about how things will develop, and people are feeling a bit unsettled in an environment that is unfamiliar ... The thing to try to do is to keep peoples' minds (including your own, of course!) focussed clearly on what you are all trying to achieve, and then somehow much of the clutter of day to day frictions can be seen in a proper context ... you will also I am sure have numerous frustrations, difficulties and awkward people too, and all this just has to be handled calmly and sensibly.

Will's diary continues:

Mon 1 May. FOB Price, Gereshk.

Patrol into Gereshk this morning. Patrols Pl had overwatched canal last night and then moved in on foot to secure area of District Chief's HQ. Screen force on edge of town. Good meeting with the Chief who seemed OK though one never really knows. Then started to move out – something of a cluster – patrols did not get into depth as I had directed and the street we were on proved to be a dead end; some lessons there I think. Corrected that, balanced and moved off ... engaged by a burst of 4 or 5 rounds of 7.62mm which kicked up the dust at the southern end of the RV – first time someone has shot at me! Fortunately it was very wide and not aimed; no way to identify firing point and no further rounds. Heading into town again would have been chaotic, thus pulled out swiftly and called in Harriers to provide top cover which they did 40 minutes later. Serious after action review back in camp ... Gereshk is proving to be a nasty little place, not helped by the location of the FOB – telegraphing whenever we leave it, lack of Intelligence and shortage of helicopter hours. Searching my brain for novel ways of doing business; lots of nervousness higher up about armour for our light vehicles. But with lack of helicopter hours we are stumped if we can't use them to deploy. Not really the way to go about operations!

Tues 2 May.

Tom Fehly's platoon went out on patrol in the afternoon. All went well though comms problems again, very frustrating. Mixed reception but instances of welcoming, which is good.

Sat 6 May.

Received quite specific threat warning of Taliban clearing villages up the valley and a 'massive' attack planned for Gereshk. On the basis of this, altered plans to do extended base plate patrols and some vehicle stuff. Had B52 in support which we got to cruise about low enough – 15,000ft – so that all would know it was there, and fired mortar illumination. Guard alert stepped up a notch.

Sun 7 May. FOB Price, Gereshk.

Day started off well with the discovery of a radio-controlled (RC) IED intact that leader of the bomb disposal team (ATO) was able to look at, providing useful technical intelligence. But then the task we had planned to recce the hospital and then deliver things to the school began to unravel. DfID [local representatives from the British Department for International Development] refused us permission to go anywhere near the hospital because a Non Governmental Organisation (NGO) – is already involved there. But they are so slow; what equipment they have provided remains in its packaging, never any sign of their presence and meanwhile the hospital remains in a filthy condition – we feel we must provide something tangible quickly. Then the helicopter support for the school evaporated, making the task pointless. Very frustrating ... You must have a unified command that links military and civil in a coherent way, delivering quick and tangible security and benefits to the people and addressing their grievances. Therefore empower the lower levels of command to achieve both. The environment is complex but the command arrangements need not be. Still, in hope that the next few weeks will bring excitement and of course all the blokes want to do is to get stuck in to the Taliban.

In a letter home, he comments:

Because DfID and NGOs obsess about separation, they become easier targets for the insurgents, who then wreck their work, thus they stop working and no development takes place – whereas if they would only embrace a civil-military concept ... then they could work within a security blanket that the insurgent would find hard to penetrate, and thus tangible benefits would come to the people ... What is so frustrating is that it is so obvious and simple that this must be the way. It is this approach and not military activity alone that will finally finish off the Taliban. I hope they will come more onside but am not optimistic. People are allowed to exercise their agendas and it is the Afghans who suffer. The soldiers are all well and relishing the tasks.

On 7 May, Hew writes:

Had a long chat with Patrick Cordingley yesterday [Patrick is just back from a visit on behalf of the BBC], he seems to have found his visit very informative, and was much impressed by the approach that you are all taking to the challenges of the mission. He especially noted how little information let alone intelligence you have as a basis for planning and action, but as James Bashall [a senior operations staff officer in the MOD and Hew's former MA] himself has commented when I mentioned it to him, that is a pretty normal situation for us to be in as an Army, and we build up knowledge and intelligence steadily by the way in which we operate. The risks involved, however, can be considerable and this is what I guess you will need to watch – the sudden change of atmosphere from benign to hostile.

Will's diary:

Mon 8 May. FOB Price, Gereshk.

Patrolled into town with Paddy Blair and C Company officers. Patrol was very hot and exhausted and dehydrated on return. Later on, the FOB Robinson (Sangin) Contingency plan kicked in – intelligence received that it might be attacked, so we were reduced to 30 minutes notice to move (ntm). Had a run in with the Padre about 'morale' in the Company! Spoke to Al and the girls – great to hear them.

Tues 9 May. FOB Price. Gereshk.

Patrols Platoon went out to the South of the river to do some OP work, but one of the Chinooks landed heavily, smashing its forward front undercarriage and rupturing one of its fuel tanks. Thus patrol did only a short time before we had to extract them; the parlous state of our support helicopter force strikes again.

Wed 10 May.

Looks like we are off to Sangin on 15/16th which may be rather sporting. Running through the tactical desires and logistic reality bits – water and batteries are the key concerns, as ever.

10 to 17 May is spent in reserve at Camp Bastion, planning for the Sangin operation. Then on the 17th, with the Sangin preparations for the Company more or less completed, reports arrive of the police station and town of Musa Qaleh being threatened by Taliban forces. By the following day the threat seems to have receded and with the Sangin operation cancelled, Will comments that 'we had planned to make the Taliban start to react to us and not the other way round.'

20–21 May, Camp Bastion-Sangin area-up to Kajaki.

A pretty grizzly day today. Contacts reported in the Sangin area from early in the morning. Picture gradually became clearer. A French/US/ ANA column had left Kajaki and headed south towards Sangin ... US was supposed to mark a turning to head the column east into the desert but this was missed in the dust cloud and so they headed straight down the main track through the high threat areas to the north of Sangin. Appears to have been a spontaneous ambush covering about a 10 km stretch of track – lots of locals, including women, firing at the convoy from as close as 25 metres. French lost two dead, left at the scene, and a number of vehicles, and US ECM kit was left in three of the vehicles. Some ANA dead and missing. US Escort just cracked on. Two Chinook loads of my blokes despatched to try to locate the vehicles, ECM and Frenchmen. Something of a cluster on the Landing Site (LS), as the whole sequence of events all happened in a manic rush. Got back to Bastion after dark having seen the ground but little else. Made a plan for Sunday and briefed soldiers around midnight. Took off at about 0600 in three Chinook with two Apache helicopters as escort and flew up to Sangin. Had French bloke with me to identify key areas and pass info on the contact the day before. Found vehicle No. 1 – burnt out, no bodies, no ECM. Found ANA vehicle, stripped bare. Found vehicle No. 3 (French) on side beneath trees about 10km south-west of Kajaki. Difficult to tell the degree of damage, presence of bodies, ECM kit, etc so planned to put 2 Platoon on the ground after refuelling ... Chinook put them down at wrong grid, then developed an engine fault ... so could not guarantee an ability to pick them up again. Thus took decision to order Apache to destroy vehicle and all [equipment] inside, which it did with Hellfire missiles and 30mm – good work and first use of British Hellfire on operations. No doubt the ECM kit is on its way to Pakistan by now, anyway. Very bad to have two dead out there somewhere, and who knows if they can be recovered. ANA missing were found to be dead, mutilated and dumped on a road near FOB Robinson. Thus a grim day, made worse by the increasingly irresponsible risks we are taking, mainly due to (lack of) Helicopter resources. The task for the Company was very high risk and tomorrow B Company are moving to Kajaki and Naw Zad to establish Platoon houses. Not a good idea, with such tenuous air resources. I do not think that the Helmand Task Force have a clear idea of the threat and we are not taking the resource issue seriously enough. Rather depressing and we remain reactive.

22 May. Camp Bastion.

Long chat with Huw Williams (Battalion Second in Command – 2IC) about what we are doing wrong.

1. No unity of command – triumvirate of military, Foreign Office (FCO) and DfID does not work. Thus command through negotiation and personality – fine until they disagree, and the personalities, especially DfID, are unsuited for their task.
2. The internal command structure is wrong. This strains communications, incurs needless staff work and splits the G2 (intelligence) effort.
3. Not enough troops. This is a Brigade task, minimum. We have one Battalion group.
4. Not enough on the development side. Have yet to see anyone from an NGO, and DfID don't go out. Yet this is the development arm that is the route to success.
5. Not nearly enough Support Helicopters – we could do with three times the number. This has massive implications for our freedom of action; clearly we can work through this and do so, but it hardly helps!

Sad really but if we cannot resource properly we shouldn't be doing it; after all this is a war of choice. We seem to ignore all the lessons of the past and especially those of Templer in Malaya. Irresponsible at the political/military strategic level. We cannot continue in this reactive posture, since it doesn't achieve anything and gives all the initiative to the Taliban. French and ANA bodies turned up, badly mutilated and burnt.

However, as an example of 'plus ça change', at around this time Will receives a letter of support from Major General Mike Walsh, who commanded A Company at Suez and again in the Radfan, in which he says: 'We also had only the support of a couple of Scout helicopters who in the heat at that altitude could carry only limited payloads of water and ammunition.' Will replies to him setting the scene of 'a torchlit letter writing session in a rather dodgy town on the banks of the Helmand River'.

On 22 May he writes to Al and the children:

It is extremely dusty and the sand here is like talcum powder and goes everywhere – there are sandstorms and whirlwinds like twisters every day – sometimes so bad that you can hardly see and we are all pretty grubby. I now have about 30 Afghan soldiers attached to the company which is interesting! They are quite keen but not very well trained, so we shall see how they get on, a rather enthusiastic if motley crew! Yesterday was their first time in a helicopter and lots of them were green and sick! But they enjoyed it nonetheless.

Tues 23-Wed 24 May. Camp Bastion.

Usual round of exaggerated reports of Taliban 'massing', and massive contacts, all of which peter out in no time, but not before we have stood up, stood down and stood up again, probably cancelling something along the way and in the end do nothing. However this afternoon appeared that we could have a task that might actually go in. District Chief up in Baghran Valley – far north of Helmand Province –with his 20 Afghan National Police (ANP) were in danger of falling into Taliban hands and needed extraction. Confirmed rough scheme of manoeuvre with CO – 2 × Apache, 2 × Chinook, only 25 blokes as we have to bring back 20 or 21 Afghans. Simple plan – Signals Intelligence assets (SIGINT) and Apache to identify, Chinook to land on – deploy from helicopters – identify individuals – secure them – extract. But didn't really know about Taliban pressure or where exactly the Chief was. Fortunately we had his phone number, which we called and got SIGINT to fix his location, asked him questions about his compound, key characteristics being a blue flag and a white/blue gate. Asked about Taliban in area and it seemed permissive, though no guarantee. Told him to prepare a bonfire to light when he is told to do so. Ran through detailed plan until about 2am so only three hours sleep, then onto LS at 5 am for arrival of Apache and Chinook. Aircraft close down and we phone Chief again: SIGINT get different location this time, so now three possible locations – Bodey, Doyle and Carter. Otherwise no change. Run through joint mission brief with pilots, then at around 7 am with Apache leading 10 minutes ahead, set out north to Baghran. Ground changed from desert to much higher ground and razor ridges running north-south with one especially severe escarpment. Followed Baghran River up to objective area then hooked in from the west. Apache looked at Bodey and Doyle, and found both to be 'No Go'. Then after 3 PARA Main HQ had made another call, clocked the bonfire at Carter. No sign of enemy activity, so with Apache covering, the Chinooks put down about 100 metres from the compound. We ran straight off with my Tac HQ, Fire Support Team (FST) and FAC, 1 Platoon and some snipers. We quickly secured the area and made contact with the Chief. Got all his blokes together and were back on the aircraft within 10 minutes and on the way home. Thus rather successful and all did well.

So a good day for us but we must have a plan that we then stick to. One senior British commander is quoted in the papers saying, 'we are impartial and not here to help solve problems.' What bollocks, we are very partial and on the side of the Afghan Government, and must solve some of their problems.

Sat 27 May. Camp Bastion.

Another possible task from Helmand Task Force tomorrow in Washir – far afield and vague at best – task so far is to go to Washir and have an effect!!

What effect, and where, and on whom?

Had a good lunch with some of my ANA soldiers today and chatted about this and that – not ill yet!

Package from Al with picture from Amelia and photos as well as other bits and pieces – very welcome.

Mon 29 May. Camp Bastion.

Did a small trial on some new types of Body Armour – Kestrel and Osprey. With the new large plates they weigh 26 and 24 lbs respectively. This is half the total recommended combat load for an infantryman – 55lbs, including all his ammunition and so forth … the soldier is thus more vulnerable, since his agility and natural senses are so dulled by the weight of kit and extreme heat. One cannot even bring the weapon into the shoulder! But the difficulty once the stuff is in theatre becomes political, so we all get ordered to wear it regardless. Anyway at present we do not have enough sets of it to go round. Wrote a paper for the CO, judging each type; the old system in my view is best.

We have a strike option on a compound somewhere, due to go in on 5th June, probably some middle ranking Taliban and cronies.

Tues 30 May. Camp Bastion.

Received target pack for strike option on 5th – kill or capture mission. Very exciting and not often that these come round for rifle companies – so a fantastic opportunity. Compound just outside Naw Zad, more cordon and search stuff but always potential for a scrap. Should be good. On for 4th June.

Corporals Lane, Jarvie and Wright promoted today – good news.

Sun 4th June. Now Zad.

Cordon and search operation on compound approx 1.5 km east of Now Zad, just west of a main north-south wadi and in an extreme 'bocage-like' area – lots of orchards, elephant grass, 15ft high walls, compounds, and Taliban! Didn't know about the latter before launch. Plan was to insert the Company with Battle Group Tactical HQ in four Chinooks to fields immediately bracketing the compound to the north and south west (Landing Sites (LS) 1 and 2), covered by two Apaches. Meanwhile Patrols Platoon in armed landrovers (WMIKs) and elements of the Gurkha Company would move from the Platoon house in Now Zad to occupy outer cordon positions to west and east respectively. Priority was compound search, not arrest. Fortunately the original Chinook crews have changed over to a much better lot – Mike Woods in charge – a great guy and the impact of his leadership is profound – also Nicol Benzi the lead pilot and on exchange from the RN – v capable and cool customer – have a strong bond with them that we lacked with the previous lot.

Landed at 1210 and whilst there was no fire coming from the compound there was firing to north west, west and south west. Due to high walls and vegetation, it was impossible to identify locations and clear that it wasn't directed at us though it may have been at the aircraft. 1 Platoon were landed in the wrong place, about 400m due west where they came under immediate contact and had a short, fleeting engagement – possible hits to Taliban? They followed up into a compound where they found no males but women and children being pushed forward. They then moved swiftly to take up their positions on the south side of the search compound. Meanwhile the Patrols Platoon to the west had run into a contact that went on for some time, about 4–500 metres west and south west of the compound – at least three separate contacts (AK, RPG, RPK) in which lots of fire went both ways, with certain kills to Taliban. Apaches fired a lot of 30mm at targets indicated by Patrols Platoon with smoke or ILAW. Some kills and blood trails were identified. This contact went on for some time. Pte Ali received one round to his body armour plate but was fine. Meanwhile the Gurkha group was ambushed on its way to the east of the compound – about 2 km north of our location – receiving RPG and AK fire, and returning fire, killing some, with Apaches in support probably killing more. Thus quite a lot going on in that first hour but sporadic, platoon level engagements in which the Taliban lost heavily, partly due to our ground fire and also due to the Apaches, which were an excellent asset.

In the compound the search started and continued all afternoon. Lots of drugs, small arms ammunition and some grenades found, but nothing especially significant. CO joined me on the ground and stayed with me throughout. We kept getting Sigint hints for a key personality, about 4–500m away, and being asked by Brigade HQ to go and arrest him. This would involve fighting our way out through very complex terrain to arrest someone only identified through Sigint, so easier said than done. Anyway, with the search going well and the cordon secure I despatched 2 Platoon out to sweep the area of the Sigint hit, 400m west of the compound. At about 1530 2 Platoon (Tom Fehly) headed out with my Forward Observation Officer (FOO) and Forward Air Controller (FAC) – Matt Armstrong and Corporal of Horse (CoH) Fry. They ran, predictably, into contact very quickly and had a running battle supported by Apaches and A10 ground attack aircraft for the next hour and a half, also a couple of low passes by a B1 bomber – nothing dropped. Heavy fire ensued and at least four Taliban killed. The platoon broke contact when I ordered their return and used the A10 to clear a wood line 50 m from them. A10 put lots of fire down, very close and all enemy fire stopped from wood line. 2 Platoon was recovered back into the cordon without casualties. Cleary – sniper – did very well – one very good head shot. Meanwhile Taliban were heard moving close to 1 Platoon on the south side. The Pl ambushed an RPG team killing two and then had a nasty scrap amongst compounds to the south, at least two more enemy killed, probably more. Cpl Poll and Hugo Farmer's platoon did excellent work while coming under heavy fire supported by grenades. I dashed about north and south to check things and control the platoons, occasionally having to take to the dirt when the snaps overhead became rather close. At about 1700 I pulled 2 Platoon back in and the search was complete. Apaches back on station and Chinooks on their way. Collapsed the cordon and patrolled out east across the wadi to an LS in open, defendable ground and covered by Apaches and Harriers. All off the ground at about 1730.

In all at least twenty enemy were killed, probably more and many wounded. We picked up one wounded Taliban who was being pushed away in a wheelbarrow. He was badly shot up in the legs but was very stoic, very hard, little complaint or noise but will almost certainly lose his leg. He is being treated in our hospital. Enemy were good and bold, in 5–6 man teams with AK, RPK and RPG. They were quick to react to our landing and had no hesitation in putting in attacks, with good use of ground in difficult terrain. Fortunately most of their fire was very high. My blokes did superb work, fantastic to see them just getting on with it in a calm professional way. Junior NCOs doing sterling work and both platoon commanders did marvellously. My FOO and FAC were quite excellent, controlling the Apaches and fast air with aplomb, especially A10 fire 50 metres away. Snipers were also first class. I have immense pride in them all, the first time for us all in contact and I have about thirty brand new soldiers straight out of training. Good drills and good junior leadership pays off and we killed many with no killed or wounded in our own ranks. Very difficult terrain in which to fight and the risk of blue on blue was high. Gave the platoons strict limits of exploitation to ensure we did not get into a messy running battle through the woods and compounds ... Apaches and close air support, and Chinooks were all superb and a massive enabling effort. The enemy proved swift and capable but we were better – the blokes were f***ing excellent and the day ended with huge pride and huge relief that all were coming home without a scratch.

Wed 7 June. Camp Bastion.

Saw the Brigadier today who told me he was getting updates on the scrap as he watched cricket in Kabul! Spoke to Al this evening and to Amelia. All are well and Amelia has now mastered the bicycle, gaining a merit from Mrs Crouch, her teacher.

Thurs 8 June.

Press came today to lap up our operation on the 4th, obviously a bit miffed that they had not been involved! Paul Wood from BBC and a girl from Jane's Defence Weekly. Christina Lamb is coming next week. Did some stuff for the cameras with a collection of the blokes and they did very well, no glorification and good answers.

Fri 9 June. Camp Bastion.

No real thought is going into what we are doing and why. We have done next to zero 'pacification ops' amongst the people and these we must do if we are to win the people over. Our resources are limited and so we should keep ourselves to an area that we can influence in a coherent manner rather than spreading ourselves about the Province in an incoherent, uncoordinated and not mutually supporting way. The ground area that I think we should be dominating is the lozenge that runs from Lashkar Gah up through Gereshk, Sangin to Kajaki. This is an important valley that should be 3 Para's legacy. Pacify this and you have a line of departure to exploit north up to the Baghran valley, which can be 3 Commando Bde's objective [3 Para and 16 Air Assault Brigade's successors in October 2006]. At present we are delivering little tangible benefit. Firmly believe that we should concentrate our efforts in the Sangin lozenge ... We were on the BBC Today programme today which apparently went down well. Spoke to Al, Mummy and Daddy, Arabella and Justin, and Emma today – all well. Lots of emails today. Amelia doing very well on her bicycle.

Sat 10 June. Camp Bastion.

Lieutenant General Richards [NATO commander of the International Security Assistance Force in Afghanistan (ISAF) in Kabul] came to visit this afternoon – chat about the 4th and then with the blokes. He is clearly on our wave length and vice-versa.

Sun 11 June. Camp Bastion.

7 RHA Captain was killed, Capt Jim Philipson [he is buried very close to Will's great-grandfather Reggie Tompson in the grounds of St Albans Abbey], a Bombardier (Thomas Mason) seriously wounded and a WO2 (Andy Stockton) lost an arm to an RPG. For whatever reason a patrol at FOB Robinson (Sangin) tried to recover a UAV which had crashed on the west bank of the Helmand River. This involved crossing the Helmand just south of Sangin on ferries probably controlled by the Taliban to then try to find a polystyrene aircraft in a known Talib hot spot. Having failed to find the UAV they returned by the same route and were ambushed. The QRF set out from Robinson and appears to have split into three parties, then quickly ran into trouble. Philippson was killed and Stockton lost an arm to an RPG. Terribly sad and probably avoidable – we wouldn't have gone to look for it in the first place since a 'model aircraft' is hardly worth the risk to life! Secretary of State [Des Browne] here today with Chief of Defence Staff [Air Chief Marshal Sir Jock Stirrup] – OK visit but rather overshadowed by last night. PJHQ getting all arsy over some photos we gave to the BBC apparently breaking protocols – apparently I am being accused of 'selling' photos – complete bollocks and very annoying. In any case none of the photos is remotely sensitive.

Tues 13–Thurs 15 June. 20 Kms S of Musa Qaleh.

Heard that US element in contact south of Musa Qaleh. A loggy [logistic] unit that had driven its big, unwieldy vehicles down the main track south from Musa Qaleh towards Sangin, a track that is very high risk for IED/Ambush. The inevitable happened – the convoy was IED'd, shot up and RPG'd. Three vehicles destroyed, one US soldier killed. They had been told not to drive down this track but had done so anyway. We were tasked at very short notice to go and dig them out of the shit. Rush job, had three Chinook loads and set off, landing near about one hour before sunset. No contact on LS but activity in built up area to east and a near miss with an RPG against one of the US Apaches. Patrolled south to some high ground that dominated the built up area and met up with the US convoy commander, a Captain, clearly pretty useless. There was some dominating high ground 50 yards from his position but he had not occupied it and had just taken hits all day. Anyway sunset was upon us and so I got him to move his vehicles onto the high ground and then occupied a perimeter, bedded in the mortars and settled down to an uncomfortable and sleepless night. It was just not practical to do anything else, given the nature of the US troops and their vehicles. Planned to stay there until first light, then patrol the vehicles out due west to open desert where we could take stock in relative security. Was sitting back to back with my stand-in CSM (Turner) [Leong was on R&R] having a chat about whether the Talibs would or wouldn't have a go when the inevitable happened. At about 2300 we received 12.7mm HMG, RPG and small arms (SA) fire from two positions. One of the RPGs struck the northerly US Humvee, wounding two of the crew, one seriously. Pte McKinley was in the most forward position and despite being under heavy fire himself ran straight to the scene and saved his life, Cpl Roberts our medic (CMT) there shortly after. McKinley is proving to be a little like George McDonald Fraser's Private McAusland – a liability in barracks but quite handy in the field. Mortars, directed by Cpls Cartwright and Wright (MFCs), steadily brought on with very good fire as close as 100 metres from the perimeter. Contact died away quite quickly. About an hour later Cpl Wright (1 Platoon) clocked movement to his north-east and engaged a group of gunmen, probably killing two or three. 1 × CH47 managed to get in to us to extract the wounded and bringing the welcome sight of 7 Pl C Coy and a resupply of Mortar Rounds and water. Reconfigured the perimeter, resupplied the Mortar line with HE and Illuminating rounds and settled down to wait for first light. In the early morning two Blackhawk and two Apache (US) arrived – good to see. Blackhawk extracted another five US soldiers plus the one soldier killed. At about 0500 we started to move swiftly across country over fields and irrigation ditches – Taliban wouldn't expect this and I thought this would have been difficult given the large size of the US logistic vehicles but it proved surprisingly straight-forward – and onto an escarpment leading to open desert plateau, with dominating views all round. What followed was a hot and frustrating day.

It looked at one point as if we were going to have to spend another night with the US loggies. Everyone was very tired after having zero sleep for over 24 hours, very hot and water quickly running out. We were resupplied around midday. A US relief column arrived around 1700 and took over the defence of area. Finally around midnight we extracted back to Bastion. A rather uncomfortable experience compounded by having to take significant risk in order to dig US troops out of a position they should never have got themselves into. Nor did we get any thanks from them. [Pte McKinley was awarded the MC for his life saving actions.]

Sun 18 June. Camp Bastion.

A mad day today. We were due to leave for Musa Qaleh at midnight. By 1400 the convoy was in line – about forty vehicles, communications checked and kit loaded. At about 1700 with daylight fading, news came that the nephew of a senior policeman in Sangin (and a mate of Province Governor Daoud) had been seriously wounded in the stomach by the Taliban in Sangin and taken to the hospital there. A few hundred yards away was the family compound with the rest of the family plus their militia guards. Meanwhile the ex-Chief of Police in Sangin had raped a girl in the town. Taliban and locals were in uproar, and he, the current Chief of Police, and thirty ANP/Militia were holed up in the compound to the south of the bazaar. The area was heavily occupied by Taliban. We were given one hour to be on the LS and ready to go. This meant stripping of kit from the vehicles, but we were ready in 40 minutes. The aim was not clear but it seemed to be to rescue the nephew, his family and possibly ANP, all in a high risk area, just before last light, with insufficient resources. Charming! Fortunately by this time a little sense had prevailed and instead the High Readiness Force was sent to FOB Robinson to assess the situation. The debate went up to the British Ambassador. Stayed up till 4 am planning. Clear that the risk was very high for a very questionable gain. Move to Musa Qaleh cancelled.

Mon 19 June–Tues 20 June. Camp Bastion.

Things went a bit manic and found myself with the Company in Sangin from 21 June for two weeks. Thought we were only going for two hours, thus did not take diary, but kept notes anyway although not much time for writing.

Continued pressure from Prime Minister Karzai and Governor Daoud to deploy into the District Centre (DC) in Sangin, reporting of significant Taliban pressure and of the District Centre being overrun. Apparently up to forty policemen have been killed and some dragged through the streets.

Visits from Major General Peter Wall (PJHQ Northwood) and Brig Ed Butler (Commander of 16 Air Assault Bde). Initially they were not keen at all to deploy. Opposed entry was thought likely and a significant risk, all to extract the probably corrupt nephew of a probably corrupt official – all rather unsavoury. It was unclear where exactly he was and in what condition. The numbers and whereabouts of his family members were somewhat vague, too. Lots of chat all night – the blokes had a warning order but little else and no plan. The BG HQ, CO and I went through a lengthy risk assessment in order to identify where the main threats would emanate from and how many casualties we might expect to take as we fought our way into the

District Centre. This was a pretty surreal discussion and I sent Martin Taylor (my excellent Coy 2IC) to bed to save his eyes from growing on even longer stalks! It did though form the basis of the CO's judgement on the risks that he then presented to Brigadier Ed Butler and also informed the artillery and air fire plans that would cover our insertion. Most of us thought that it would probably get called off but then the mission went green about thirty minutes before launch at first light, thus a mad scramble to get the blokes up – nearly missing the Doc which would have been a disaster – a very hurried brief on the LS and then off.

Wed 21 June. Sangin. Dawn.

Nicol Benzi was again the lead pilot. We landed by the river in Sangin, about 500 metres south west of the District Centre – four Chinook loads. Being on the first Chinook into the LS every time is the place I must be but it gets a little more concerning every time. Landed on and initiated a rolling fire base by each platoon. The area is dominated by the river to the west and then small irrigated fields bordered by tree lines that give way to a canal and clustered compounds, small orchards and the town itself. We encountered no opposition and occupied the District Centre (DC) within a few minutes. My key weapons and snipers immediately occupied positions on the roof which gave commanding arcs of fire in most directions. One of the platoons established themselves in positions around the compound itself. The District Chief was there, called Haji Khan Mohammed, whom I told to get the nephew here and also to arrange a Shura so that we could talk to the people. The nephew arrived and the Doc [RMO] sorted him out. About two or three hours later the Chinooks returned, bringing in some combat supplies for us and extracting the nephew and various other hoods. We were now to stay in the DC for at least ninety-six hours. Once into these places it becomes hard to leave, mainly due to the politics involved and the fear that the Taliban will claim that any 'pull out' would be as a result of their pressure and thus a victory for the insurgent.

Sangin was not a particularly comfortable place or situation in which to be dropped. We knew that Sangin was a bad place – strong linkage of Narco/Taliban and a significant number of key leaders – Mullah Sazhaddin and Koo Agha for example; thus a considerable and credible enemy threat. However we could cope with this. More worrying was the fact that apart from FOB Robinson, with a 105mm Lt Gun troop and loads of ANA, the nearest help was about 60 kms away. There was no easy way of driving in since the IED/ambush threat on those routes was extreme – thus to get in would require a forced convoy probably as a BG deliberate operation – and the helicopter LSs had to be very close, since we only had two Quad

191

bikes and trailers to clear stores with. The LSs were predictable and vulnerable. The DC was not a protected compound, so one had to turn the site into a defended locality. The ground around especially east and south was close, thus limiting fields of observation and fire, but giving the enemy covered approaches. Since there seemed no likelihood of getting the required road resupply with Engineer Plant and Field Engineers any time soon, we had to receive repeated

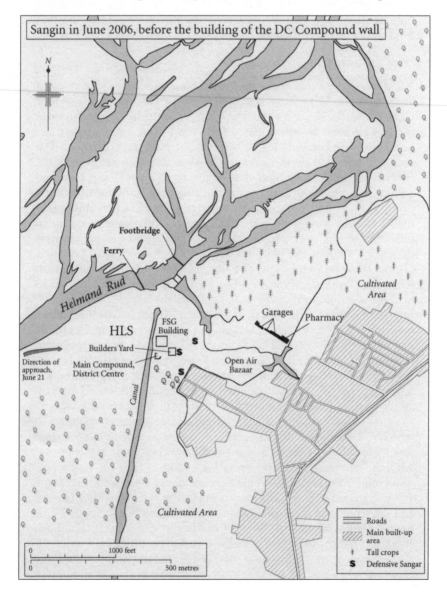

Sangin in June 2006, before the building of the DC Compound wall

N

Footbridge

Ferry

Helmand Rud

HLS

FSG Building

Builders Yard

Direction of approach, June 21

Main Compound, District Centre

Canal

Garages

Pharmacy

Cultivated Area

Open Air Bazaar

S

S

S

Cultivated Area

	Roads
	Main built-up area
ǂ	Tall crops
S	Defensive Sangar

0   1000 feet

0   500 metres

helicopter resupplies, each time requiring us to clear the LS, move to the LS to clear the stores, and then ferry all back in – a process that could take as much as a couple of hours. Naturally the pilots did not want to fly into the same LSs too often and so increasingly Apaches were required to cover all landings – and the risk to aircraft grew. Thus the initial strain of our stay in Sangin came from this slight feeling of 'abandonment' in a barely viable location with lots of enemy about. Dien Bien Phu came to mind on occasion, and it was hard personally, though I could see the rationale for staying – the soldiers were less convinced. The other great concern was the balance of patrol tasks, especially at night, with the risk of casualties and the difficulties of casevac extraction. The RMO was deployed forward with us for this reason, but even so it was a worry. The light levels were such that the aircraft couldn't really fly at night – there was not enough ambient light for their Night Vision Goggles (NVGs) to work. There was also the risk to crew and airframe to be considered.

The 21st June passed swiftly, our main preoccupation was achieving some sort of coherent defence prior to darkness. This was largely achieved, though with limited resources, only about 200 sandbags but did manage to collect various materials from a couple of building sites. Key concern was the area to south east and east, which was very close country and did not provide very good fields of fire.

I had about 116 soldiers broken down as:

Company HQ including signallers and interpreters	10
Fire Support Team (FST), FOO, FAC and MFC parties	8
LEWT (Light Electronic Warfare Team) including interpreter	5
Fire Support Group (FSG) 2 × .50 HMG 2 × GPMG SF 1 × Javelin	12
Mortar Section 2 × 81mm Mortar	8
Snipers 3 × .338, 1x L96 Rifle	4
RMO, Medical Sgt, Medical Orderly	3
Intelligence Sgt	1
2 × Rifle Platoons	about 30 each
ANA and Liaison Team	5
Additional Interpreters	3

The FSG established a fire base in the northern building. This was a dominant position but also quite vulnerable since it remained an 'open' building site, and one feared Taliban gaining access to the lower floors of the building. Over time we wired, sandbagged and claymored the area. The Mortars under Cpl Hope bedded in within the courtyard and we were to become very accustomed to the Mortars firing only a few feet away, the Illuminating rounds much louder than the HE and makes one jump every time. We were fortunate in having Harvey Pynn, the RMO and Medical Sgt with us as well as Cpl Roberts, my own Coy medic. Sgt Hughes, my excellent Intelligence Sgt who had been with us in Iraq, started 'investigating' straight away. The two rifle platoons were full of quality, 1 Platoon commanded by Hugo Farmer and 2 Platoon by Tom Fehly, though in the process of handing over to Andy Mallett. Hugo seems to thrive in combat and is first class [he receives the Conspicuous Gallantry Cross after the tour.] Andy is brand new but has stepped up to the mark quickly and is proving excellent.

Sometime in the afternoon I had my first chat with the District Chief, Haji Khan Mohammed. He seemed a reasonably genuine sort of chap, and he had about twenty or so guards, suspect that these were his own men, not policemen, and in effect his bodyguard. All came from Gereshk, his home town where he had been Chief of Police. It was clear that whilst he had some credibility, due probably to his tribal or family links, he was largely ineffective as the District Chief. This was not really his fault, since he had been given absolutely nothing with which to exercise rule in Sangin – no cash, no staff, no vehicles, no communications, no trustworthy police. Even in providing useful information he was woeful, but I quite liked the Chief despite his lack of utility. I asked the Chief to sort out a Shura for the 22nd so that I could explain why we were in Sangin. After I had been round the positions a few times, we stood to and then bedded down for our first night.

Thus 22 June. DC Sangin.

Main event was the Shura. About 60 or so attended including the District Chief and Chief of Police. The Shura started by me giving them a chat on what we were doing in Sangin and why, very much emphasising that we were there to help, initially with security, then paving the way for reconstruction. I also stressed that we were not at all interested in narcotics. Then general chat, the main theme seeming to be that they would rather we went away, since our presence would guarantee a fight with the Taliban, which would affect business in the bazaar. They would rather live under the coercive terror of the Taliban than actively help us, or the Afghan Government. I stated that we had no intention of leaving and that our presence was the first indication of the Afghan Government commitment to reconstruction in the area. This didn't seem to convince them, with some justification, since the Afghan Government has done basically nothing for these people in four years and is seen to be largely corrupt. The lesson is clear – we must demonstrate a tangible benefit of Afghan governance to the people. After about 45 minutes I was invited to leave so that they might continue the discussions amongst themselves. Afterwards the District Chief told me that none of the key local leaders attended, because all the local power brokers are either Narcos or Taliban. Thus they sent the 2nd XI as a fact finding mission and would hold further Shuras, including talking to the Taliban, to establish a course of action. Thus other than being able to send out a few messages I did not expect the Shura to have achieved a great deal. Still, one had to start somewhere and it was interesting – lots of old boys with long grey beards sitting on carpets beneath a tree in the compound, all with prayer beads and all listening intently. Only a few spoke and occasionally there was a burst of animated debate. The atmosphere was guarded rather than hostile and one could sense the impact of Taliban coercion. We set a date of the 24th for the Shura to reconvene, to be attended by Governor Daoud and the Helmand Chief of Police, although we didn't tell them this.

Following the Shura I took a patrol out into the bazaar with 2 Platoon and got the District Chief to come along as well – rather reluctantly and claiming old war wounds! Eventually he agreed and so with him and a few of his hoods we set off. The bazaar is quite small but with wide dirt streets, hundreds of stalls lining the streets selling or making more or less anything. Lots of people were about either among the stalls or sitting in groups on carpets drinking 'chai'. Rather like at the Shura the mood was guarded rather than openly hostile, though there were a few rather menacing groups around. The District Chief seemed to enjoy himself and seemed to know quite a lot of people, which was heartening. We finished off at the Hospital just north east of the compound, run by a Pakistani and with a female doctor, which was unusual. It seemed OK though the NGO (Ibansemeer – Italian) that is supposed to support it had not been seen for over two years. The RMO had a good scoot about and good first relationships were made with the doctors, all of whom spoke English. Our route in cut across the dry wadi immediately north of the DC. Each Thursday Kuchi nomads with their hardy sheep come into Sangin from the west, from the grazing by the Helmand River, over the rickety, straw/stick footbridge that is washed away by the floods in winter, and into the wadi where there is a livestock market. Thus lots of tribesmen and sheep, a typical Afghan scene. Sadly this area was to become something of a firezone shortly, and much 'normal' activity ceased as the innocents fled the fighting.

We continued to build up the positions throughout the day, various NCOs competing for the best bunker! We had no specific intelligence but all we have gathered from various sources including the LEWT confirms that the Taliban are in numbers – some talking about 1000 – in the villages immediately to north and south of us.

General habit was to move into the bazaar by night from safe locations to intimidate or attack. At night all our night vision equipment, especially thermal, was focussed on threat areas, roof tops and potential firing points. Quiet night.

Fri 23 June. DC Sangin.

The religious day, so we decided not to patrol the bazaar. Frequent calls to prayer throughout the day. Work on our positions was continuous; with no engineers and few sandbags, self-help and improvisation were the key. We spent $1000 on bricks (breeze-blocks) from a local brick factory just outside the DC, with these we could at least create enough depth to stop small arms fire, and around the hard core we placed what few sandbags we had. We also used empty ration boxes and any other containers to fill with sand. However we had a problem with overhead protection, but did as much as possible using planks of wood – not ideal. Steadily as we got more stores in, things improved. In this game the threat was 360 degrees, and all sangars had to be as well protected at the back as the front and sides.

One thing that worried me was the risk of being overrun – a deeply unpleasant prospect. The worst case scenario (my assessment) saw the police (in league with the Taliban) acting as a sort of Trojan Horse followed by a rushed assault by Taliban. I think we would have beaten off such an attack but it caused me most concern. My section commanders were tremendous though – Cpls Poll, McDermott, MacLachlan, Wright, Curnow, Budd [he is killed in action after Will's departure] and Waddington. They engaged with every task and did all well, they were all 'human' in command, very professional and demanding of high standards but popular and respected. I can think of no bad words for any of them and since they are the engine room of the Company it meant that the Company worked well. We had been together for two years in most cases, including Iraq, and the guiding principle in all things was to build confidence; there was lots of trust amongst all.

We tightened the position up and stood to at last light. We didn't stand down until after midnight and then only to 50/50 manning. No attack materialised. Had a mutton and bread dinner with the District Chief.

Sat 24 June. DC Sangin.

The day of the Governor's Shura. Governor Daoud apparently had not been keen to come, very unhelpful considering that we were there largely to shore up his credibility. With him by helicopter came the Helmand Chief of Police and various media people including

Christina Lamb. The Shura became a diatribe by the Governor, telling the locals not to support the Taliban, but he failed to provide them with anything that might encourage them to do his will, nor did he ask the District Chief what resources he might need in the town. The people here are not remotely convinced by words – they need actions.

This Shura I think marked the end of the talking. Those there were then to continue their discussions and return their verdict to the District Chief in a couple of days. Essentially the village's position remained unchanged – they would rather we left so that there would be no fight with the Taliban, which would harm business in the bazaar. So the stage was set for whatever was to come.

During the day we received various reports of people leaving the town, of groupings of up to thirty fighters each operating to the south, ambushes being prepared to attack our patrols and so forth. I stressed again to the CO that we must get a road convoy in with a large quantity of combat supplies and engineer plant to dramatically improve the compound. Also that we needed a significant number of ANA/ANP in the DC that could be used to secure the bazaar. I didn't get the impression that any of these things would happen soon – far too much talking and not enough action.

Sun 25 June. DC Sangin.

With each passing day the situation becomes more ominous. Threat reporting continues, none specific but the general trend is clear. The steady move out seems also to include the District Chief's men, whose numbers have dwindled considerably since we arrived, from thirty to less than half that number. The District Chief himself is also suddenly talking about how he must go to Gereshk to see his family. The Police Chief is equally awkward, he claims to be ill every time I ask him to the HQ, and he does nothing. We are also sure, by our own observations and EW intercepts, that the Police may as well be Taliban. It is immensely disquieting to have such an 'enemy within'. My demands for policemen to join our patrols have yet to be honoured. But why, I suppose, should they show loyalty to a Government that shows so little loyalty to them and gives them so few resources, sometimes not even paying them?

Mon 26 June. DC Sangin.

Cpl Shimmins, my MMG Section Commander, was struck on the right hand side of his face after a single high velocity round was fired at his position, fortunately missing him but striking the breezeblock just to the right of his head and causing shards to hit his face. The first shot to be fired at us here, and a warning about movement and cover

197

in exposed positions. No one heard the shot, which seemed to be from some distance away, and no fire was returned.

Lots of chat about a recce to FOB Robinson, about 6 kms south of Sangin. Quite why this particular location was chosen is a mystery, since it is not in the most dominating position but simply a base in the desert that requires soldiers to man it. There are about two hundred ANA soldiers there but all they do is sit in their sangars. They do not patrol and would be far more handy in the DC with us. Also and much more usefully there is a troop of 105mm guns from 7 RHA. More threat reporting, some of the key names appearing, such as Koo Agha, Jumma Gul, Niamalullah, Mullah Sazhaddin and others – all key Taliban commanders that seem to be concentrating around Sangin.

Tues 27 June. DC Sangin.

Woke up to something of a hornet's nest kicking off about 3kms to our south, and apparent immediately that it was the Special Forces (SF) strike/lift op going in. There was a lot of fire going down, including the 105mm guns from FOB Robinson. Targets were Mullah Sazhaddin (leader of Taliban in Sangin), Matiullah, Sheragha and Abdul Zatar. All were lifted initially but then all went wrong. The locals reacted and so the withdrawal became a fighting withdrawal, harried by bands of Taliban. During the melee Mullah Sazhaddin and Matiullah were killed and the other two managed to escape. The SF lost two killed, one of whom I had met a few times recently. The Quick Reaction Force (QRF) from Robinson was ambushed and thus ineffective. As we learned on 4th June, the whole area can light up, and suddenly one is faced with gangs of twelve to fifteen Taliban roaming about and trying to have a go. Thus whilst Special Forces skills would get them into the compound to seize targets, they need more conventional size and skills to get out in one piece. In this game one SF troop is not nearly as capable as a full company [from a battalion]. The latter would have been able to secure a corridor through which the SF lot could have been extracted and it is possible that the enemy would have seen what they were up against and pulled back. Whilst the result was good – District chief very happy indeed – the cost was very sad and might have been avoided – a lesson there for conventional/SF joint planning.

That evening Predator (UAV) was up and it clocked the funeral of almost certainly, Sazhaddin. This, linked with the Sigint, placed a considerable number of key leaders at the site, only a few kilometres from the DC, and discussion resulted at higher levels as to what to do. The issue of bombing funerals was inevitably somewhat sensitive, and fraught with downstream consequences, so the bombing did not go in. At about 2300 we were hit by a considerable weight of small arms, RPG and MMG fire, mostly directed at our FSG building to the north. In response we fired most natures from 5.56, 7.62, .50, 81mm and 105mm. I think we had B1 and A-10 air support but neither dropped anything. 81mm and 105mm were brought in to within about 200 metres of our positions and our machine gunners and snipers were very busy indeed. Things quietened down at about 2 am, when we went to 50/50 manning. This was the first major attack on our positions – whether planned or a reaction to the day's events – and had met with a fierce response.

Wed 28 June. DC Sangin.

More ominous reporting – EW intercepts of Taliban meetings in the town, also of fully prepared 4x4 vehicle-borne suicide IED in Sangin. Reports of 'hundreds' of Taliban in the bazaar were now common-place. Heard that a US Apache had come down slightly to our west – mechanical failure I think. I wouldn't much want to be in the crew of a downed Apache out there!

In the early hours of 29th we received the second instalment of Taliban effort, not dissimilar to last night and fortunately equally ineffective, though it only needs one lucky RPG or bullet strike. Again the focus was our FSG building to the north. They selected similar points from which to attack, all of which are now firmly registered with our 105mm guns and 81mm mortars, both of which were on target within a couple of minutes of contact, as well as a fierce return of fire from all systems that could be brought to bear. Whilst we emerged unscathed and they must have suffered, the feeling of the besieged grows and it is not pleasant. Moreover, we remain constrained by self defence Rules of Engagement (ROE) – essentially, we must wait for them to fire first – although there is talk of putting us onto Measure 429 – in essence, war fighting ROE.

Thurs 29 June. DC Sangin. Imme's Birthday.

Had my first proper wash for over a week – went down with Zac Leong (the Company Sergeant Major – CSM), also washed clothes and socks. Nice to have a shirt that bends again after my salt encrusted cardboard version was washed. It was immensely refresh-ing and one felt much better afterwards, not only cleaner but also slightly less drained by the constant pressure of our situation, when one needs to question the pros and cons of everything one decides, even the safety of the 'bathing pool' for everyone. I am extremely fortunate to have Zac Leong and he helps my confidence so much. He always has good advice and usually we agree anyway. And I do not have to worry about loose ends when he is there, as I know that all behind me will be efficiently 'sheep-dogged' by the CSM. There is a canal that breaks off from the river just by the DC and at this point it is very fast flowing but only about waste deep – it is also surprisingly cold and rather clear. There are steps leading down to a small basin, this is the usual washing point, only observed from the immediate vicinity. Initially, of course, the blokes were completely naked and splashing about, which upset Muslim sensitivities a bit, so now it is shorts and T shirts at least, when washing.

Spent a lot of the day thinking about Imme and her birthday. Fortunately we have a satellite telephone here so was able to ring later on, rather swift and hard to be chatty whilst standing in a compound that could receive enemy fire at any time.

Later that night we received the usual going over with small arms and RPG fire. During the days we are working on the positions and patrolling, and at night it is becoming usual to be stood to or fighting for extensive periods. There is little respite.

Fri 30 June. DC Sangin, later FOB Robinson.

In the morning I got the District Chief to summon the Chief of Police, mainly because he is failing to do anything we ask of him – no information, no policemen for our patrols, no knowledge of police patrols and so on. Eventually after all his excuses he stated that unless ordered by the Governor he would not play. This again shows the impotence of the District Chief. Afghanistan remains dominated by the 'politics of the biggest bribe', whilst we fritter away our strength by penny-packeting small groups here and there, none of them strong enough to make a real difference. We must concentrate strength if we are to have a lasting effect.

In mid-afternoon two Chinook came in on a resupply sortie, also to pick up some blokes going on R and R [leave in UK] as well as me, to go to FOB Robinson to recce the place with the BC (Gary Wilkinson) – the purpose of the recce was to have a look at how the place was being run and how it and the UK & Afghan forces there (about 200 in total) could be more useful since at the current time, other than the 105mm from 7 RHA and the UAVs, the forces there added little value. It is only 6 kms away from Sangin yet it might be a million miles away. Landing there felt like arriving in some safe oasis away from the dangers and tensions of the DC but it was clearly being run in a slap dash and deeply unprofessional way – it was all shorts, sky TV and blokes getting ready to watch the world cup games – seemingly little idea as to the threats and yet almost within viewing distance we were experiencing intense combat – whilst you cannot quite see the DC from the FOB, due to the shape of the ground, you can see the dust cloud that is kicked up by a landing helicopter. Worried about my blokes in Sangin without me, though in good hands.

At about 9pm the DC was hit quite hard by probably 107mm rockets, RPG, MMG and small arms fire. This went on for some time, much was thrown back and the Taliban would have suffered heavily from our direct fire plus 81mm mortars and 105mm and artillery (from here at FOB Robinson), now with very accurate defensive fire (DF) tasks and very quick into action. Javelin also fired. The Anti-tank section saw four Taliban on a roof top, checked to see whether the seeker head on the missile would lock onto humans – it did – and off went the missile. Snipers also busy. An unpleasant feeling listening to it all on the net. Things died down around midnight.

Sat 1 July.

A pretty fraught day on the air side with many requirements and not enough aircraft! Finally just before last light a Chinook came in to pick me up and take me back to Sangin, others to Bastion, just as England were starting their World Cup Quarter Final. It was dusk when we got into the aircraft, which had one Apache flying as escort, then lifted to fly the short hop into Sangin. The Chinook approached and landed and I jumped off into the dust cloud and found it slightly odd that no one emerged from the gloom. Anyway the dust cleared and I found myself completely alone somewhere near the river. But also near some compounds about 1 km south of the DC. There were two Afghans with a pick-up beside the LS who I said salaam to, in the dawning realisation that I had been dropped right in the shit. It was a rather frightening realisation that I was completely alone and somewhere very close to Taliban villages beside the Helmand River. I must have been some way from the DC for I could not make out any of the building landmarks that would have given me my location, thus I didn't have an accurate fix of where I was. I switched on my 349 [small short-range tactical commander's radio], but knowing that it just did not have the range to be useful. Worth trying anyway and started sending distress calls over the net – to no response. I think I used the words 'oh f***' repeatedly, and I started to run westwards towards the river to try to get some distance between myself and the village fringe only about 100m away. The two Afghans disappeared and some locals close to a compound about 100m away had obviously seen the aircraft land and could only see me and were thus becoming increasingly interested. The Chinook had disappeared and it was getting dark and I thought that I was now a dead man. Despite this I was rather calm and made my way as fast as I could away from the fringe of compounds, trying to put as much ground and obstacles between myself and any pursuers. I nearly ran into a Kuchi nomad with his sheep and nearly shot him but he waved his hands in 'peace' so I travelled on. At this stage the Apache appeared in the vicinity and

I began to feel better but I couldn't be sure that he had spotted me in the gathering darkness. I started to flash my torch at the AH and since he didn't disappear, I assumed I was now identified. I found myself at the river's edge and secreted myself down in the reeds with some cover from the bank, where I could continue to signal the AH and cover the growing crowd of Afghans about 300m away. After about fifteen minutes the Chinook returned, and far more slowly than I would have liked wandered down the river line, seemingly ignoring my torch flashes, but eventually it turned and landed. I was much relieved to clamber up the ramp to be greeted by a worried looking Gary Wilkinson. The loadie then asked if I was OK and I think I responded with 'How the f*** do you think I am?!'

Like many such things the experience was more terrifying after it had happened. At the time one is concerned only about self-preservation and doing things that will help this, there is therefore no time to think about what might have been. These one thinks of afterwards and are not pleasant. Had I been captured the mind boggles, there is no way I would have survived but it is more the manner of one's death that frightens, and the aftermath – perhaps strung up in the bazaar! Then of course you wonder if you would have been taken alive – certainly I would have fired every last round and thrown every grenade prior to capture. But would I leave a round for myself and would I have been able to do it? Most distressing was the fact that I had come within a hair's breadth of widowing Al and leaving the girls with no father, and all because a Chinook pilot couldn't find the right LZ. Thank God for the Apache pilot who clocked the mistake by the dust cloud in the wrong place and hung around to check; the Chinook was heading home. Had there been no Apache escort – often the case if two Chinooks are flying as a pair – then I would be history. I was very pleased to be back in the DC and had a very welcome brew and a smoke! Also a card there from Simon Hall [ex-Headmaster of Milton Abbey School] which was a welcome surprise.

Having been updated about the plan for the night, we settled down into the routine. Not long afterwards there was an enormous explosion in the Fire Support Group building to the north. Initially we assumed RPG but it was much larger and turned out to be a 107mm rocket. Following the blast there were a few moments of silence – very ominous – and then the cries for 'medic'. Then the .50s and GPMGs opened up and all hell broke loose for most of the night. We had heard about Taliban groupings, civilians moving out and the 'big plan' to overrun the DC. So the gloves really came off. The rocket that marked the opening sequence skimmed the roof of the building and then exploded against the wall of the small blockhouse in the centre of the roof that covered the stair well. The blast blew all the support weapons crews out of their bunker, wounding six, none seriously, and narrowly missing the snipers who were on the roof of the blockhouse. But it impacted on the LEWT who were inside, killing Cpl Thorpe and LCpl Hashmi more or less instantly. Dowood their interpreter was also killed. Pte Brown had lacerations to his legs, Cpl Cartwright a piece of shrapnel in his backside, Cpl of Horse Fry (my FAC) received a wound to his hand. Scott and Evans minor scrapes, and LCpl Hadfield (sniper) deafened by the blast. This toll explains the pause before the returning of fire. The CSM, Zac Leong, was tremendous; as we were getting a picture of things he dashed up to sort out the wounded and was met by a grisly scene. The LEWT team destroyed, one with signs of life but died very soon, awful head injuries, the hole in the wall was enormous and the roof in turmoil. Leong sorted all out, getting the dead and wounded down quickly and efficiently, restoring order to the shocked roof top. He returned to the Ops room shortly afterwards, covered in blood.

All movement was now taken as hostile and engaged. The MSTAR and Thermal Imaging picked up various groupings at distance and these were engaged with 105mm and 81mm. The machine-gunners, snipers and mortars were busy throughout and at some stage we received an AC 130 on station which added its 105mm to the fray and bringing in fire at suspect groupings or possible forming up places (FUPs). The bunkers dominating the approaches from the bazaar engaged fighters emerging from the side streets; the night was characterised by insurgent movement on three sides, but there was no serious attempt to breach our perimeter – possibly because they couldn't get close enough. The northern roof top was the most unpleasant place to be; they had sustained a significant strike but now just cracked on with dogged stoicism, shocked and shaken as they must have been – Cpl Shimmins (MMG Section commander), the snipers, CoH Fry(FAC) and Cpl Wright (MFC) were fantastic, doing their jobs extremely well in the face of enemy fire. CoH Fry returned to that awful roof with his hand bandaged to continue controlling aircraft [he is later awarded a MC] and Cpl Wright continued with his MFC work after the other MFC, Cpl Cartwright, had been wounded. [Cpl Wright is later to be awarded a posthumous George Cross for his courageous and utterly selfless actions when his team find themselves caught in the middle of an old Soviet minefield.]

Matt Armstrong, my FOO, and in command of the Fire Support Team (FST), was excellent too, ensuring the indirect fires were applied where most required and de-conflicting this with air support – mainly the AC-130, B1 bomber and A-10 close air support. All movement was Taliban, of this there was no doubt, and there were lots of them.

Our dead were the first from 3 Para BG and I think my initial contact report shocked the Battalion Ops Room. It is dreadful but one had this awful relief that the dead weren't A Company but Royal Signals attached, and of course I didn't really know them in the same way as my own. I decided with RMO advice that our wounded should wait until the next day for casevac. None of their injuries were life threatening.

This was a night when the Taliban were trying to turn the screw. We met them with greater resolve and although it felt very odd to be bringing in significant fire so close and to be engaging all movement, it was also well within our Rules of Engagement (ROE.) The attacks reflected the intelligence we had had, too – of over a thousand Taliban massing in the area, of ten significant leadership figures, of the 'big plan' to roll over the DC, the movement of 'innocents' out of Sangin and of others to the safety of mosques. The sound of the AC-130 overhead and firing its 105mm is fantastic and rather eerie, with a definite rumble on the ground when it hits. It is a fabulous platform and we should have some & also A-10s – much much more useful than the Eurofighter! I will always remember the awful silence after the first blast, the .50 opening up, and Zac Leong the CSM returning from his task covered in blood.

Sun 2 July. DC Sangin.

Summoned the Police Chief so that I could explain my severe disappointment about the general conduct of the Police. The Chief could not come because he had a 'headache', so he sent a couple of dodgy subordinates, one of whom was the brother of a significant Taliban leader. They were pretty useless and it was a waste of time – I think they only came to judge what damage their mates the Taliban had caused the night before – enemy 'battle damage assessment'!! At around midday a resupply including mortar ammunition arrived in two Chinooks, also bringing in the CO and his Tac HQ, and extracting our dead and wounded. Took the CO round the position starting on the roof and the 107mm impact point. Then we sat down to discuss the situation. I stressed to him that I did not think that the position was tenable without significant logistic effort, an Engineer Field Troop with lots of stores and plant and a good quantity of reasonably trusted ANA and ANP. Without these things the position was simply in 'survival mode' and whilst we could hold our own there would be a steady trickle of casualties. He seemed to agree to all this and of course the politics meant that we must stay in Sangin. The CO also said that he had decided to relieve us with B Company, very welcome news, having been here nearly two weeks and been in contact every night since the 27th, we were quite happy to let someone else have a go.

The Brigadier has now got the Province Governor to order the Chief of Police to provide the support that is asked of them – not that this is likely to come to much. Following this the CO and RSM decided to show what good blokes they were by filling some rather superfluous sand bags on the southern side of the DC roof! In the course of this, at about 1900 (still light) we received small arms fire from wood lines to the south west. Thus CO and RSM scrabbling about on the roof with rounds nipping over their arses! So tonight activities started early and for the first time in daylight. We had a lot of air on station including the AC-130, Apache, A-10 and a B1 bomber. The night followed a similar pattern to the 1st – small arms, RPG and fortunately inaccurate 107mm from three sides throughout the night. We using our direct fire weapons, 81mm, 105mm, Javelin and air assets to kill suspicious movement before it could close with us. Cpl Poll at the front sangar had a few vehicles and fighters emerge to advance on his position, straight into the frontal arcs of his GPMG, with predictable consequences. He also hosed down the Chief of Police's car – what a shame! We on the ground were now on war fighting ROE but the air were still operating under more restrictive measures. Thus the Apache had to be told that a target was a definite risk to life before he would engage. A bit tedious.

Mon 3 July. DC Sangin.

Advance parties of Giles Timms' B Company arrive. By late afternoon all had been briefed by their counterparts. Prepared for a similar night to the last two and with that settled down. First contact at about 2200, a 107mm rocket that missed and hit the ground near the outer perimeter wall, followed by the usual flurries of small arms and RPG fire, from three sides. Fired a Javelin missile at a vehicle retreating from the suspected 107mm firing point. Vehicle destroyed. Sporadic engagements through to about 0200 hrs, with the usual response from our small arms, HMG, 81mm, 105mm and air fires.

Tues 4 July. DC Sangin.

In the morning we received a group of village elders from the north, an area that had borne the brunt of much of the fighting. Essentially they wanted us to stop! They were unwilling to do anything to assist in securing peace in Sangin but just kept asking us to stop firing our weapons. I was quite blunt with them and pointed out quite forcefully that security within Sangin will only be achieved through a partnership between us and the local people – I told them that they needed to do more – such as providing us with information or arranging groups of volunteers to build community opposition to the

Taliban. But I fear they will not move in our direction until we are clearly more powerful than the Taliban, have much greater strength, have a reasonable police force and have started development work; then they might decide to take our side. One of the old boys gave me a huge kiss at the end! We have shown ourselves to be a pretty fine tribe over the past two weeks and the Taliban must have suffered well over 100 casualties. Thus a certain grudging respect perhaps? As this mini Shura concluded, we received quite sustained small arms fire from the south west.

Later on I was extracted with most of the Company to Bastion, Hugo Farmer's 1 Platoon and a few others staying at Sangin under OC B Company until their third platoon could be extracted from Musa Qaleh. Felt awful leaving some of my blokes there, but little point in having two company commanders there and I was needed for the planning of a strike option in a few days time – Op Augustus. With the feeling of guilt one also had a feeling of relief at escaping from Sangin, a miserable place and a pretty unpleasant two weeks. Went to see Andy Cash who was piloting the Apache on the 1st July that had clocked the messed-up drop-off and effectively saved my life. I was very grateful and thanked him rather a lot. There was then time to shave off two weeks growth of beard and mull over the last couple of weeks. We seem to be stretching ourselves dangerously and things seem to be run in a rather haphazard way, the strain being mostly felt by those placed in unpleasant places. Clearly there is always risk, but it is the risk of unnecessary death, with little being done to minimise the risks which made me angry. Combat is not pleasant and I have found that the 4th June was rather an odd day, 13th June was rather unpleasant and Sangin was deeply unpleasant. In all we have given a good account of ourselves and accounted for a lot of Taliban. But it remains a deeply unpleasant experience and naturally one thinks of the girls and of Alison, both from whether it is all fair to them but also whether you want to continue to risk not seeing them again. It brings such questions well forward and I suppose one rationalises it all with the importance of the task but also with the realisation that I'm quite good at it. It is strange that the dangers and risks are not really an issue whilst one is deployed. It is before and afterwards when you have time to think and mull things over that you really feel the fears and risks.

In the evening we had the Memorial Service to Cpl Peter Thorpe, LCpl Jabron Hashmi [the first Muslim soldier to lose his life in the campaign] and Dowood the Interpreter. Very sad but well attended.

Wed 5 July. Camp Bastion.

Finding that fresh rations have a destabilising effect on the bowels! Spent first half of the day marshalling thoughts and started writing the after-action review. Resupply sortie due to go in to Sangin later in the day. Just prior to this heard that there had been a contact in Sangin and a friendly casualty. This turned out to be Pte Damien Jackson, whom sadly died of his wound. Basically his platoon (1 Pl) had been out securing the LS to the south of the DC when they ran into a team of Taliban. Fire was exchanged and Jackson was hit in the stomach by a 7.62 round. This did severe damage and he died more or less immediately. The RMO was on the scene but could do nothing to save him. Very sad but also not unexpected. Jackson was one of the more senior 'Toms' [Private soldiers] in the Company, a very good Geordie from South Shields, 19 years old and due to be 20 on 9th July – a strong runner for promotion, too, and a great loss. Due to the risk to the LS the resupply could not go in and Jackson's body could not be recovered today.

6–13 July. Camp Bastion.

Rather a strange period, dominated by trying to extract my elements from Sangin and insert B Company's, and by the preparation for Op Augustus. While all this was going on there was the need to get over the demands and pressures of Sangin, come to terms with Jackson's death and hand over the Company to my successor. [Under a system that has since allegedly been adjusted, Will's two years with his company are up, and he is required to move to his post-Staff College staff appointment, in his case on the Afghanistan desk in the MOD, thus making way for his successor to properly fit in his own two years as a company commander. The importance of continuity during operational deployments seems to have been seen as less important than rigid adherence to the necessary but inflexible process of succession planning.]

It took a while for all to start smiling again once out of Sangin – all were pretty shocked, strained and had lost a lot of weight. It was not really about the casualties but about the general position there, the feeling of isolation and of being 'surrounded' and the long nights stood to. One was also deeply struck by how magnificent the blokes had been, never a complaint, always cracking on and doing the very best they could; fantastic in contact, lots of initiative, drive and courage too – in particular the section commanders were all quite superb. It really is a deep honour to be fortunate enough to be in command of them.

We had a Memorial Service for Jackson on the 9th – his 20th Birthday – in which the Padre spoke well, I did the tribute and the CSM, Zac Leong, the remembrance. The cookhouse was packed to the gunnels and it all went off as well as could be expected. Afterwards I gathered the Company and we spent 15 minutes together, outside under the stars remembering one of our own, and then putting him away and refocusing on challenges to come. It was an important 15 minutes.

In his tribute to Jackson, Will says they should all remember 'Jacko's wiry, slightly gawky frame. His awful set of teeth that required repeated trips to the dental centre. His Geordie wit, his love of football and extensive knowledge of the sport he loved. His prowess as an athlete. His welcoming and outgoing personality; he was always the first to make the newer soldiers feel at home in the Company ... carry with you a picture of Jacko the man, the Geordie teenager who was a first-class soldier and a friend to all. Your duty to him now is to apply his legacy with added resolve.'

The diary continues:

Op Augustus is now the focus and being used as the final flourish of the US-led Operation Mountain Thrust. The US Commanding General (Freakly) came down to see us. Essentially it is a deliberate search and arrest operation focussed on two compound areas about 4 kms north of the Sangin District Centre. This is Taliban heartland and there have been numerous (hundreds) of Sigint hits on these compounds, suggesting that Koo Agha himself may be there. It was thus a kill or capture mission and A Company was to have the lead. The operation was due to go in on 12 July, but none of the assets that Freakly had promised materialised and the weather (dust in the air, etc) meant that aircraft and sensor viability was reduced below tolerable levels. Our date slipped to the very early hours of 15 July, my last day in command and one way to spend such a day!

We lifted in darkness at about 0210 on the 15th. My Company in the first 3 Chinooks with Paddy Blair and C Coy just behind in a further 2 aircraft. I again shared the lead aircraft with Nicol Benzi the lead pilot. Apaches had preceded, with AC-130 and Predator already on station. Not much more Intelligence but we knew that Koo Agha was in the immediate vicinity.

Our Chinooks routed out to a holding point where we went into a low-level circuit whilst AC-130 and Apache scoped the LS and target area. Despite having a significant number of surveillance capabilities looking at this tiny area they could spot nothing of great significance – yet we knew that there were substantial numbers of Taliban there. After some frustrating delay the green light was given. We had a five minute run-in and as we came in to touch down all hell broke loose and we began to receive fire from at least three sides. My three Chinooks pressed in whilst the follow- on pair with C Coy aborted. Hard to tell when inside a Chinook but the door gunner to my immediate right started to send large amounts of fire back in a north-westerly direction. We hit the ground and blokes started piling off the back straight into a deeply channelled and wet field. Thus something of a cluster and a lot of fire coming in, small arms and RPG. But everyone working to the mission and moving to the first two compounds. Fortunately for us the fire was at the aircraft (no fun for the crew!) and was not coming from the closer compounds, so once on the ground one was shielded a bit, though still a lot buzzing about. Pte Jones was hit whilst still in the aircraft, a round through his upper left arm, nothing important hit. He tried to get off the aircraft and crack on but was ordered to stay on board. As my aircraft lifted off, an RPG passed over my head and landed beneath it and exploded – very lucky. Once the Chinooks were clear the AC-130 and Apaches started brassing up the main compounds, mainly to the West. On the ground I thought that we were going to have a spell of pretty intensive fighting before the air assets and ground forces combined fought off the Taliban so that the follow-up company (C Company) could land. Hence the importance of gaining the two nearest compounds quickly, since their thick walls and parapets would allow us to fight off threats from all sides. 1 Platoon were quickly into theirs, mousehole charge on the main gate, massive explosion and then they were in, throwing grenades and clearing rooms. No one inside and the compound swiftly secured, with good fields of fire from it. 2 Platoon were a bit slower, with a mousehole charge against the wall, but little damage despite 8 sticks of P4 explosive, indicating the thickness of these mud/wattle walls. Anyway after a couple of minutes they were in and again the compound was unoccupied. As we were securing it, AC-130 and Apache were engaging depth targets with 105mm and Hellfire missiles. There was little incoming fire and after a short spell it seemed that the enemy had decided that discretion was the better part of valour.

By the time C Company arrived it was getting light so I took the opportunity to make myself a cup of tea to welcome the strengthening light. As the search operation progressed and the day grew hotter, I had established my HQ in a typical compound of mud and wattle walls, with a sleeping platform, amongst chickens and goats and a heap of opium stalks. We sat on the roof waiting for C Company to finish their task and eventually started to extract. After about 12 hours on the ground some of the blokes with heavier kit, weighing up to 90lbs, were beginning to struggle with the heat (50 degrees C). The decision was therefore made, rightly in my view, to return to Bastion to regroup before going in to reinforce Sangin the following day, to enable a road resupply of defence materials to get there. Very good to be back in Bastion after an op that could well have been much bloodier. Most expected us to take some killed in action on this one, yet fortunately Jones was the only casualty. I went to see him shortly after we returned and he was in good spirits. His main concern was getting his shirt back complete with bullet holes.

I spoke to the Company that evening – a somewhat brief farewell – but thanked them all personally. If there was one major thing I had learned, it is the fantastic professional forbearance and toughness in adversity that the Toms and NCOs have displayed in abundance over the past few months.

16–18 July. Kabul.

Flew to Kabul on 16th. Bumped into Mike Woods and Nicol Benzi and the rest of the Chinook crews who had just been replaced and were also on their way home – told them that they had been great and if it were up to me I would give them all a maroon beret. Then on to Brigadier Ed Butler's HQ (HQ BRITFOR in Camp Souter). Very odd feeling. The place feels a million miles from Helmand and everyone here talks about 'going down south' in awestruck terms. Everyone though is interested and impressed, which is nice. Went across to the Afghan MOD with the Brigadier to see the Afghan Secretary of State for Defence. He struck me as a rather idle and ill-informed sort of bloke, but Ed Butler seemed to like him. He was an old Mujahaddin commander. The Brigadier wanted me to give him my assessment of Sangin which I did, but awkward since the Minister didn't really say anything. Thus something of a one-way conversation. The British Embassy, where we also went, was a bit weak and disappointing I thought. The strategic direction of UK operations in Afghanistan seems ad hoc, poorly co-ordinated, and not very well thought through. There seem to be rival strands – military, FCO, DfID and so forth all with their own lines of management, agendas and processes. None seem to be fused very well at the strategic level so that direction downwards is equally incoherent. This is no real surprise having viewed it at the lowest level. There does not seem to be a UK plan for Afghanistan or Helmand. Hopefully I can bring some reality to the MOD?

Flew back to UK on 18th via Cyprus and Germany in the clutches of the dreadful movements staff, who never fail to disappoint and treat their charges like cattle. Flight made more bearable by having Phil White and Ralph Wooddise to chat with. They got off in Germany. Arrived back at Brize Norton at about 10pm – awfully nice to see Al. Back to Aldbourne – nice and rather odd to be home.

By the end of the tour, eighteen soldiers and one interpreter of the 3 PARA battle group have been killed, and forty-six wounded.

After less than a year working on the Afghanistan desk in the MOD, Will resigns from the Army.

Roll of Honour, 3 PARA Battle Group, April–October 2006

Sergeant Paul Bartlett	Royal Marines
Corporal Bryan Budd VC	The Parachute Regiment
Private Andrew Cutts	Royal Logistic Corps
Corporal Oliver Dicketts	The Parachute Regiment
Ranger Anare Draiva	Royal Irish Regiment
Captain Alex Eida	Royal Artillery
Lance Corporal Jabron Hashmi	Intelligence Corps
Lance Corporal Jonathan Hetherington	Royal Signals
Private Damien Jackson	The Parachute Regiment
Second Lieutenant Ralph Johnson	Household Cavalry Regiment
Lance Corporal Luke McCullough	Royal Irish Regiment
Lance Corporal Paul Muirhead	Royal Irish Regiment
Lance Corporal Ross Nicholls	Household Cavalry Regiment
Captain David Patten	The Parachute Regiment
Captain Jim Philippson	Royal Artillery
Lance Corporal Sean Tansey	Household Cavalry Regiment
Corporal Peter Thorpe	Royal Signals
Corporal Mark Wright GC	The Parachute Regiment

Epilogue

Most wars can be blamed on the fallibility of man's judgement one way or another, though often there are evil elements at work, creating difficulties which simply cannot be overcome without recourse to fighting. Whilst force should always be the last resort, therefore, it can sometimes prove necessary, although even in these cases, with the wonderful gift of hindsight we can see where things might have been handled differently, especially in the months or years before the stone begins to roll towards conflict. When we look at the spectrum of wars experienced by my family in this book, some wars, like the South African War, were justified at the time by the demands of Empire, and although controversial even then, are now viewed more critically still. The same can be said in a minor key about such operations as the Aro Expedition and, much later, the Radfan – both colonial-style 'punitive raids' of a kind. Other wars, like the Second World War and Korea were clearly justified on grounds both of International Law and moral rectitude. And whatever the diplomatic misunderstandings and mistakes that preceded it, the same can be said of the Falklands War. For despite the sad loss of 255 British and possibly as many as 700 Argentine lives, in addition to the hundreds who were wounded, the conflict emphatically left the Falkland Islands, Britain and Argentina better places. The First World War remains more problematic, so that one can only sensibly observe that at the time, few participants other than pacifists, or those like the poets Siegfried Sassoon and Wilfred Owen, haunted by their own terrible experiences, doubted that this dreadful catastrophe must be seen through to the end. I am certain that the likes of Reggie, Bridgy, Frank and Cuthbert felt this way.

The wars of the twenty-first century seem to be posing challenges as much to do with governance and reconstruction as with tactical military actions, having about them also a moral and political ambivalence that just makes the job of the soldier even more difficult, but no less dangerous. Will's account of the rapid descent into fighting in Afghanistan in the summer of 2006 thus highlights the extent to which the military role is only one part of a broader strategy, demanding an equal or greater commitment of civil and economic resources, if success is to be delivered. As Paddy Ashdown put it in a recent commentary, 'Breaking up the Taliban by winning over the moderates is a far better route to success than bombing and body counts.'

And so we come to the soldiers, who leave their families to go off and do the nation's business, sometimes mighty unpleasant and poorly rewarded business, too. Few of them are 'heroes' in the hackneyed headline sense, but most of them do their duty by their comrades and in this sense vindicate the words of St John's Gospel: 'Greater love hath no man than this, that a man lay down his life for his friends.' Most of those who do sacrifice their lives, do so as part of a close-knit team, in which each man relies on the support of the others and each understands that they must risk their lives if the team is to prevail. In this sense, duty and sacrifice become synonymous. 'Never did I think the valour of simple men could be so compelling,' writes Thomas Little of the Dublin Fusiliers from the Somme in 1916. 'I have chosen to stay with my comrades. I am calm and happy and desperately anxious to live.' Nor can the frequency of accident and mischance be forgotten in this 'province of uncertainty', as von Clausewitz describes war, where men and women so often lose their lives in circumstances that seem to contribute nothing whatever to the cause of success – Hew Tompson's death being a prime example of this; Goldie, one of Reggie's comrades on the Aro Expedition, killed in an accident on the Western front, being another.

Kipling famously recognized the public's and Government's historic neglect of soldiers in the 'piping days of peace' – 'It's Tommy this, an' Tommy that, an' Tommy go away, But it's "Thank you, Mister Atkins" when the band begins to play'; and Winston Churchill also understood these dangers, writing of the Army:

If it is bullied, it sulks;
If it is unhappy, it pines;
If it is harried, it gets feverish:
If it is sufficiently disturbed, it will wither and dwindle and almost die;
And when it comes to the last, serious condition, it is only revived by lots of time and lots of money.

All this rings true today, of course, and it is cold comfort to be reminded that there is nothing new in it. Reggie's speech in 1934 at Merton College about the surgeon and the rusty table knife perfectly makes the point about the resources needed by soldiers, that are so often missing. Will's company arrive in Helmand in 2006 still highly vulnerable to Improvised Explosive Devices (IEDs), and are issued with some equipment for the first time, despite their intensive pre-deployment training in Oman. Their flexibility and responsiveness is also critically constrained by the lack of helicopters. Early in his political life in the 1850s, Lord Salisbury wrote in the *Saturday Review* about the way the Army was 'looked upon as a sort of luxury, like a private gentleman's carriage, which is naturally "put down" when times are bad'. Equally timeless is his response as Prime Minister in 1885 to a request from General Sir Frederick Roberts for an increase in the size of the British garrison in India so that Kandahar could be recaptured and Herat secured against the Russian threat 'as soon as possible'. 'Our people require to have it driven into their heads,' he wrote, 'that if they will not submit to a conscription they must submit to a corresponding limitation of their exploits.' For 'our people' read 'democratically elected British governments in the early twenty-first century', who are so markedly failing to balance military resources with commitments.

And what, finally, of the families of our under-resourced and over-committed soldiers? Warfare is, of course, timeless in this respect, too. Timeless in terms of the partings and the constant anxieties, and timeless in terms of the strong desire to communicate, these days made almost too easy and immediate, so that the letters that say so much about person and place have now largely given way to the urgent immediacy and shorthand of the e-mail, the text message and the mobile telephone. Timeless, too, are those terrible moments when the news arrives of death or serious injury, and the grieving that follows. Yet with the grieving should come pride; pride that an example of courage, discipline and a strong sense of duty to comrades and friends have been shown, and can never die. After the Falklands, we travelled the country visiting the families of those who had been killed, and every household we went to reflected this pride; pride in the remembrance of past ambitions and achievements at school, on the sports field or in the Army. Every member of the family seemed to be in the Regiment too, rooting for their 'own particular anxiety', in Bridgy's words, marching with him, cheering him on to the end. And naturally they all had a picture in pride of place, just like Hew Tompson's on our own table at home.

'A nation is not merely a place where we happen to be. A nation is also a narrative of which we are a part. Society is a contract between the dead, the living and those not yet born.'

'Oh dear, what comfort can I find?' writes Rudyard Kipling of his son Jack, missing at the Battle of Loos in 1915:

> None this tide,
> Nor any tide,
> Except he did not shame his kind –
> Not even with that wind blowing and that tide.
>
> Then hold your head up all the more,
> This tide
> And every tide:
> Because he was the son you bore,
> And gave to that wind blowing and that tide.

Glossary of Abbreviations

AA	Anti Aircraft.
AC-130	See C-130.
ACM	Anti Coalition Militia. Generic term for any element opposed to the International Coalition in Afghanistan. In broad terms, this means the Taliban.
AH	Apache attack helicopter, equipped with rockets, 30mm cannon and MGs; excellent for observation.
A-10	A slow-flying but extremely effective aircraft designed for close support of ground troops, equipped with rockets and MGs. Sometimes called Warthog or Tankbuster.
AK	Kalashnikov. One of the world's most successful and widely used short-barrelled assault rifles.
ANA	Afghan National Army
ANP	Afghan National Police.
ATO	Ammunition Technical Officer. Often called a Bomb Disposal Officer. Normally a member of the Royal Logistic Corps (RLC).
B-52	Huge US bomber.
Basha	An improvised shelter in the field, often made from a poncho and rubber bungies. A basic essential to surviving the elements.
BC	Battery Commander.
Bde	Brigade. Normally three or more infantry battalions and/or armoured regiments. A Brigadier's command.

BEF	British Expeditionary Force. Also proudly known as the 'Old Contemptibles' in the First World War after the Kaiser had described the BEF as a 'contemptible little army'.
BG	Battle group. A combined arms force, often including infantry, armour and engineers, of battalion size.
BGS	Brigadier General Staff. Senior staff officer in a Corps HQ.
Blue on Blue	An accidental engagement of fire by friendly forces.
Bluey	Air mail letter form. Can also be an 'ebluey'.
Bn	Battalion. Normally 600–700 men strong, though sometimes more in wartime. Usually comprises a number of companies, each commanded by a captain or major. A Lieutenant Colonel's command.
Bocage	Originally describing the close, raised banks and hedges of Normandy, now used more generally to describe terrain of limited visibility where fighting is at fairly close quarters.
Bofors	A light air-defence gun.
Bombardier	A corporal in the Royal Artillery. Hence, also, Lance Bombardier is a Lance Corporal.
Bowman	Generic name for communication system used by the British Army in the twenty-first century. According to some cynics the acronym stands for 'Better Off With a Map And a Nokia'.
Bren	Second World War vintage .30-inch light machine gun, magazine fed.
Bty	Battery. A unit of artillery, generally supporting infantry and/or armoured regiments with indirect fire. Usually comprising six to eight guns, and a major's command.
BV	The BV202 or Bandwagon. A tracked, articulated, over-snow vehicle, consisting of a prime mover and a trailer, built by Volvo. Although designed for work over snow in the Arctic, this diminutive but gutsy little vehicle

proved excellent in the Falklands peat bogs, too
– as did the Scorpions and Scimitars.

BW   Black Watch. An infantry regiment.

Casevac   Casualty Evacuation (process of).
C-130 Hercules   Large transport aircraft carrying sixty-two
                       paratroops or slightly more airlanded troops.
                       The AC130 is a US Air Force C130 gun ship, an
                       exceptionally effective Close Air Support
                       platform, generally used at night. It mounts
                       105mm, 40mm and 20mm weapons systems, all
                       controlled by sophisticated sensors. The morale
                       aspect of having the AC130 overhead at night is
                       significant.
CCRA   The Brigadier commanding the artillery
                       resources at Corps level.
CCS   Casualty Clearing Station. A relatively static
                       facility in the chain of casualty evacuation from
                       front line to rear, where surgery can be carried
                       out.
CDS   Chief of the Defence Staff. Professional head of
                       the three armed services.
CH-47 Chinook   Large twin-rotor support helicopter carrying
                       thirty to forty men or a payload of 10 tons of
                       stores or weapons, sometimes underslung.
Chai   Tea.
Churchill   Infantry tank with heavy (6-in) armour, armed
                       with 6-pounder gun (Second World War).
CIGS   Chief of the Imperial General Staff. Now just
                       CGS – the Imperial was dropped in the 1970s.
                       The professional head of the Army.
Claymore   A shrapnel-scattering mine for area defence.
CMT   Combat Medical Team.
CO   Commanding Officer. Normally used for a
                       regimental or battalion commander. Officer
                       Commanding, 'OC', is usually used for a Major's
                       command (e.g. squadron, battery, company).
Cdo   Commando – a Royal Marine battalion.
Corps   Normally two or more divisions make up a
                       corps. A Lieutenant General's command.

CoH	Corporal of Horse. A rank in the Household Cavalry corresponding to Warrant Officer.
Company	Infantry sub-unit of about 100 men, commanded by a Major. Often abbreviated to 'Coy'.
Comms	Communications.
CP	Command Post.
CRA	Commander Royal Artillery. Normally a Brigadier's position, commanding a number of regiments supporting a division (e.g. the Commonwealth Division in Korea).
CSM	Company Sergeant Major. The senior non-commissioned rank in a company.
DAQMG	Deputy Assistant Quartermaster General. A staff position dealing with logistics.
DfID	Department for International Development (British).
Div	Division. Normally of three or more brigades. A Major General's command.
DSO	Distinguished Service Order. Generally awarded to officers in command positions in the face of the enemy, normally at Major (e.g. Frank Thicknesse, 1917) or Lieutenant Colonel level (e.g. Willie Pike 1943). Sometimes awarded to more junior officers for conspicuous gallantry (e.g. Reggie Tompson, 1902), but these days, with other awards available, notably the Conspicuous Gallantry Cross and the Military Cross, this is most unusual.
DC	District Centre.
DCLI	Duke of Cornwall's Light Infantry. An infantry regiment.
ECM	Electronic Counter Measures.
FAC	Forward Air Controller. Officer or NCO moving with forward troops, with communications to guide aircraft on to targets.
FCO	Foreign and Commonwealth Office (British)

Fd	Field. normally describing an artillery regiment (e.g. '77 Fd Regt'). Equipped with eighteen or more guns for close support of armour and/or infantry units.
Fire Team	An infantry team of four soldiers, often including a LMG.
FOB	Forward Operating Base.
FOO	Forward Observation Officer. A Gunner (RA) officer moving with the armour or infantry to observe and adjust fire, and to advise on fire support.
FSG	Fire Support Group (e.g. HMG, ILAW and MILAN teams).
FST	Field Surgical Team. In some situations deployed well forward of the Field Hospital.
FUP	Forming Up Place. The area behind a start line (SL) in which assaulting troops shake out into their positions for the attack.
GHQ	General Headquarters.
GOC	General Officer Commanding.
GPMG	General Purpose Machine Gun. Belt-fed 7.62mm weapon, normally one per section (eight to ten men) in British battalions. Can also be used in the Sustained Fire (SF) role with a heavier barrel, when longer uninterrupted bursts are possible.
Group	e.g. 'Company Group'. An all-arms group, including supporting elements other than purely infantry ones.
GSO	General Staff Officer. GSO 1 is a lieutenant colonel, GSO 2 is a major, GSO 3 a captain. However, this is now old terminology and has been superseded by NATO terms.
Gunner	Used in conversation to describe an officer or soldier of any rank in the RA. Also the equivalent rank of Private, e.g. Gunner Milligan.
HAC	Honourable Artillery Company. A Territorial Army regiment with traditions dating back to King Henry VIII.

Harrier	RAF aircraft used in close support of ground forces.
HE	High Explosive.
Hercules	See C130.
HF	High Frequency communications. Skywave communications, with greater ranges but more static interference, especially at night, compared to VHF or UHF communications.
H-Hour	The time at which the first assaulting troops cross the Start Line (SL), or leave their landing craft to assault a beach.
HRF	High Readiness Force.
Humvee	US 4 × 4 broad chassis jeep.
ICOM Scanner	Small hand-held scanner that scans and picks up insecure voice conversations.
IED	Improvised Explosive Device (e.g. roadside bomb). RCIED is a radio-controlled IED.
ILAW	Shoulder-operated anti-tank rocket in current service (2008) in the Army.
Illum	Illumination. Normally describing illuminating ammunition.
Indirect fire weapons	Those that are not aimed directly at their target, notably artillery and mortars.
ISAF	International Security Assistance Force in Afghanistan.
Jaeger	German light infantry troops.
Javelin	The successor to MILAN. It is a fire-and-forget', guided, anti-tank missile with a particularly good TI night site. However, the missiles remain in very short supply for front-line troops.
Jebel	Arabic word for rocky, mountainous or hilly area in the Middle East.
KIA	Killed in action.
LAD	Light Aid Detachment. A small team providing REME support well forward.

221

LAW	Also called M72 or the '66' (mm). A light, shoulder-controlled anti-tank rocket that proved invaluable as a bunker buster in the Falklands fighting. Range up to 300 metres.
LCU	Landing Craft Utility. Carries 100 men or 22 tons of stores. Four carried by each LPD.
LCVP	Landing Craft Vehicle and Personnel. Carries thirty men. Four carried by each LPD.
LEWT	Light electronic warfare team.
LPD	Landing Platform Dock. Assault ship. In the Falklands, HMS *Fearless* and HMS *Intrepid*.
LS	Landing site – for helicopters and troops.
LSL	Landing Ship Logistic. Roll-on, roll-off ships crewed by the Royal Fleet Auxiliary (RFA).
LZ	Landing zone. Same as LS.
MA	Military Assistant.
Madrasa	A mosque school.
M and AW Cadre	Mountain and Arctic Warfare Cadre. RM specialists in these skills.
MFC	Mortar Fire Controller. A NCO moving with the forward infantry, advising commanders and controlling the fire of a battalion's 81mm mortars, normally six to eight.
MG	Machine gun. Thus L for light, M for medium, H for heavy MG.
MGO	Master General of the Ordnance. Member of the Army Board responsible for the provision of weapons and munitions
MILAN	Wire-guided anti-tank missile, with a range of up to 2,000 metres and excellent for bunker-busting.
MSTAR	Man-portable (in theory but not really in practice!) Surveillance and Target Acquisition Radar. Deployed as part of a FOO party. Excellent for picking up movement in depth and thus an understanding of what is going on 'out there'.
MSR	Main Supply Route.
MT	Motor Transport. MTO is the Motor Transport Officer in a battalion.

NCO	Non-Commissioned Officer.
NOK	Next of kin.
NGO	Non-governmental organization (i.e. groups, including charities like the Save The Children Fund, working in a theatre of operations, that are not financed or sponsored by national governments).
NVG	Night Vision Goggles. Image Intensification (II) light-gathering goggles.
ODA	Operational Detachment Afghanistan. A US Special Forces Group.
O Group	Orders Group. Term used at all levels of command to describe the team to which formal orders are given out by a commander.
OMLT	Operational Mentoring Liaison Team.
OP	Observation Post. Very often used by the RA for forward observation and adjustment of fire onto targets. A Gunner OP party includes the FOO and his signallers.
PARA	The Parachute Regiment and its battalions, known as 1, 2 and 3 PARA. 4 PARA is a TA battalion.
PJHQ	Permanent Joint HQ, Northwood. Responsible to the MOD for the operational direction and management of all national contingents to allied or coalition operations worldwide.
Platoon (Pl)	Infantry sub-unit of thirty men, normally commanded by a Lieutenant, sometimes these days by an experienced Colour Sergeant.
PNG	Passive Night Goggles. Image-intensifying (II) goggles used by helicopter pilots to fly at night.
Predator	A UAV. Can be equipped with Hellfire missiles.
PTI	Physical Training Instructor.
QRF	Quick Reaction Force.
RA	Royal Artillery. At the time of the First World War, the terms used were often Royal Garrison Artillery (RGA) or Royal Field Artillery (RFA).

RAMC	Royal Army Medical Corps.
RAP	Regimental Aid Post. Where the RMO and his small team provide the first line of care for casualties evacuated from the front line. Normally well up behind the fighting.
Rapier	British land-based, surface-to-air AA missile system.
RE	Royal Engineers.
REME	Royal Electrical and Mechanical Engineers.
RF	Royal Fusiliers. An infantry regiment.
RHA	Royal Horse Artillery. Thus '7 RHA' means 7th Parachute Regiment, RHA, the parachute-trained gunner regiment that supports the battalions of the Parachute Regiment.
RHQ	Regimental Headquarters.
Rifle Company	A manoeuvre company, normally of three platoons.
RM	Royal Marines.
RMA	Royal Military Academy, Woolwich, also known as 'The Shop', where all officers going to the RE, RA and Royal Signals were trained. It closed in 1939.
RMC	Royal Military College. This was the title of Sandhurst until the Second World War, where all cavalry and infantry officers were trained. After the Second World War it became the RMA and started to train all officers, as it still does today.
RMO	Regimental Medical Officer. .
ROE	Rules of Engagement. The rules governing decisions on opening fire that must be made in the field. These will vary from theatre to theatre and often within theatre, too.
RPG	An anti-tank rocket of Russian origin. An excellent weapon.
RPK	Soviet era 7.62 LMG. Widely available round the world. Range up to 500 metres.
RSM	Regimental Sergeant Major. The senior Warrant Officer in a battalion or regiment.
RTR	Royal Tank Regiment.

RUC	Royal Ulster Constabulary (now the Police Service of Northern Ireland (PSNI)).
RV	Rendezvous.
RWK	Royal West Kents. An infantry regiment.
SA fire	Small-arms fire. Includes high-velocity rifle and MG fire.
Sangar	A protective wall of stone or peat built on ground too hard to dig, or where trenches are flooded.
Sapper	Describes a soldier of the Royal Engineers, of any rank, when used as 'a Sapper'. Also the equivalent of Private soldier (e.g. Sapper Jones).
SAS	Special Air Service.
SBS	Special Boat Service.
Scimitar	Also called a CVR (Combat Vehicle Reconnaissance). A light, tracked, armoured recce vehicle with a crew of three and equipped with a 30mm cannon. Crewed in the Falklands, like the Scorpion, by the Household Cavalry.
Scorpion	A CVR similar to the Scimitar but equipped with a 76mm gun.
Scorpion	Tracked mine-clearing vehicle (Second World War), based on a Sherman chassis. Fitted with an axle in front, round which chains swung as it progressed, to detonate mines. Worked well, but slow and the chains soon wore out.
SEAC	South East Asia Command.
Sea King	A medium-lift helicopter with the capacity to carry about twenty men and/or loads underslung in nets. Vital in the Falklands for moving the guns (artillery) as underslung loads.
SF	Generic term for Special Forces (e.g. SAS, SBS). But see also 'Sustained Fire' under GPMG.
SH	Support helicopter. Generic term normally used to describe troop-carrying medium or heavy lift helicopters such as Chinook, Puma or Sea King.
Shura	Meeting.
SIGINT	Intelligence gained from signal intercept or location finding.

SL   Start line. The line of departure for an assault. For example, the line of a stream or track. Now redesignated 'Line of Departure'.

TA   Territorial Army. Part-time Army volunteers.

Tac   Tactical. Of an HQ, it means a small, mobile, forward HQ.

Tac Sat   Tactical Satellite Communications System.

TF   Task Force. A military grouping of specialized skills for a particular task, at any level.

TI   Thermal Imaging, i.e. systems for detecting objects through their heat at night or in poor visibility.

Tiger   German heavy tank. It weighed 56 tons and mounted an 88mm gun.

Time   Falklands Time is four hours behind GMT and the war was fought on GMT or 'Zulu' time in military parlance. However in this account all timings used are local. First light was at about 0630 and last light at about 1615.

2IC   Second in command. Can be used at any level but often refers to the regimental/battalion 2IC.

UAV   Unmanned Airborne Vehicle. Normally for battlefield surveillance (e.g. Predator).

Utrinque Paratus 'Ready for Anything' – the motto of The Parachute Regiment.

VSI   Very seriously ill (SI – seriously ill).

Wadi   Arabic word for dry river bed often subject to sudden flash flooding in the rainy season.

WIA   Wounded in action.

WLs   Wagon Lines. Where artillery transport is held.

WMIK   Weapons Mount Improvized Kit (e.g. Land Rover WMIK). A Land Rover customized to be able to mount either a HMG, anti-tank system or grenade launcher.

WRNS   Women's Royal Naval Service (WRENS).

Index

Note. Ranks given are generally those held at the time, not the ultimate rank reached. Initials or first names/nicknames are sometimes missing, where these are not known.